Str Enr Planning:

A Dynamic Collaboration

How higher education leaders can align mission, vision, and values with shifting market needs and expectations

DISCARD

Edited by Jim Hundrieser, PhD

Noel-Levitz®

ISBN: 978-0-9854281-0-5

Printed and bound in the United States of America.

First Edition: November 2012
10 9 8 7 6 5 4 3 2 1

Copyeditors: Jim Hundrieser, Sher Jasperse, Pam Jennings, Angie Pederson, Lewis Sanborne, and Brandon Trissler

Design: Curt Muntz

Noel-Levitz, Inc.
2350 Oakdale Boulevard
Coralville, Iowa 52241
and
6300 South Syracuse Way, Suite 645
Centennial, Colorado 80111

Visit our Web site at www.noellevitz.com

CONTENTS

Strategic Enrollment Planning: A Dynamic Collaboration

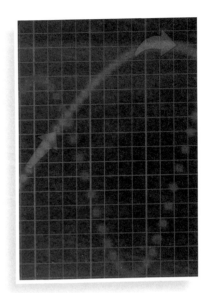

Noel-Levitz has been providing enrollment management consulting to higher education for almost 40 years. Prior to 2008, the plans that we helped colleges and universities develop were primarily focused on developing annual marketing/recruitment and retention plans. During the latter part of the past decade, the demographic and financial realities facing higher education forced institutions to move away from this annual focus and instead think of enrollment management holistically over a multiyear period.

The mission of Noel-Levitz, "…to provide strategic enrollment solutions to our college and university partners so they fully realize their institutional mission," led us to develop the strategic enrollment planning process described in this book.

As with any project of this magnitude, many people contributed their talents to the book. Before I give thanks, I need to first acknowledge that the idea to create this planning process originated with Dr. James Mager, formerly the associate vice president for enrollment management at The Ohio State University and associate vice president for consulting services at Noel-Levitz; and Kent Hopkins, vice provost for enrollment management at Arizona State University and formerly vice president and principal at Noel-Levitz. Without either of these gentlemen, the foundation for this book and the planning process it outlines would not have been created. It is the culmination of their detailed experience within enrollment management that validates the data-informed approach to enrollment management and distinguishes the strategic enrollment planning process from annual planning. Without data, there is no plan.

In addition, there are several Noel-Levitz team members to acknowledge. Kevin Crockett, Craig Engel, Lewis Sanborne, Pam Jennings, Brandon Trissler, Curt Muntz, Catherine Carpenter, Angie Pederson, and Jody Heid, all played instrumental roles to ensure this book happened. In addition to the Noel-Levitz team, the book was edited for grammar and formatting by Sher Jasperse.

Lastly, each of the authors provided their individual expertise and guidance to this book, and I offer them my thanks.

−Jim Hundrieser

Strategic Enrollment Planning: A Dynamic Collaboration

By Jim Hundrieser

We live in confusing times—many of the features that gave structure to our lives are disappearing or changing in dramatic ways. Institutional structures that we relied on throughout our careers are no longer so sure or so certain. More than a decade ago, Charles Handy discussed the need to find a sense of structure or order in uncertain times (1998). We may think this great wave of change and uncertainty has passed, but higher education may be facing a more uncertain future than ever. Financial constraints caused by a rapidly rising and falling economy have resulted in dramatic shifts in federal and state funding support and college affordability. At the same time, higher education continues to struggle to meet the needs of an increasingly diverse student body, challenging our ability to graduate more students. Unless we move with urgency, today's young people will be the first generation in American history to be less educated than their predecessors (*College Completion Agenda*, College Board, 2011).

> **Strategic enrollment planning (SEP) refers to a complex and organized effort to connect mission, current state, and changing environment to long-term enrollment and fiscal health, resulting in a concrete, written plan of action.**

Based on current estimates, in order to reach the goal of 60 percent of adults with postsecondary degrees by 2025, a challenge posed by the Obama Administration and the Lumina Foundation, the U.S. higher education system must produce 23 million more college graduates than are expected at present rates of production (Lumina, 2010). While the principles and concepts described in this book do not solve the challenges higher education faces as it strives to achieve the goal of producing a competent, credentialed workforce for 2025, they offer a context for planning that will help institutions evaluate their current state and establish measurable institutional goals for the future. For most institutions, this planning process should initiate a dialogue making it clear that current practices will not be sufficient to meet the demands of the majority of learners by 2025.

Strategic enrollment planning (SEP) refers to a complex and organized effort to connect mission, current state, and changing environment to long-term enrollment and fiscal health, resulting in a concrete, written plan of action. While some within the academy would prefer to keep the focus of SEP on enrollment, the authors of this book agree on the basic principle that academic and co-curricular programs must be linked to enrollment planning and aligned with the organization's fiscal health as an essential component of this process. The initial strategic planning process typically takes 9 to 12 months. This time is needed to collect, analyze, and utilize the relevant environmental and internal information and data that are required to inform an institution's strategies and future directions.

After the strategic enrollment plan has been developed, the corresponding strategic enrollment management (SEM) process is implemented as part of the institution's ongoing/routine planning process to ensure that the plan's strategic vision and goals are effectively and efficiently achieved. Progress with respect to action strategies and tactics must be continuously monitored, evaluated, and modified as appropriate. As the internal and external environments change, additional information and data must be collected, analyzed, and integrated into the ongoing planning process.

Strategic enrollment planning versus long-range planning

Chapters 2, 3, and 4 provide insights into the difference between strategic planning and long-range planning. At the core of this difference is the SEP focus on the role that enrollment management plays in linking curricular and co-curricular trends, demands, and capacity data with enrollment planning. In many cases, this will mean that institutional leaders can no longer allow legacy programs to consume institutional resources (unless mandated by charter or mission), while other programs with opportunities for growth fail to be supported at a level that enables them to reach their maximum potential. In addition, we believe SEP must link with physical plant, human, and technological resources to ensure student engagement and achievement of outcomes that will prepare them for career or further graduate education opportunities. If a campus is not yet prepared to address this challenge to connect all the elements of the institutional experience, this book offers suggestions for ways to create a long-range enrollment plan with a focus on recruitment, financial aid, marketing, persistence, and completion strategies. These long-range plans aim to connect these elements to provide a view of the student enrollment funnel that encompasses all stages from inquiry through completion, rather than inquiry through enrollment.

While some might consider SEP an activity designed simply to refine marketing, recruitment, and student success initiatives, our work tells us that quality academic and co-curricular programs lie at the heart of a strong enrollment management program. A thorough assessment of these areas should drive strategy development to create marketing activities, new student enrollment operations, and retention and persistence-to-completion activities, rather than the other way around.

Planning approach

Traditional planning approaches are not equipped to meet the challenges facing higher education today and in the future because they generally lack systemic coordination and campuswide engagement. Frequently, they also fail to effectively take into account the impact of external environmental factors and changes in competitive relationships. We share the view expressed in *Strategic Change in Colleges and Universities* that institutions can engage in effective planning processes that will lead to strategic management and the use of strategic planning can play a proactive role in shaping the future of the institution (Rowley, Lujan, and Dolence, 1997).

Without a systemically coordinated and sustainable process in place for strategic enrollment planning, colleges and universities take a significant risk that their future enrollments will not fulfill their institutional mission and vision, eventually jeopardizing their fiscal health. Given this enormous potential impact, SEP should be among the top institutional priorities.

The following offers a visual summary of the approach recommended by this book:

Figure A-1: Strategic Enrollment Planning Phases

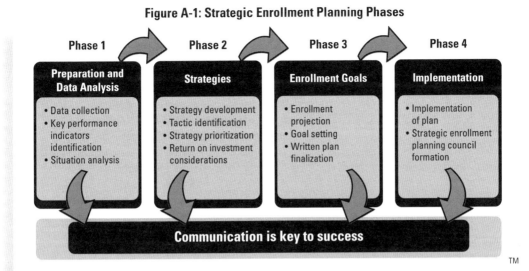

Essential to the successful SEP process is the establishment of a strategic enrollment management council. This council ensures the plan is implemented and tracks plan progress through the monitoring of key performance indicators established during the planning process. To be effective, this council must be led by high-level institutional leaders and not relegated to "committee" status. This council must push the institution to change and insist that priorities are established, included in the budget, and implemented. What is ultimately at stake is the quality of the educational experience an institution offers its students and, in turn, the level of its attractiveness to prospective students, faculty, and staff.

Considerations as you read the book

Each chapter of this book is designed to address a specific topic and can stand alone as a discussion of one component of strategic enrollment planning. The book has three sections. The first section (Chapters 1-3) sets the stage by discussing the imperative to plan, the need to build trust and collaboration, and the fundamental elements of SEP. The second section (Chapters 4-9) provides explanations and illustrations of the planning process and the essential elements needed to complete a strategic enrollment plan. The last section (Chapters 10-12) offers a more in-depth look at fundamental concepts related to recruitment, marketing, student persistence, and completion. It is intended to provide readers with specific strategies to consider as they compare their practices and data with best or emerging practices.

Chapters 4 and 9, in particular, identify key members of the institutional community who should be included in the planning process. The SEP process is *not* a time to attempt to convince the non-believers of the purpose or value of strategic enrollment planning. From the outset, it requires buy-in from committed institutional members who are eager and ready to engage in a data-informed planning process that links strategy with data and determines institutional priorities that will yield the best return on investment.

Some campus leaders have suggested that the planning process is more important than the actual plan itself, and we at Noel-Levitz have observed this firsthand. Campuses with strong institutional leadership actively engaged in the planning and implementation process succeed at high rates. While this book offers suggested approaches to the planning process, we emphasize that campuses are most successful when their planning processes are customized to match their institutional culture. Success is highly likely as long as the process remains data-informed and uses data and return-on-investment considerations to drive action.

At the conclusion of most chapters, the authors have provided two- to three-paragraph summaries or lists of questions campus leaders may find helpful in prompting discussion within the campus community related to the topic or phase of the planning process described in that chapter. These concluding thoughts emphasize the importance of sharing the information and data learned through creation of the plan. These data may lead to immediate actions that can be implemented during the planning process. The dialogue may identify potential implications and/or challenges faced during the planning process and suggest ways to communicate these opportunities or challenges.

Strategic Enrollment Planning:

A Dynamic Collaboration

Section One: The Future Is Strategic Enrollment Planning and Management

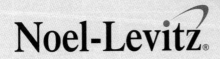

CHAPTER 1

The Future of Higher Education and the Strategic Enrollment Planning Imperative

By Kevin Crockett

Chapter highlights

- **Changing enrollment patterns**

- **Enrollment forecasts to 2020**

- **Retention and completion take center stage**

It is always dangerous to look into a crystal ball with respect to the future of American higher education. Whenever the academy seems on the brink of fundamental change or institutional closures/consolidations are predicted on a broad scale, we are reminded that our colleges and universities are remarkably resilient. Indeed, since World War II, the industry has either prospered from or suffered through events such as the introduction of Title IV aid programs, the substantial impact of Vietnam on both enrollment levels and campus culture, a massive expansion in the community/technical college sector, booms and busts in the number of high school graduates, large increases in the number of adult learners, explosive growth in the for-profit sector, the introduction and growth of online learning, and relatively severe recessions in the 1970s, 1980s, and 2000s.

Each of these events created winners and losers in our postsecondary system, but, for the most part, the system itself grew and prospered. Indeed, most of these events resulted in increased access to higher education, and that has led to more people than ever before attending college and holding postsecondary credentials. In 1949, there were 2.4 million individuals enrolled in postsecondary institutions, 70 percent of whom were men. By fall 2008, those figures had increased to 19.1 million students, 57 percent of whom were *women* (NCES, 2010). During this same period, the number of degrees conferred on an annual basis increased from 497,000 to more than 3.1 million, a 528 percent increase in approximately 60 years (NCES, 2010). Importantly, the percentage of young adults (age 25 to 29) with a bachelor's degree or higher increased from 8 percent of the population in 1950 to 32 percent by 2010 (NCES, 2010). To say that the last 60 years have been a gilded age for American higher education is an understatement.

As the United States and other developed nations struggle to emerge from the worst economic downturn since the Great Depression, perhaps our colleges and universities will emerge stronger than ever; or maybe economic and demographic changes will lead to a fundamental transformation of our postsecondary system. In either case, institutions that develop strong strategic enrollment planning (SEP) systems will have the best chance of capitalizing on an increasingly turbulent environment. Those that fail to adapt may find themselves closed, consolidated, or considerably weaker.

The purpose of this chapter is to briefly review some of the issues and trends confronting enrollment planners as we enter the second decade of the new millennium and discuss why these trends make strategic enrollment planning an imperative for colleges and universities that wish to thrive in the years ahead.

Slowing enrollment growth

Table 1-1 shows the enrollment growth of American higher education by type of institution. It also displays the market share for each sector. Between 1963 and 2009, total fall enrollment increased 327 percent from 4.8 million students to 20.4 million students. This growth was largely driven by the emergence of the public two-year sector, which grew by 860 percent and increased its market share from 15 percent of total enrollment in 1963 to 35 percent in fall 2009. While the growth in the public two-year sector is impressive, it is worth noting that, as a share of total enrollment, this group of institutions achieved its maximum market share in 2000 (37 percent), and that figure has since declined to 35 percent. In an era of escalating college costs, it is interesting that our lowest-cost providers were experiencing a modest decline in their share of total enrollment as we entered the worst portion of the recession in 2009.

Meanwhile, the four-year public sector experienced growth of 229 percent during this period, while its share of total enrollment declined from 49 percent to 38 percent. The growth rate in the four-year private sector mirrored the four-year public trends, with 227 percent overall growth and a decline in its share of total enrollment from 33 percent to 25 percent. Regarding private colleges, their erosion in market share continues a long trend. If you look at the data as far back as 1950, enrollments in public and private institutions were within a few thousand students of each other (NCES, 2010). Today, public institutions control 73 percent of the market, and that share would be greater were it not for the emergence of the private for-profit sector during the past decade.

Table 1-1: Total Fall Enrollment in Degree-Granting Institutions by Type of Institution: Selected Years, 1963 Through 2009

Year and type	Total enrollment	4-year public	Percent of total enrollment	2-year public	Percent of total enrollment	4-year private	Percent of total enrollment	2-year private	Percent of total enrollment
1963	4,779,609	2,341,468	49%	739,811	15%	1,587,780	33%	110,550	2%
1970	8,580,887	4,232,722	49%	2,195,412	26%	2,028,780	24%	123,973	1%
1980	12,096,895	5,128,612	42%	4,328,782	36%	2,441,996	20%	197,505	2%
1990	13,818,637	5,848,242	42%	4,996,475	36%	2,730,312	20%	243,608	2%
2000	15,312,289	6,055,398	40%	5,697,388	37%	3,308,460	22%	251,043	2%
2009	20,427,711	7,709,197	38%	7,101,445	35%	5,197,108	25%	419,961	2%
Growth percent	327%	229%		860%		227%		280%	
Compounded annual growth rate	3.2%	2.6%		5.0%		2.6%		2.9%	

Source: *2010 Digest of Education Statistics*: Table 198

The data in Table 1-1 mask an important trend, namely the explosive growth of the for-profit sector within the private college arena. As Table 1-2 shows, since 1980, the for-profit sector has grown from 111,714 students to 1,851,986 students, for a compounded annual growth rate of 10.2 percent, and its share of total college enrollment has increased from just under 1 percent to 9 percent. This increase in market share appears to have largely come at the expense of the public sector, which lost 4 percentage points of market share between 2000 and 2009.

The slowest growth sector over the last 29 years is the independent not-for-profit group, which has seen its share of total enrollment decline to 10 percent, while the other portion of the not-for-profit sector, religiously affiliated schools, experienced a relatively healthy 80 percent increase in fall enrollment. The growth in the latter group is divided almost equally between institutions affiliated with the Roman Catholic Church and institutions affiliated with various Evangelical Protestant denominations (NCES, 2010).

Table 1-2: Fall Enrollment by Control and Affiliation of Institution: Selected Years, 1980 Through 2009

Year/control and type	Total enrollment	Public institutions	Percent of total enrollment	Independent not-for-profit	Percent of total enrollment	Religiously affiliated not-for-profit	Percent of total enrollment	For-profit	Percent of total enrollment
1980	12,096,895	9,457,394	78%	1,521,614	13%	1,006,173	8%	111,714	1%
1990	13,818,637	10,844,717	78%	1,474,818	11%	1,285,409	9%	213,693	2%
2000	15,312,289	11,752,786	77%	1,577,242	10%	1,532,177	10%	450,084	4%
2009	20,427,711	14,810,642	73%	1,953,136	10%	1,811,947	9%	1,851,986	9%
Growth percent	69%	57%		28%		80%		1,558%	
Compounded annual growth rate	1.8%	1.6%		0.9%		2.1%		10.2%	

Source: *2010 Digest of Education Statistics*: Table 205

In summary, over the last 46 years (1963-2009), enrollments have increased 327 percent for an annual compounded growth rate of 3.2 percent. That growth was initially fueled by the rapid expansion in the two-year public sector during the 1960s and 1970s, followed by growth in the for-profit sector during the last decade. Since 1980, the public sector and independent not-for-profits have been losing market share to both the for-profit sector and religiously affiliated not-for-profits.

Enrollment forecasts: 2009 to 2020

According to the *Projections of Education Statistics to 2020*, total enrollment is expected to increase from 20.4 million in 2009 to 23.0 million in fall 2020. This represents growth of 12.7 percent overall and a compounded annual growth rate of just 1.1 percent, compared to 5.6 percent between 1963 and 1980 and 1.8 percent between 1980 and 2009. While these declines may appear modest at first glance, they represent decreases of 80 percent and 39 percent in the respective compounded annual growth rates. Here's another way to look at the data: Between 2000 and 2009, total enrollment grew 33.4 percent, compared to projected growth of 12.7 percent through 2020. That's 62 percent less growth than colleges actually experienced over the last decade (NCES, 2011).

The projections do not forecast any significant shifts in market share among sectors, but that may have more to do with NCES methodology than anything else. It is difficult to imagine existing market share ratios remaining relatively stable over the next decade given past changes. That said, there are some significant changes projected in the underlying student populations. Specifically, enrollment is expected to grow more rapidly among part-time students (+15.9 percent), women (+16.4 percent), graduate students (+17.7 percent), and non-Caucasians (+31.2 percent). These are displayed in Table 1-3. The growth in non-Caucasian students is driven by a projected 45.5 percent increase in Hispanic students and 24.5 percent growth in Asian/Pacific Islanders (NCES, 2011).

Table 1-3: Actual and Projected Enrollments in All Postsecondary Degree-granting Institutions: Fall 2009 Actual Versus Fall 2020 Projected (in Thousands)

Year/student category	Full-time	Part-time	Male	Female	Under-graduate	Graduate	Caucasian	Non-Caucasian
2009 actual	12,722	7,705	8,769	11,658	17,565	2,862	12,731	7,697
2020 projected	14,090	8,927	9,450	13,566	19,649	3,368	12,921	10,095
Growth percent	10.8%	15.9%	7.8%	16.4%	11.9%	17.7%	1.5%	31.2%

Source: *Projection of Education Statistics to 2020*, pages 66-69

If the preceding forecasts materialize, then higher education will have to adapt to slower growth rates, especially among undergraduates, Caucasians, males, and full-time students. This will represent a paradigm shift for many institutions that have relied on enrollment growth to fund campus improvements and academic and co-curricular program expansion. It also underscores the importance of localizing the preceding trends in your enrollment planning efforts.

I am routinely amazed at how little schools know about the market share trends in their student markets or how their growth patterns compare to those of major competitors. I recently visited a college that was experiencing enrollment declines in its adult undergraduate programs. Although campus leaders were convinced they were losing market share to several for-profit competitors that had entered their primary recruitment markets, they had no data on the size or scope of this erosion in market share.

Moreover, it is also rare for institutions to have developed enrollment forecasts based on current and projected market share data in their region. These data are foundational to the SEP process. Strategic enrollment plans cannot be based on what you would like to see happen or what you might need to strengthen your institution's financial position. Rather, they should be based on an empirical analysis of past trends and future forecasts in your markets.

Demographic shifts

Coming demographic shifts will lead to regional variations in enrollment levels and ongoing challenges in student preparation and ability to pay for college. The preceding data on projected college enrollments do not include regional projections, but it is safe to assume the underlying projections of high school graduates by geographic region will have a significant impact on college enrollments. The vast majority of college freshmen enroll at colleges/universities within 250 miles of their home, and transfer students tend to be even more local in their enrollment behavior. Enrollment of young adults (age 24 to 30) in both undergraduate and graduate programs is also impacted by these projections, although they tend to lag the high school projections by six to eight years.

Tables 1-4 and 1-5 show the projected change in public high school graduates from 2007-08 through 2020 by geographic region and race/ethnicity. Although these tables only display public high school graduates, the private high school trends mirror the changes in the public school data, but they are on a much smaller scale and the declines are more severe. Between 2007-08 and 2020-21, private high school graduates are expected to decline 27 percent, from 312,263 to 228,340 (NCES, 2011).

Table 1-4: Actual and Projected Numbers of Public High School Graduates by Region: 2007-08 Through 2020-21

Region	2007-08 actual	2014-15 projected	Percent change (from 2007-08)	2020-21 projected	Percent change (from 2007-08)
Northeast	552,289	490,680	-11.2%	481,850	-12.8%
Midwest	721,220	665,870	-7.7%	674,900	-6.5%
South	1,031,610	1,028,350	-0.3%	1,103,230	+6.9%
West	694,389	682,500	-1.7%	721,610	+3.9%
Total	2,999,508	2,867,400	-4.4%	2,981,170	-0.6%

Source: *Projection of Education Statistics to 2020*, pages 50-52

The number of public high school graduates increased nationally by 32 percent between 1995-96 and 2007-08, from 2,273,109 to 2,999,508 (NCES, 2011). A decrease of 4.4 percent is expected between 2007-08 and 2014-15, after which graduates will rebound slightly for a net loss of less than 1 percent by 2020-21. However, the regional variations are substantial, with modest increases expected by 2020-21 in the West and South and substantial decreases expected in the Northeast (-12.8 percent) and Midwest (-6.5 percent). It is important for institutions to look inside these regional trends by focusing on their own student catchment areas. For example, in the Northeast, New York state's projected decline by 2020-21 is 14 percent, whereas New Jersey is expected to decline by only 1 percent. In the South, Texas is expected to grow by 26 percent, whereas Louisiana is projected to decline by 2.1 percent. In the West, California is expected to decline by 2.8 percent, while Colorado is projected to increase by 21 percent (NCES, 2011).

If your institution serves large numbers of transfer and adult students, population projections are typically available from state planning offices. These can be used to infer future enrollments based on your current and projected market share of students within specific age groupings. For example, if your state had 1,000,000 persons age 25 to 29 with 50,000 enrolled in college, and your institution enrolled 500 of those students, your market share would be 1 percent of the 25- to 29-year-old college population. These data can be compared to future population projections to infer potential changes in enrollment based on changes in the age cohorts of the general population.

Table 1-5: Actual and Projected Numbers of Public High School Graduates by Race/Ethnicity: 2007-08 Through 2020-21

Region	2007-08 actual	2014-15 projected	Percent change (from 2007-08)	2020-21 projected	Percent change (from 2007-08)
Caucasian	1,916,642	1,703,760	-11.1%	1,707,400	-10.9%
Black/African American	435,920	422,650	-3.0%	425,940	-2.3%
Hispanic	453,383	521,950	+15.1%	575,060	+26.8%
Asian/Pacific Islander	161,164	189,720	+17.7%	234,550	+45.5%
American Indian/ Alaska Native	32,401	29,740	-8.2%	32,690	<1%
Total	2,999,508	2,867,400	-4.4%	2,981,170	-0.6%

Source: *Projection of Education Statistics to 2020*, page 48

Note: Detail may not sum to totals due to rounding. The high school projections for African American students do not support the 18.6 percent projected enrollment increase cited above. This is because there are larger cohorts of African American high school graduates leading up to 2020-21 before starting a relatively steep decline in 2019-20.

The race/ethnicity data also contain significant underlying trends, namely a projected 10.9 percent decline in the Caucasian population (by 2020-21) accompanied by substantial increases in the number of Hispanic and Asian/Pacific Islanders (Table 1-5).

The increase in Hispanic high school graduates coupled with the decline in Caucasian students is significant as it relates to preparation for college. According to data from the American College Testing (ACT) Program, in 2011, Hispanic test takers had an average ACT composite score of 18.7 versus 22.4 for Caucasian students. Moreover, while 31 percent of Caucasian students met all four ACT college-readiness benchmarks in 2011, only 11 percent of Hispanics met all four benchmarks. These benchmarks are based on achieving specific scores on ACT sub-tests, which correlate to the statistical probability of achieving a C or higher in college course work (ACT, 2011).

Meanwhile, the increase in Asian/Pacific Islanders is encouraging, at least as it relates to the Asian portion of this population. Forty-one percent of Asian students met all four college readiness benchmarks, the highest of any group. Meanwhile, only 15 percent of Pacific Islanders met all four college readiness benchmarks (ACT, 2011).

When it comes to remediation, 31 percent of first-year Caucasian students took a remedial course in 2007-08. The corresponding figure for Hispanic students was 43 percent and 45 percent for African American students. The figure for Hispanic students in 2003-04 was 38 percent, so not only are more Hispanic students

> *" It is fair to conclude that institutions that will serve growing numbers of non-Caucasian students will need to allocate additional resources for developmental education programs and related academic support services in the years ahead."*

graduating from high school and enrolling in college, but an increasing percentage of them require remediation (NCES, 2010). Thirty-eight percent of Asian students required a remedial course in 2007-08 despite their relatively strong ACT composite and college-readiness statistics. It is fair to conclude that institutions that will serve growing numbers of non-Caucasian students will need to **allocate additional resources** for developmental education programs and related academic support services in the years ahead.

Finally, demographic shifts are likely to place additional pressure on students' ability to pay for college. In 2010, median family incomes were highest among Asian families ($75,486), followed by Caucasians ($68,961), Hispanics ($39,538), and African Americans ($38,500). Indeed, Hispanic and African American families earn approximately 43 percent less than the typical Caucasian family (College Board, 2011). This promises to place additional strain on federal, state, and institutional financial aid resources as we experience a contraction in Caucasian students and substantial growth in Hispanic students. The projected increase in Asian families could somewhat mitigate this effect, but the sheer decline in Caucasian students coupled with the increase in Hispanic students will make the college financing environment particularly challenging in those regions of the country where these shifts are most pronounced.

Rapidly changing economic models

The traditional economic model for both public and private institutions is changing rapidly. While enrollment growth rates are projected to slow over the next decade, it is highly likely that resources to fund the enterprise will also contract. Indeed, in virtually every sector, reliance on net tuition revenue has increased while state and federal support has either contracted or increased only modestly. As Table 1-6 shows, at all types of institutions except private doctoral universities, the average share of revenues coming from net tuition and fees increased between 1998-99 and 2008-09 (College Board, 2011).

Table 1-6: Percentage of Institutional Revenue Per FTE Student in Constant 2009 Dollars at Public and Private (Non-profit) Institutions by Revenue Source: 1998-99 Versus 2008-09

Institutional type	Federal appropriations and federal, state, and local grants and contracts		State and local appropriations		Net tuition and fee revenue	
	1998-99	2008-09	1998-99	2008-09	1998-99	2008-09
Public doctoral	25%	34%	49%	34%	25%	32%
Public master's	11%	14%	56%	43%	33%	43%
Public bachelor's	13%	17%	56%	42%	31%	41%
Public two-year	14%	15%	64%	57%	22%	27%
Private doctoral	38%	38%	1%	1%	61%	61%
Private master's	7%	5%	1%	0%	92%	95%
Private bachelor's	9%	7%	0%	0%	91%	93%

Source: *Trends in College Pricing 2011*: page 20, figures 12A and 12B

Note: Revenues from private gifts, investment returns, and endowment income are not included in these percentages.

These shifts were most pronounced in the public sector, where reliance on net tuition and fee revenue increased by 10 percentage points in the master's and bachelor's degree-granting institutions and 5 to 7 percentage points in the two-year and doctoral institutions. These trends over the past decade reflect a longer-term shift in the financing of public postsecondary education, changing what was once a largely public entity to one that is increasingly financed by students themselves. Looking across all public institutions, in 1985 net tuition revenue as a percentage of public higher education total revenue was 23 percent. By fall 2010, that figure had increased to 40 percent. Moreover, in constant dollars, the amount students contributed to finance public postsecondary education through net tuition and fees increased 205 percent during the period, from 16.5 billion to 50.2 billion (SHEEO, 2011).

Meanwhile, net tuition revenue constitutes a much larger percentage of revenues for private non-profit colleges and universities than for public institutions. The bachelor's and master's degree-granting institutions derive nearly 95 percent of their revenue (excluding gift and investment income) from net tuition and fees, while the doctoral institutions are somewhat less dependent on net tuition revenue.

So if we assume colleges and universities will continue to be increasingly dependent on net tuition and fee revenue to finance operations, what are the prospects that students and families will be willing and able to pay an ever-increasing share of college costs?

It is well documented that college costs have risen faster than both family incomes and the consumer price index for at least the last 30 years. As Table 1-7 shows, the average annual percentage increase in *inflation-adjusted* published tuition and fee prices has increased in each of the past three decades. While price increases have slowed in the private college sector, especially during the past 10 years, they are accelerating in the four-year public sector as state support has contracted.

Table 1-7: Average Annual Percentage Increases in Inflation-adjusted Published Prices by Decade, 1981-82 Through 2011-12

Institution type	1981-82 to 1991-92	1991-92 to 2001-02	2001-02 to 2011-12
Private non-profit four-year	4.8%	3.1%	2.6%
Public four-year	4.5%	3.2%	5.6%
Public two-year	6.1%	0.5%	3.8%

Source: *Trends in College Pricing 2011*, page 13, Figure 4

However, published prices are a less meaningful figure than net tuition and fees, the amount that students actually pay after subtracting grant aid from all sources and federal education tax credits and deductions. As Table 1-8 shows, over the past 15 years, net prices have actually declined in the two-year public sector while increasing 30 percent in the public four-year sector and 22 percent in the four-year private sector. Remember, all figures are adjusted for inflation. It is also important to recognize that large increases in federal Pell Grants and veterans' benefits in 2009-10, combined with the 2009 implementation of the American Opportunity Tax Credit, had a significant impact on the net prices paid by students who benefit from these programs (College Board, 2011). In the case of tuition tax credits, it is debatable whether these funds truly impact student enrollment decisions because families experience these "savings" within the context of their individual tax return, not when they are initially evaluating college costs and financial aid offers.

Table 1-8: Net Tuition and Fees in Constant 2011 Dollars for Full-time Undergraduate Students: 1996-97, 2006-07, and 2011-12 (Estimated)

Institution type	1996-97	2006-07	2011-12
Private non-profit four-year	$10,630	$13,520	$12,970
Public four-year	$1,910	$1,330	$2,490
Public two-year	$510	$30	$-810

Source: *Trends in College Pricing 2011*, page 15, Figure 7

Nevertheless, these relatively modest increases in net tuition and fees have come at a price, especially in the four-year private sector where tuition discount rates have been on the rise. In fact, between fall 2000 and fall 2010, the average tuition discount rate increased from 37.3 percent to 42.4 percent for first-time, full-time freshmen while increasing from 33.6 percent to 37.1 percent for all undergraduate students (NACUBO, 2010). When more than 40 cents of every tuition dollar collected is returned in the form of institutional financial aid (and it is not uncommon for individual institutions to be above 50 cents on the dollar), we are clearly seeing price resistance manifested in the form of increased discounting.

Finally, student borrowing has also been on the rise over the last decade. About 56 percent of students who earned bachelor's degrees in 2009-10 from the public four-year colleges at which they began their studies graduated with debt. Average debt per borrower was $22,000, up from $19,800 (in 2010 dollars) a decade earlier. Meanwhile, about 65 percent of students who earned bachelor's degrees in 2009-10 from the private non-profit, four-year colleges at which they began their studies graduated with debt. Average debt per borrower was $28,100, up from $22,600 (in 2010 dollars) a decade earlier (College Board, 2011).

> " Given the federal budget deficit and very tight fiscal conditions in the states, the best-case scenario is probably static funding at the state and federal levels, and even that might be optimistic."

In my judgment, the next decade promises to be very challenging for colleges and universities as they attempt to help students manage net cost of attendance. The industry received some necessary relief in 2009 with increased Pell Grant funding and the American Opportunity Tax Credit, which expanded the number of families eligible for tuition tax credits. Moreover, federal stimulus funds provided some relief to public institutions that might otherwise have had to increase their tuition at an even faster rate. Given the federal budget deficit and very tight fiscal conditions in the states, the best-case scenario is probably static funding at the state and federal levels, and even that might be optimistic. What does this mean for strategic enrollment planners and students?

Four-year public institutions are likely to continue increasing tuition rates at well above inflationary levels, assuming policy makers do not constrain their ability to do so, as is happening in some states. This will require them to adopt financial models more akin to the private four-year sector, charging some families more so that they can provide adequate financial aid to families with lower incomes. Private institutions, which have already experienced erosion in net tuition and fee revenue, are likely to face a prolonged period of very modest growth in net tuition revenue, forcing them to make difficult choices regarding program offerings and the types of students they serve.

Community colleges continue to offer the most favorable financial proposition for students. This is unlikely to change in the years ahead, but they will also contend with contractions in state support, which may require them to curtail their enrollment levels.

It will be important to aggressively monitor student borrowing levels across sectors in the years ahead. According to the New York Federal Reserve, outstanding student loan debt now exceeds the outstanding debt on both credit cards and automobile loans. There is also growing evidence that students and their parents have reached the upper limits of their willingness to borrow to finance postsecondary education. A recent Pew Research study found that "a majority of Americans (57 percent) say the higher education system in the United States fails to provide students with good value for the money they and their families spend. An even larger majority (75 percent) say college is too expensive for most Americans to afford" (Pew Research Center, 2011).

> **" Despite decades of increased focus on student retention and completion, little progress has occurred in improving either retention or graduation rates."**

If we are indeed witnessing increased price resistance, this will further constrain institutions of all types from increasing tuition at the rates necessary to contend with stagnant or declining state and federal support. Finally, there is growing pressure at the federal level for institutions to slow the rate of growth in tuition and fees. In a 2011 speech, Education Secretary Arne Duncan pushed higher education officials to "think more creatively, and with much greater urgency, about how to contain the spiraling costs of college and reduce the burden of student debt on our nation's students" (*New York Times*, 2011).

This environment makes it imperative that enrollment planners understand how various segments of their student population pay for college and develop targeted financing strategies for these student populations in the years ahead. Indeed, it is far too common for colleges to raise tuition and fees in the context of their own internal cost pressures with little regard for how various student groups will finance those cost increases. Therefore, a central focus of SEP in the years ahead will be devising multiyear strategies to make certain that the target student markets have a viable means of managing their portion of college costs.

Growing pressure for improved retention and completion rates

Not only are we facing a difficult demographic and financing environment, the demand for public accountability is on the rise, especially in the form of improving college completion rates. The Obama Administration has a stated goal of increasing the percentage of young Americans with a college degree from 41 percent in 2009 to 60 percent by 2025. If successful, that would produce about eight million more college graduates than the two million that are currently projected through modest growth in college enrollments (U.S. Department of Education, 2011). Large foundations, such as Lumina and the Bill and Melinda Gates Foundation, have aligned themselves with the President's completion agenda and are investing tens of millions of dollars in programs aimed at helping to increase college access and attainment rates. State legislatures and higher education coordinating boards are also demanding increased completion rates from the institutions they fund and oversee. Dozens of states have announced plans to increase college attainment rates, and with that comes increased pressure on enrollment planners to develop viable strategies for reaching these goals.

The focus on increased college attainment has strong rationale. In a 2011 blog post, Dewayne Matthews, vice president for policy and strategy at Lumina, summarized the most recent data from the Organization for Economic Cooperation and Development (OECD) on international educational attainment. "Here are the highlights:

- The U.S. has slipped to 15 in the proportion of young adults (25 to 34) who have obtained a two- or four-year college degree. Last year, the U.S. was tied for eighth.

- The reason the U.S. attainment rate appeared to fall so dramatically is because the U.S. rate dropped by 1 percent (from 42 to 41 percent) while other countries increased. The U.S. also lost one position due to the addition of Israel to OECD this year.

- The top three countries are the same as last year: South Korea, Canada, and Japan. South Korea's attainment rate (age 25 to 34) increased by an astounding 5 percent, from 58 percent to 63 percent.

- For all adults (age 25 to 64), the U.S. ranks fourth at 41 percent, behind Canada, Israel, and Japan.

- In four-year degrees for young adults, the U.S. now ranks only 11. In 2010, we ranked seventh.

- At 9 percent, the U.S. ranks 20 (out of 33) in two-year degree attainment." (Matthews, 2011.)

On a macroeconomic level, if the United States wishes to remain competitive with the rest of the world, it cannot afford to have a workforce that is significantly less educated than other developed nations—hence the sharp focus on increasing attainment rates at the federal level. At the state level, we are likely to see increased accountability in the form of funding mechanisms that reward institutions on the basis of course and degree completions instead of enrollment levels, which have driven these formulas in the past. For example, the state of Tennessee recently adopted a funding formula for its public institutions that does not include student enrollment-level data at all. Rather, it focuses on student progression, degree production, efficiency, and other important institutional functions (Deaton, 2011).

At an institutional level, strategic enrollment planners will be motivated by more than just state and federal calls to improve completion rates, especially if they are in markets with flat or declining demographics. Indeed, if you are faced with a shrinking student market, one way to maintain existing enrollment levels is to increase student retention and graduation rates as a means of mitigating potential losses in new students. Unfortunately, this is no small task, but one that can be accomplished when data are used to create specific strategies.

Despite decades of increased focus on student retention and completion, little progress has occurred in improving either retention or graduation rates. Table 1-9 displays data from ACT on the retention rates of first-year students at four-year colleges from 1990 to 2010. Among all institutions, the first- to second-year retention rate has dropped from 74.8 percent to 72.9 percent with a slight improvement at public institutions and a decline at private institutions.

Table 1-9: Percentage of First-year Students at Four-year Colleges Who Return for a Second Year: 1990-2010 (in Five-year Increments)

Institution type	1990	1995	2000	2005	2010
Public institutions	71.4%	71.4%	72.1%	72.7%	73.9%
Private institutions	76.2%	74.8%	75.1%	75.3%	72.4%
All four-year institutions	74.8%	73.8%	74.2%	74.4%	72.9%

Source: *ACT 2010 Retention Completion Summary Tables*

Table 1-10 contains data on the five-year graduation rates among first-year students at four-year colleges by year. Among all institutions, just slightly over half (52.3 percent) of first-year students who begin at a four-year school graduate within five years.

Table 1-10: Percentage Four-year College Students Who Earn a Degree Within Five Years of Entry: 1990-2010 (in Five-year Increments)

Institution type	1990	1995	2000	2005	2010
Public institutions	47.9%	46.1%	41.9%	42.3%	43.4%
Private institutions	57.8%	57.5%	55.5%	57.4%	57.2%
All four-year institutions	54.9%	54.0%	51.2%	51.8%	52.3%

Source: *ACT 2010 Retention Completion Summary Tables*

While ACT does not provide year-to-year data on the two-year sector, they do report that, between 1983 and 2010, fewer than 6 in 10 students at two-year colleges returned for their second year. Moreover, after peaking in 1989 at 44 percent, the three-year graduation rate at two-year colleges had declined to 28 percent (ACT, 2010). Of course, this does not consider students who move on to a four-year college prior to completion of an associate's degree as a success, and more states are counting this as a successful two-year student. Nevertheless, it represents a significant attainment gap when fewer than one in three full-time, degree-seeking students at two-year schools successfully complete a degree within three years. This is especially troublesome given the Obama Administration's focus on the two-year sector for achieving its goal of America having the highest proportion of college graduates in the world by 2020.

Faced with pressure from state and federal governments to improve student success rates and the declining numbers of high school graduates in many regions of the country, strategic enrollment planners cannot afford to ignore the critical issues surrounding persistence, progression, retention, and completion in their work. In fact, it is likely that these issues will consume an increasing portion of the SEP agenda on most campuses, whereas, in the past, they have all too often taken a backseat to in-take strategies.

Changing learning modalities

The enrollment data in Table 1-11 should come as no surprise to anyone in higher education. The modalities for learning are changing and are providing both an opportunity and a challenge. The growth in undergraduate online learning has been substantial over the past decade. As recently as fall 2002, less than 10 percent of all students were taking at least one online course. By fall 2011, that figure had increased to 31 percent, with more than six million students taking at least one online course. However, it is interesting to note the dramatic disparity between the growth rates in online learning and the growth rates in total enrollment. Between fall 2003 and fall 2010, the mean annual growth rate in online learning approached 19 percent, whereas the mean annual growth rate in total enrollment was just over 2 percent. This suggests a growing student preference for online courses, but it also underscores the limitations of online learning in developing new student markets.

Noel-Levitz recently worked with a group of institutions that had placed a lot of emphasis on building their online delivery capacity as part of their effort to reverse a multiyear enrollment decline. However, as their online enrollments grew, they were experiencing commensurate declines in their other learning modalities. Therefore, as strategic enrollment planners consider the role and scope of online learning in crafting their academic strategy, they should bear in mind that, unless an online program represents an entirely new academic program or is targeted to an entirely new student market, the potential to cannibalize existing enrollments is high.

Table 1-11: Total and Online Enrollment in Degree-granting Postsecondary Institutions: Fall 2002-Fall 2010

Year	Total enrollment	Annual growth rate total enrollment	Students taking at least one online course	Online enrollment increase over previous year	Annual growth rate online enrollment	Online enrollment as a percent of total enrollment
Fall 2002	16,611,710	NA	1,602,970	NA	NA	9.6%
Fall 2003	16,911,481	1.8%	1,971,397	368,427	23.0%	11.7%
Fall 2004	17,272,043	2.1%	2,329,783	358,386	18.2%	13.5%
Fall 2005	17,487,481	1.2%	3,180,050	850,267	36.5%	18.2%
Fall 2006	17,758,872	1.6%	3,488,381	308,331	9.7%	19.6%
Fall 2007	18,248,133	2.8%	3,938,111	449,730	12.9%	21.6%
Fall 2008	19,102,811	4.7%	4,606,353	668,242	16.9%	24.1%
Fall 2009	19,524,750	2.2%	5,579,022	972,669	21.1%	28.6%
Fall 2010	19,641,140	0.6%	6,142,280	563,258	10.1%	31.3%

Source: *Going the Distance: Online Education in the United States*, 2011, page 11

There are also significant gaps between attitudes and implementation of online learning by institutional type. For example, in its survey of campus leaders, the 2011 study *Going the Distance* found that, while two out of three reported that "Online education is critical to the long-term strategy of my institution," the percentage that had distance education in their strategic plans was 60 percent for private for-profit providers, 48 percent for publicly controlled institutions, and 35 percent for private non-profit institutions (Allen and Seaman, 2011). This suggests a fairly significant gap between perceived importance of online learning and what is actually making it into institutional strategic plans.

It is also clear that faculty skepticism regarding online learning remains a problem. In fact, only about one-third of the survey respondents in the *Going the Distance* study reported that, "Faculty at my school accepts the value and legitimacy of online education." This percentage was 21 percent at private non-profits, 36 percent at public institutions, and 49 percent at private for-profit providers, and these percentages have not changed significantly over the past decade (Allen and Seaman, 2011).

Finally, any discussion of online learning would be incomplete without commentary on student satisfaction and retention. Unfortunately, we still lack normative national data on the retention and graduation rates of students in online courses. Since retention and completion rates are tracked by student cohort, and many students take a mixture of online and face-to-face, or hybrid, courses, there is simply no reliable source of data on student success rates in online courses. The lack of national normative data makes it even more important that strategic enrollment planners evaluate student success metrics in their own online courses compared to students enrolled in more traditional course delivery formats.

The Noel-Levitz Priority Survey for Online Learners™ (PSOL) provides some insight into the satisfaction of online learners and suggests areas that represent challenges to institutions offering online course work (Noel-Levitz, 2011). In our *2011 National Online Learners Priorities Report*, we identified both the strengths and challenges for online learners as a whole. Strengths were defined as those items ranked above the mid-point in student importance and in the top quartile of satisfaction. The following strengths were identified by online learners as a whole (in order of importance):

- Registration for online courses is convenient.
- Instructional materials are appropriate for program content.
- Billing and payment procedures are convenient for me.
- Adequate online library resources are provided.

Challenges were areas ranked above the mid-point in importance and in the bottom quartile of satisfaction—in other words, the top quartile of performance gaps. Listed in order of importance, the following were the top challenges identified by online learners as a whole:

- Student assignments are clearly defined in the syllabus.
- The quality of instruction is excellent.
- Faculty are responsive to student needs.
- Tuition paid is a worthwhile investment.
- Faculty provide timely feedback about students progress.

These high-level findings suggest that schools have done a good job of perfecting the transactional aspects of online learning such as registration, billing, and making instructional resources available to online learners. On the other hand, students are expressing dissatisfaction with some important parts of the actual learning experience, including instructional quality, faculty responsiveness, and the overall value received for tuition paid. These are significant issues that should be addressed in any SEP process, especially for schools that are exploring significant expansion of their online offerings.

Conclusion

In this chapter, I have outlined some of the major trends impacting higher education. They can be summarized as follows.

- Enrollment growth is projected to slow over the next decade. This means institutions that have previously relied on enrollment growth to fund campus improvements and academic and co-curricular program expansion may have to adapt their thinking based on likely student demand in their primary student catchment areas.

- Demographic shifts will lead to regional variations in enrollment levels and ongoing challenges in student preparation and ability to pay for college. The traditional student cohort is becoming more ethnically diverse, less able to pay for college, and less prepared for the rigors of postsecondary education. These trends need to be localized and strategies developed to respond to the needs of future students. Schools should also develop programs to serve the needs of students in their 20s and 30s. These students fueled enrollment growth over the past decade and will have needs for graduate education as well as continuing education in the years ahead.

- The traditional economic model for both public and private institutions is changing rapidly. Public institutions will become increasingly reliant on net tuition and fee revenue and the privates will have to contend with slower growth in net tuition revenue than they are accustomed. This environment makes it imperative that enrollment planners understand how various segments of their student population pay for college and develop financing strategies for these student populations in the years ahead.

- Pressure to improve retention and completion rates will intensify. For some institutions, this will represent an economic imperative based on the demographics of their primary student markets. For others, the pressure will come from legislatures and higher education coordinating boards discontent with the lack of meaningful progress in improving student success rates over the past several decades.

- Online learning will offer both opportunity and challenge. Schools that learn to harness online technology to develop new academic programs and open new markets will prosper. Those that simply shift students from one learning modality to another may see their cost structures increase as they attempt to maintain multiple delivery systems without any significant increase in enrollment and net tuition revenue.

As the United States and other developed nations struggle to emerge from the worst economic downturn since the Great Depression, perhaps our colleges and universities will deal with the challenges outlined above and emerge stronger than ever; or maybe these structural economic and demographic changes will lead to a fundamental transformation of our postsecondary system. In either case, institutions that engage in meaningful strategic enrollment planning and shift institutional thinking from annual planning to strategic enrollment management with a longer-range (three- to five-year minimum) focus will have the best chance of thriving in this environment. Those that rely on traditional planning models, with their inherently inward focus, are likely to fall victim to the market forces described above.

I hope this chapter both motivates your campus to engage in an SEP process and provides some initial guidance about the environmental data you should be collecting in the first phase of that process. In closing, it is well to heed the admonition of the 19th-century English essayist and reformer John Ruskin: "What we think, or what we know, or what we believe is, in the end, of little consequence. The only consequence is what we do."

CHAPTER 2

Strategic Enrollment Planning Coalition Building: A Trustful Mediation

By Douglas Christiansen and Thomas Golden

Chapter highlights

- **Essential need to build trust**

- **Importance of alignment to mission**

- **The college/ university as an ecosystem**

Every autumn, in a time-honored tradition, faculty across thousands of university and college campuses will watch a new class of students join the college ranks. However, today's class is notably different from those of the past. It is the most ethnically diverse, most economically challenged, and most technologically engaged of any generation of college attendees in history (Pryor et al., 2011). Yet, in many respects, it is also perhaps the least prepared for an economy that will challenge it in ways no other generation has experienced (see Babcock and Marks, 2010; Bowman, 2010; or Prensky, 2002). While the incoming class indeed differs from its predecessors, soon these students will join an epistemic tradition inherited not just from recent generations, but from medieval Europe. According to David Bleich, (2008), "In its identity as a group of 'masters and scholars,' in its curriculum, and in its structure of faculties, the institutional identity of the university has remained stable over eight centuries."

As outlined in Chapter 1, outside the college or university, the rumble for accountability and reform amplifies the pressures of increased public management, globalization, and market positioning (differentiate or perish) already felt by senior leaders inside higher education. Ironically, college freshmen and college presidents both find themselves in the tenuous position of having to do much more with much less. Presidents face the demand to broaden college access while public and private funding narrows and students confront their own mounting expectations to achieve, precisely when the hours spent studying in high school have dropped to their lowest point in 30 years (Pryor et al., 2010; Babcock and Marks, 2010). In each case, a failure to "do more" will have significant repercussions for our national trajectory and that of our nation's students.

A recent report by the Lumina Foundation (2010) found that the growth of the American economy is driven less by "home runs (such as securing a new manufacturing plant)" than it is by expanding the knowledge and skills of the American work force. For the newest generation of first-year students, the strain of doing more with fewer resources to support enrollment in higher education has taken its toll. Debt continues to increase and access and affordability are raising more alarms.

Genghis Khan and permanent whitewater

While the university has undergone profound organizational changes since World War II, the inner culture of academia remains unchanged in its faith in autonomy, collegial democracy, and intellectual freedom (Mora, 2001). Indeed, the aforementioned societal characteristics and challenges are often complex and novel in nature, while our nation's universities are all but novel and innovative. Inside the professional confines of higher education, scholarship and mastership advance steadily within an autonomous hierarchy developed in the same era as the signing of the Magna Carta and the rise of Genghis Khan. The Carnegie Foundation for the Advancement of Teaching recently confirmed this in a detailed report proposing sweeping policy and pedagogical changes to a medical school and residency curriculum that has not substantially changed in more than a century (Cooke, Irby, and O'Brien, 2010).

Einstein reportedly remarked, "We cannot solve our problems with the same thinking we used when we created them." Similarly, the ability of the college/university to meet current challenges will depend largely on the ability of campus leaders to partner and collaborate in unprecedented ways, particularly with respect to enrollment, revenue, and curriculum delivery. This chapter will review old and new thinking on how partnerships are forged through the strategic enrollment planning (SEP) process, not only on a structural level, but also, and perhaps more importantly, on a personal and emotional level. Based on our research findings and professional experience, it is our assertion that, without a culture of trust, the collaborative synergy that is the core of effective SEP cannot occur, rendering even well-resourced strategies incapable of generating meaningful and lasting change. Through our work, we have often found that the planning process is more important than the plan itself. The process is the place where trust is built and the community sees how enrollment management aligns with institutional mission, vision, and a desired future state grounded in institutional values.

Higher education's troubles may be new and evolving; however, the fact that higher education has formidable challenges is nothing new. Indeed, Kent Farnsworth, former president of Crowder College, aptly refers to the seemingly perpetual vulnerability of the American academy as "permanent whitewater" (2007).

Even so, within the American public there exists a rising chorus of unprecedented questioning of higher education's value, motives, and good faith. Most recently, such a refrain echoed in a National Center for Public Policy and Higher Education study in which 60 percent of those surveyed indicated that colleges today are more like businesses and "care mainly about the bottom line" (Immerwahr, Johnson, Ott, and Rochkind, 2010).

Indeed, the financial viability of an institution has dramatic impacts on its ability to implement strategic initiatives. Our purpose here is not to chronicle the challenges facing higher education today, but rather to note that these obstacles are complex and evolving and, thus, will require an equally comprehensive and determined response. While the college/university tradition of autonomy and academic freedom must be upheld in research labs and classrooms, a new convention of interdependent synergy, trust, and collaboration must take root in higher education if it is to meet these profound challenges. In part, it is this belief that is the foundation for SEP.

> " *[The academy is] always in a state of crisis in someone's mind, making it all the more difficult to assess when the condition actually exists, and even more difficult to convince others of that condition once present.*"
> **Kent Farnsworth**

The case for connectivity and alignment

SEP is the alignment of an institution's strategic planning core with the collective mission, vision, and values of the college/university with the intent of generating meaningful collaboration to achieve common goals and integrated strategies. It is tempting for the casual observer to compartmentalize the influence of a well-functioning SEP enterprise within an institution in spheres surrounding the student application and enrollment processes. In fact, the fully realized SEP engages the entire mission, vision, and values of an institution in aligning academic and co-curricular programming with the student life cycle from initial interest through completion. Figure 2-1 illustrates the central role of the institutional mission, as well as the interconnectedness of the SEP on every level of college/university management.

Figure 2-1: The Interconnectivity of Effective SEP Planning

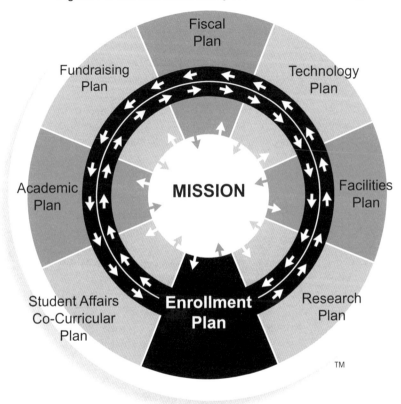

This level of interconnectedness ensures each functional unit is integrated so the academic, co-curricular, and enrollment plans, in effect, become a unified whole. For example, a community college might establish a mission of outreach to a local neighborhood with a large Kurdish immigrant population. If only embraced by the admissions staff, a few local open houses and community events may take place, but the resulting outreach has minimal effectiveness. However, if also embraced by the foreign language department as part of its educational mission, native speakers from the department may begin educational programming in the community while the alumni office engages young alumni from that neighborhood to host campus tours.

In an authentic sense, a well-crafted SEP process answers *who* we educate, while the academic plan establishes *how* we will educate them, and the co-curricular plan seeks to link together an expanded community experience. The bottom line is that these three concepts (SEP, academic plan, and co-curricular plan) are interrelated and must be viewed in this manner to realize the educational goals of the institution. While answers to these questions form the essence of an organization's purpose and are at the center of mission-driven SEP effectiveness, they are only part of a complex process of interdependent SEP leadership. In order to foster innovative collaboration, the bond felt by a campus community to the academic mission of the institution must extend beyond the surface to provide engagement at a deeper, human level.

The structuralist focus

Much of the literature on how to generate campuswide collaboration focuses on identifying and constructing the optimal institutional structure and the strategic planning practices necessary to ensure the sustainability and success of that structure (Henderson, 2005). From the original conception of enrollment management, the fulcrum of success hinged on a structure that would generate synergy among college/university enrollment functions such as admissions, financial aid, and retention programming (Henderson, 2005). Today's chief enrollment officer leads an immensely sophisticated network: steering committees of high-level administrators and deans; planning groups with enrollment management directors; marketing task forces; retention roundtables; and a range of formal and informal partnerships with external constituents, alumni, parents, and students. The current state of shared governance seeks to draw in key campus voices to the enrollment management process, thus requiring their "skin in the game," which moves them toward mutual accountability. As described by Henderson, this "structuralist" viewpoint, with its focus on which office should report to which division of the college/university, falls short of the need for a comprehensive solution to our challenges for two primary reasons.

First the organizational structure it seeks to address is that of a highly decentralized and comparatively non-hierarchical academic institution. In contrast to officers of a corporation, the military, or other government agency, university faculty and administrators have considerable leeway in the pursuit of their work (Tierney, 2006). In this environment, assigning a tenure-track assistant professor to an enrollment management task force may heighten his/her awareness of the enrollment process, but may not cause him/her to feel responsible for that process or its outcomes. Dolence, Rowley, and Lujan (1997) propose four hierarchical levels of strategic enrollment management (SEM)—considered the theoretical predecessor of SEP. These levels begin with a nominal level (the identification of a need for SEM), advance to a structural level (the identification of an appropriate SEM structure), proceed to a tactical level (the identification of proper implementation actions), and finally reach a strategic level (the integration of SEM with the deeper values and mission of the university) (Dolence et al., 1997).

The power and autonomy granted to academic deans, lay trustees, and faculty within the academy make the advancement of a true college/universitywide enrollment planning process very difficult beyond Dolence's nominal level. In other words, it may be relatively easy for a college/university community to coalesce around a need for enrollment planning, but actually doing it is another matter. For example, an academic dean may readily admit that her institution needs a better enrollment structure, but may concurrently draw the line at allocating a percentage of her top professor's time for a student recruitment council (structural level). This same dean may balk at the notion of eliminating a long-standing yet low-enrolling major within her college while simultaneously acknowledging the need for calibrating offerings to prospective student demand (tactical level). Finally, this same dean may protest the promotion of graduation and job placement rates to prospective students, as these may appear to discount the pure undergraduate educational mission of the university/college (strategic level).

The second drawback of a structure-centric solution to enrollment management lies in the fact that an institution is, above all, composed of human beings. No doubt, anyone reading this can recall an instance in which individuals within an organization resisted meaningful collaboration despite a structural imperative to do so. Why is this? Human behavior is complicated, especially when considered in the context of a complex and decentralized organization like a college or university. The human mind utilizes a plethora of mental shortcuts, biases, attributions, and emotional associations to sort through the wilderness of information it must process in the span of a day (Moskowitz, 2004). A study by the University of California at Berkeley estimates that approximately 18 exabytes (that's with 15 zeros) of new electronic information is generated each year—the equivalent of three times the data storage needed to record and store all the words ever spoken on earth over the entire history of mankind (Lyman and Varian, 2003). This condition of perpetual "cognitive busyness" forces a compartmentalizing of a person's mental resources, focusing mostly on matters perceived to be the most threatening and immediate (Moskowitz, 2004).

" While the SEP process does not answer all questions, it does force key institutional leaders to think beyond silos."

Within the context of a highly complex institution where an employee's experience is itself largely compartmentalized, individuals readily accept that they simply cannot know every piece of relevant information about the organization. Staff and faculty, even at the middle and senior levels, perpetually operate with incomplete knowledge of the scope and depth of the broader organization. Therefore, it is not surprising that these staff members do not readily or frequently consider their daily actions as interdependently linked to the greater mission of their college/university, a basic condition of SEP. Psychologists and researchers Bolton and English (2010) refer to this phenomenon as "bounded rationality," in which a person operates in an environment of great uncertainty over the full consequences of his or her decisions. In other words, no one person has the complete picture or the full set of answers.

While the SEP process does not answer all questions, it does force key institutional leaders to think beyond silos. At its best, the SEP process moves institutional leaders to seek ways to actively engage and connect efforts focused on the student in order to promote a learning-based experience with measurable outcomes. The goal of this process is to align enrollment efforts with other key institutional priorities and to interlink academic and co-curricular offerings with future enrollment trends and demands.

The university as an ecosystem

Current psychological research on effective collaboration and partnership identifies a mutual condition in which individuals feel comfortable acknowledging that they do not know it all, cannot know it all, and must establish trust to advance a common cause. Such an acknowledgement inherently involves risk-taking. The decision to trust, which research shows is a vital precondition for effective collaboration, is intricately related to the assessment of risk. As examples:

1. A director of admissions must first acknowledge that he may not have the capacity to evaluate the effectiveness of an on-campus open house program before he can engage the institutional research group.

2. A director of housing can more effectively tackle the challenge of integrating first-year students into campus life when she compares notes on resident assistant training programs with the campus orientation director or a first-year experience coordinator.

3. The ability for an assistant dean of college advising to ensure better counseling to undergraduates is facilitated by the dean of admissions granting access to the previously guarded admissions decision notes.

In each vignette, the ability for one campus leader to enhance service to stakeholders requires banking on the belief that, not only will another individual reciprocate in good faith, but also that they will not act out of ill will (Baier, 1995).

Classic psychological theories observe that human behavior can best be understood through an understanding of both the individual and the situation in which the individual operates (Ichheiser, 1949). We turn to these two analytical storylines to illustrate how the SEP process can support and enhance relationships within a university system through the medium of interpersonal trust. In doing so, our hope is to conceptualize SEP as a person-centered collaboration that must align with how people think and how a college/university operates.

In our analysis of trust as a mediator for campuswide collaboration, the task of identifying situational factors, as described by Ichheiser, is daunting and generally outside the scope of this chapter. Higher education has hundreds of organizational variations and thousands of unique dynamics that administrators must navigate. At its most essential level, however, a college or university is a type of ecosystem in which interconnected, yet autonomous, individuals operate under a similar set of conditions and shared resources (Bertalanffy, 1969). Within the institutional context, the application of an ecosystem paradigm has been termed "systems theory" as a means of understanding the constant interplay between units and resources. To illustrate this ecosystem analogy, consider the following fictitious case study.

A mid-sized public university welcomes a new director of undergraduate financial aid in April. Founded as the state's land-grant institution, the university consists of four undergraduate colleges, the most popular being the engineering college, which is nationally ranked and well regarded by alumni and industry employers. While the engineering college continues to see record applications and enrollment growth, the remaining undergraduate colleges (education, liberal arts and sciences, and agriculture) have struggled to meet enrollment goals. The university utilizes a central funding structure in which the university provost allocates resources according to a defined formula, factoring in each college's instructional hours and FTE enrollment as well as a percentage of external funding secured by the college. Undergraduate merit scholarships are awarded by committees within each college and administered by the financial aid office. Public criticism of the university has been intensely focused on the university's rising tuition and fees, a necessary reaction to the now five-year trend of declining state funding. Internal criticism from various board of trustees members centers on the sliding academic reputation of the university and the perception that top students in the state are selecting a peer university.

Several months into her role as director of financial aid, Jan has become accustomed to the culture of this new university. The financial aid office is located on the ground floor of the central administration building, and the staff unceremoniously refer to it as "the basement." The staff include many long-time employees, and the previous director recently retired after 28 years at the institution. Three years prior to Jan's arrival, the university had moved the office to its current location to be closer to the new vice president of enrollment management and the newly created enrollment management (EM) division. Even though Jan has met several times per month with fellow directors from admissions, the registrar's office, university research, and retention programs, she senses that relationships among the offices, and even among her and the other directors, are tepid. Stories and rumors abound about the bad blood between the EM directors and the former director of financial aid. The rest of the financial aid staff would often lament about being in the dark regarding most matters of substance in EM.

From a system point of view, we can begin to understand this case study on two levels: the university as a whole and the EM division as a sub-system. The university as a whole is struggling to meet its goals and, more importantly, its obligations to fully serve the people of the state vis-à-vis its mission as a land-grant university. While the university does have an EM structure in place, the enrollment success the university has experienced has been compartmentalized, compounded by a funding structure that promotes competition (for students and external funding), which benefits engineering. From a system point of view, this could be characterized as a sub-optimization in which one or more elements of the university atrophies while another experiences over-investment.

The university has a clearly defined mission and values, but it is unclear whether the broader university system has a vision shared by all stakeholders concerned with the needs of those the university serves. Within the EM division, the system has all of the pieces of interconnectivity. EM leadership members are meeting, setting strategy, arranging tactics, and getting plenty of face time. Roles are defined and communicated and areas of collaboration are discussed. So why isn't it working? In effect, these positive system dynamics merely set in place the conditions for collaboration and trust to occur, but leading the proverbial horse to water doesn't necessarily make it drink.

The turning point for Jan (and for the entire university) comes in a moment of desperation. Faced with a deadline from the vice president to develop a strategy for integrating the disparate elements of the university's merit scholarship program, Jan reaches out to the director of university research for assistance with a data point. In the course of the conversation, Jan discovers that university research had conducted a study projecting the positive outcomes that could result from unifying the merit scholarship portfolio, only to see it sit on the shelf of the former director of financial aid. Jan suggests the director of university research resurrect the study and serve as the project chair for the scholarship proposal, admitting that she doesn't know the data like the director of research does. In this simple exchange, Jan demonstrates authentic leadership and accomplishes more than any organizational chart could by simply issuing a signal of trust to her colleague.

" Without trust, this collaboration is nearly impossible, as relationships begin to break down and resources (both physical and emotional) become commodities to be hoarded."

The presence of a system, even one of magnificent design, does not ensure a healthy campuswide partnership. When goals intersect with shared resources (and often, shared sacrifice), which then interface with unpredictable human emotions, another side of a university system becomes visible. Samier (2010) noted, "Social action is enabled by trust, especially during change and reform processes," which we have observed in this case study. Jan's conversation with her colleague rewrote an organizational script and generated genuine goodwill. "Social action" and collaboration results in the best work from the division as partnerships are forged, collaboration flourishes, and individuals truly start exchanging their talents and gifts with each other. Without trust, this collaboration is nearly impossible—relationships begin to break down and resources (both physical and emotional) become commodities to be hoarded. One might argue that the EM division's strategy to unify the merit scholarship portfolio is a critical step toward accomplishing the university's goals. However, neuroeconomist Paul Zak would likely suggest that the most important step in the entire change process was Jan's simple outward display of trust, by seeking and truly listening to the voices around the division.

Neuroeconomics and the trust molecule

Paul Zak is a professor of economics and the founding director of the Center for Neuroeconomics Studies at Claremont Graduate University. His team's research aids our understanding of why Jan's leadership proved to be so effective. In 2004, Zak and his colleagues found clinical evidence linking the human decision to trust with the body's release of the hormone oxytocin, or the "trust molecule," as he termed it in a recent TED Talk (2011). It appears that the measurement of the brain's release of oxytocin holds the key for understanding the true nature of how trust is developed and exchanged between two people.

Oxytocin is a neuropeptide found only in mammals that has, for many years, been identified in animal research as related to nurturing and other caregiving behavior. Zak and his colleagues were able to measure oxytocin levels before and after an experimental economics game in which a participant (Subject A) was provided $10 for his or her participation in the study (Zak, Kurzban, and Matzner, 2004). Subject A was randomly assigned to another study participant (Subject B) and the two were never to see each other or interact. Subject A was asked to choose how much of his or her $10 (including $0) to send to the unknown partner under the condition that any amount selected would be tripled. If Subject B received any money from Subject A, then Subject B would be asked to choose how much of that money he or she wished to send back to Subject A (again with the available option of sending $0). Zak et al. measured pre- and post-game levels of oxytocin, theorizing that the initial amount sent from Subject A was a "trust signal" in that the participant had to "sacrifice to signal the degree of trust in the other before the other's behavioral response is known" (2004). The amount of money sent back from Subject B was theorized as a measure of trustworthiness (i.e., a kind of "thanks for trusting me" message from Subject B).

What Zak et al. found "flummoxed" economists, who questioned, "why the second person would ever return any money…they assumed that 'money was good, why not keep it all?'" (Zak, 2011). In fact, the study found the opposite effect. Ninety percent of Subject A participants sent money, and 95 percent of Subject B participants who received money sent some back (Zak, 2011). Interestingly, Zak and his colleagues observed a doubling of oxytocin levels in Subject Bs who received money (the signal that Subject A trusted them). In other words, when people receive a trust signal, their brains feel a rush of generosity from the release of oxytocin, a chemical known to promote feelings of altruism, well-being, and nurturing toward others. Motivated by that energy kick, recipients of that trust signal were much more willing to give back some of their treasure.

Effective SEP promotes the inclusion of all campus voices in the planning process because of the assumption that, in doing so, it empowers those individuals to bestow their emotional treasure— their passion—to the organization. Within the context of enrollment management, we notice many instances where collaboration is hindered by an unwillingness to exchange physical, technological, informational, or emotional assets, whether that takes the form of the vice president of information technology hoarding database access for fear of misinterpretation of information or recruitment coordinators from two colleges at the same university quietly denigrating each other to a prospective undergraduate. Recalling our case study, Zak and his colleagues explain the neurological foundation for why Jan's conversation with her colleague was so critical to the open sharing of professional gifts. The exchange of goodwill in the form of respect, openness, and honest communication likely led directly to a return exchange of pro-social behavior from the recipient. In the place of monetary exchange, however, the colleague gave his own unique gifts and talents, including the report and data supporting the benefits of a collaborative merit scholarship portfolio.

The mechanics of personal trust are measured in the often subtle willingness of others to engage in "a relationship that involves being vulnerable to another person" (Chhuon, Gilkey, Gonzalez, Daly, and Chrispeels, 2008). This is often easier said than done. In practice, the cost of personal trust and collaboration within a college/university inherently involves risk and vulnerability on the part of the leader. For example, in order to provide her signal of trust, Jan essentially admitted she did not possess all of the solutions to her division's problems. For many leaders, this appearance of vulnerability in their perceived competence is simply too great to risk. Zak et al. found a contradiction between competence and vulnerability. Many institutional leaders desire to avoid the appearance of incompetence among the very peers and subordinates with whom they wish to collaborate. The mutual need for and avoidance of vulnerability may very well hold the key to how even well-structured SEP processes can fail to synergize a team or university. It seems the basis for growth in relationships is the natural exchange of social resources and energy between two people, just as the basis for growth in a plant is the natural exchange of sun and water.

Figure 2-2: Synergy Among Campus Outcomes

The SEP process is a place where active collaboration, debate, and trust-building can occur through the analysis and understanding of institutional data compared to peer or aspirational data. Through the data collection and analysis process, the SEP planning team should be allowed to openly question data, as in our case study, and seek to better understand the implications of data and its overall effect on the institution. This analysis opens conversations, asks more questions, and seeks to build an understanding among planning members. Ultimately, the hope is that this process will also build the type of trust described in the case study.

The flywheel and stubborn symbiosis

Given the profound external challenges universities face, transformational SEP leaders must not only master the strategic and organizational framework of the organization, but also establish patterns that bring out the deep talents and gifts of the people within that organization. In the case study, we illustrated how success can emanate from a single interaction between colleagues. How then can we leverage this knowledge of human behavior into a consistent pattern of interaction? How can SEP establish a culture of trust?

A useful management construct that may apply here is the "flywheel," explained by management researcher and author Jim Collins in his executive leadership book, *Good to Great: Why Some Companies Make the Leap and Others Don't* (2001). Collins noted that effective organizations foster a culture of deliberate, consistent action toward a common goal. To illustrate this point, Collins uses the metaphor of a flywheel, "a massive metal disk mounted horizontally on an axle, about 30 feet in diameter, 2 feet thick, and weighing about 5,000 pounds" (Collins, 2001). Members of the organization attempt to rotate the disk, yet the weight of the wheel makes the initial pushing almost backbreaking. Finally, the wheel moves an inch, then two, then a quarter turn, and then, with considerable and sustained force, the wheel finally makes a full rotation. At this point, the momentum of the massive disk begins to compound the efforts, making the pushing no less sustained, but less intense with each and every push. Eventually, the wheel is humming.

> " Depending on an institution's history and experience with enrollment management, the path toward trustful collaboration may take many years."

This is the kind of disciplined culture that SEP represents and facilitates as long as trust and interdependence are fostered with the ongoing intentionality Collins describes. Chapters 3 and 4 of this book will describe the key step of building and creating lasting trust by employing an SEP model that brings the planning process to life. While many variables may differ by institutional type and governance structure, the initial movement in a truly collaborative SEP process is usually imperceptible and agonizing for all those leaning into that wheel of change. Depending on an institution's history and experience with enrollment management, the path toward trustful collaboration may take many years. In our case study, Jan's signal of trust will fade into the background of daily work, and only through steady and purposeful interactions with her colleagues can the institutional script be gradually rewritten. This is the behavior required to ensure effectiveness.

As various stakeholders and university divisions battle to avoid vulnerability and maintain control—both perceived and real—the effort needed to move the enormous disk may be prolonged. However, if we recall the profound and ever-present "whitewater" that surrounds the work of a higher education professional, then we must be equally stubborn in our insistence on a symbiotic solution to the challenges faced by the academy and, indeed, by higher education collectively.

The establishment of trust-based SEP collaboration is an important goal; however, it is not the end goal. SEP advocates for the accomplishment of sustainable success through a highly collaborative, long-term process allowing a college/university to thrive in a multitude of market conditions. A pattern thus emerges from the combined campus interactions—a type of upward spiral of increasing mutual faith, in which the level of positive empathy and cooperation grows. As the collaborative process grows, the loops decrease in circumference as the trusting process becomes easier and easier with each rotation. Research and experience consistently confirm that educational organizations featuring higher levels of trust are able to instill an ongoing confidence that the institution will act "reliably and competently" (Bryk and Schneider, 2003, as quoted in Schmidt, 2010). Trust reduces inner complexity, as individuals engage in repeated interactions where what was expected to happen has come to pass (Lane, 1998).

Conclusion

As students graduate from our institutions, they pass along unique perspectives, tenacity, and creativity to society as a whole. Those who make it to graduation are the fortunate ones, and while we cannot assure them of success, we can be certain of the existence of the thousands who do not make it to this milestone and of the struggles that likely await them. Stephen Jay Gould noted, "I am somehow less concerned with… Einstein's brain than I am with the near certainty that people of equal talent lived and died in cotton fields and sweatshops" (as quoted in College Board, 2007). While the traditions of the university/college hold steadfast, the role that the university is being asked to serve is rapidly evolving. Modern higher education, once a credentialing entity of the wealthy elite, now must pivot to serve those who would have "lived and died" without contributing their gifts to the world. To do so, higher education must find a way to mediate the nexus of the autonomous environment of the academy with a commitment to collective organizational action. This coming together to form partnerships in a setting where participation is not mandatory can only occur through an active choice to trust and an ongoing commitment to trustworthiness. No matter how well-positioned or strategy-aligned an organization may be, without trust, authentic collaboration is not possible.

The generative promise of SEP lies in the belief that success will be achieved if a university can assemble the right people, put them in the right places at the right times, and provide them with the right resources and vision. Inherent in this process of university advancement is the active interchange of resources, the unfettered flow of insight and information, and the sharing of human talents and gifts. We have contended and provided evidence supporting the premise that such exchanges cannot occur without a foundation of mutual trust. Unlike other worldly endeavors in which the lone genius can create greatness, the entire notion of SEP depends on groups of people collaborating in historic ways to confront unprecedented national challenges.

It is true that universities are traditional enterprises, embodying a centuries-old way of life. However, perhaps the greatest of these traditions is the enduring capacity of institutions to bring together the brilliance of diverse people and make it possible for them to realize and unleash their awesome creativity. The hopeful generation at the gates will rely on the trustful mediation between the forbidding currents moving against them and the unfailing promise of our values. For centuries, learners have signaled their trust in our institutions of higher learning, and now, perhaps more than ever, we must demonstrate our trustworthiness.

Dialogue

The path toward a collaborative SEP process requires the use of data and an understanding that resources need to be allocated (or reallocated) to ensure the plan is implemented. The notion of building trust throughout the process is essential as resources are exchanged for expected outcomes. What follows is a collection of questions and actions to initiate a conversation both within small leadership groups and among a broader campus audience.

- Who are the stakeholders related to SEP and SEM on your campus? For each individual, indicate why he or she holds such influence. In the effort to adopt a pattern of a trustful exchange, you must begin with identifying partners. For each individual or group, honestly assess whether you have issued a significant signal of trust that they would find meaningful.

- What voices are currently not being heard at your institution in relation to enrollment success? What could you do in the next 30 days to promote their inclusion?

- Are there any instances in your interactions where the exchange of resources (either physical or emotional) is hindered by your unwillingness to give up control or otherwise become vulnerable?

As you start the planning process, it is imperative that institutional leaders have a clear understanding of the need to build trust and community through this process. For reasons described in Chapter 1, as the campus launches the SEP process, these leaders must advocate linking the process with the larger institutional mission and vision to ensure a future where enrollment is not seen as a number, but as a way to recruit and graduate the best students aligned with institutional fit, values, cultures, and the realities of a current and future state based on internal and external data. Within this context, institutional leaders must understand and communicate the importance of transparency and trust as key institutional norms for a vibrant future state.

CHAPTER 3

Building a Culture of Strategic Enrollment Management

By Jim Hundrieser

Why is effective strategic planning so rare on campuses?

In *The Chronicle of Higher Education* in 2011, Benjamin Ginsberg, professor at John Hopkins University and author of *The Fall of the Faculty: The Rise of the All-Administrative University and Why It Matters*, stated that faculty members often view the strategic plan as "neither strategic nor a plan, but a waste of time" (Ginsberg, 2011). In a survey of enrollment managers conducted by Noel-Levitz, less than half of respondents said their institutions had a multiyear strategic enrollment plan (SEP) they would consider of good or excellent quality. One-third said they didn't have any such plan at all (Noel-Levitz, 2011).

Many institutions make student enrollment and its relevant metrics a top priority. The metrics include such things as total enrollment numbers, academic profiles, diversity profile numbers, student success measures such as retention and graduation rates, and many others. These metrics are discussed at board meetings, presidential cabinet meetings, deans' meetings, faculty meetings, and with the media. In fact, these enrollment metrics define each institution—its reputation, its learning environment, its culture, and its fiscal health.

Given this importance, most institutions should have well-conceived, multiyear strategic enrollment plans to optimize these important metrics. In reality, however, most institutions do not have effective enrollment plans, and many lack a multiyear enrollment plan of any type. Why? The fault typically lies with a poor planning process, no planning process, or a history of plans that were made but not implemented. Many times, an enrollment plan may be called "strategic" but was produced by a process that was not really strategic. The reason excellent enrollment plans are the exception is because true strategic enrollment planning is rare. Indeed, if the planning process is not done right, the plan will be a waste of time.

So how does an enrollment plan become a strategic enrollment plan? How do campus leaders get administrators, faculty, and staff to see it as an active, intelligent, realistic vision of what the campus could (and should) become? In this chapter, we will explore how to create an environment where strategic enrollment plans can thrive—from the elements of a successful plan to the acceptance of the plan by campus stakeholders.

Chapter highlights

- **People create the process**

- **Process is as important (or more important) than the plan**

- **The plan sets the direction for a future state**

Seeking alignment with a future state

In the early 1990s, President James Young of Elon University told his faculty and staff, "A fine-quality institution is never static" (Keller, 2004). The same can be said for first-rate enrollment management programs. With fast-paced changes in technology, the need to attract and graduate a more diverse student body, and the challenges identified in Chapter 1, planning must be more than a periodic exercise conducted by an organization to maintain legitimacy (Bolman and Deal, 1997). Good planning needs to shift paradigms and provide a roadmap to the future. This is not a task to be delegated. Plans should be shepherded by top leaders, well-lived through active review, and carefully monitored by institutional leaders along with key faculty, staff, and other administrators.

Chapter 1 considered the strategic enrollment management imperative, demonstrating a case for planning. Chapter 2 discussed the importance of trust in creating a campus environment that will support a platform for change. As institutions contemplate creating strategic enrollment plans for their campuses, practitioners must consider how this planning process can strengthen enrollment management and align academic and co-curricular trends, demands, and capacities with graduate academic programs, employment, and workforce needs.

SEP embodies these principles. SEP refers to a complex and organized effort to connect mission, current state, and changing environment to long-term enrollment and fiscal health. SEP is a data-informed and ongoing process that identifies, evaluates, and modifies strategies and enrollment goals in light of internal and external forces that may influence the direction of the institution. The planning process addresses:

- The institution's mission and goals, as well as its competitive position in the higher education environment;
- The institution's ability to serve students, both currently and in the future;
- The changing marketplace and environment and their relative impact on the institution's vision; and
- The potential to adapt within the context of an institution's current mission with the expected future state.

Ultimately, SEP should align enrollment goals with a stable future fiscal state that allows the institution to achieve optimal long-term enrollment levels and fiscal health.

The initial process involves innovative thinking by a cross-section of strategic planners and leaders who can determine institutional direction and allocation of resources as well as use data to inform their strategic direction and action. It also entails communicating with all constituencies and earning their confidence and support. After a strategic enrollment plan has been developed, a campus must shift efforts from planning to implementation. Strategic enrollment *management* becomes an ongoing and routine planning process to ensure the plan's strategic vision and goals are effectively and efficiently pursued. The results of action strategies and tactics must be continuously monitored, evaluated, and modified when necessary. As the internal and external environments change, additional information and data need to be collected, analyzed, and integrated into the ongoing management process.

Higher education serves a variety of markets (traditional, transfer, adult, and those seeking certification for specific skill sets), and its practitioners need to better understand the evolving marketplace in order to create a sustainable future. The current state of higher education suggests that few of the thousands of colleges and universities in existence have done enough to adapt to changing market conditions since those institutions were founded 50 to 200 years ago. Despite extensive research and high-level theorizing, higher education has made little progress toward its ultimate mission—moving more students toward degree attainment (DeAngelo, Franke, Hurtado, Pryor, and Tran, 2011). As institutional leaders prepare to launch an SEP process, they must consider the involvement of stakeholders, the realities of higher education's future, and the use of data to determine their position relative to peer and aspirational institutions.

Harvard business professor Clayton Christensen has written numerous books about innovative solutions and practices. In *The Innovative University*, he discusses the innovator's dilemma: When industry leaders focus on better serving their most prized customers and matching their toughest competitors, they may overlook what is happening among their broader base of potential consumers (students). In an educational context, this suggests that two things are likely occurring: 1) growth in the number of potential students who cannot afford an enhanced but increasingly expensive product (a college education) and thus become non-consumers of that product, either by transferring to another institution or withdrawing completely; and 2) the emergence of technologies that allow new competitors to serve this disenfranchised group of non-consumers (Christensen, 2011).

As Chapter 1 explained, focusing on the best and brightest students who have the time and ability to pay for a traditional college education has two negative outcomes for institutions. First, the non-consumer group of students is likely to grow as they are overlooked and priced out of a college education. Second, institutions pursuing an inordinate number of top-quality students may endanger their fiscal health as they have to offer steep discounts to enroll those students. The romanticized idea of four years at a residential college will still have a place in higher education, but it will be a smaller piece of the overall picture (Van Der Werf, Sabatier, 2009). It is likely this shifting paradigm will continue to cause disruptions to the higher education marketplace.

The role of SEP is to identify those disruptions and determine how the individual institution can optimize its market niche within the higher education marketplace. Institutions must hone their program offerings and key marketing messages while also aligning those offerings and messages with market demand and student preferences. They must also understand how they can distinguish their programs, services, activities, or community experience from their competition, and convey the value and benefits of their offerings to students.

> " *Institutions must hone their program offerings and key marketing messages while also aligning those offerings and messages with market demand and student preferences.* "

Finally, the campus must rethink its product and how it is delivered. In a complex market, institutions must consider multiple types of program delivery (online learning, face-to-face instruction, hybrid class offerings) and understand the implications of changing or limiting their product delivery methods. Furthermore, in seeking to find the point where market, competition, and product align, each institution must compare its own offerings and delivery modes to those of its peer institutions and aspirational institutions.

Peer versus aspirational institutions

As campuses begin the planning process, it is critical to conduct an honest and data-informed review of institutional competitors within the marketplace. Campuses should determine which institutions are considered their peers and which institutions they aspire to be more like.

- Peer institutions are those that have comparable or similar programs, similar student characteristics of those they attract and enroll, and comparable size and resources. Peer institutions become the group against which a campus benchmarks its data in order to gauge its performance.

- Aspirant institutions are those that an institution aspires to be more like in terms of enrollments, student profiles, research goals/initiatives, athletic affiliations, academic or co-curricular product offerings, size, endowments, and/or resources.

There also may be institutions that are competitors and would not be classified as peer or aspirant institutional types. For example, small privates have many prospective students who also apply to large public institutions (cross-applicants) where location, not necessarily peer or aspirant institutional classification, drives that cross-application. It is essential to base these comparisons on solid data rather than assumptions or perceptions.

Campuses need an accurate assessment of their peers, which students are cross-applicants, where those cross-applicants are also applying, and the demographics of the students applying to their institution. Numerous national surveys allow an institution to compare their data with that of both peer and aspirant institutional types. As part of the planning process, an institution must assess whether it is below, above, or at the stated averages of its peer institutions. If below or at stated averages, an institution must set goals to move above peer averages *before* it can set data goals that focus on reaching aspirant institution benchmarks.

Part of the reason for this comparison is to answer three questions:

1. Who are your competitors (peers, aspirants, community colleges, cross-applicants, institutions establishing a campus, or institutions advertising online programs in primary or secondary markets)?

2. How closely do your campus metrics align with those of your peer institutions?

3. How far are your metrics from those of your aspirant institutions?

The data comparisons should help you understand the realities of your current state and the points of difference between your campus and other institutions. For example, many campuses desire high-ability students based on national benchmark indicators (SAT and ACT scores, high school ranking). In reality, data show that only one in four traditional, college-seeking students are fully prepared in every subject area for college-level work (ACT, 2011). Institutions must fully understand the capabilities of their students and be prepared to offer them the support and services they need to succeed. Too often, institutions want to shift efforts to enroll high-ability students who align with their aspirant group's entering student profile. ACT data from 2011 indicate that, while some campuses may be able to do this, the pool of highly prepared applicants is expected to decrease in size. Campuses must accept this reality and provide the support services that will produce student success and strong outcomes.

Therefore, the SEP process aligns both the current state of a campus and its desired future state. It also provides a data-informed process for making the transition between those two states. If a campus aspires to seek a different type of student, SEP establishes comparison benchmarks that are carefully monitored while also illuminating the necessary realignment of academic and co-curricular offerings, enrollment and marketing practices, and fiscal strategies to grow revenues as the institution progresses toward that desired future state.

Figure 3-1: Peer Institution Data Benchmarks

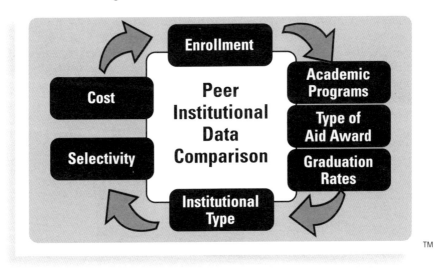

Peer institution data benchmarks are the foundation of SEP. They inform decisions in key areas of enrollment management, ensuring that these areas are aligned and working in harmony toward common institutional goals.

Engaging stakeholders

Every institution has internal and external stakeholders with differing levels of investment in the institution and in the SEP process. Some external stakeholders might welcome growth and understand its economic benefits—boards of trustees or governors, local officials, alumni, or donors within a smaller community who see the institution as a positive contributor to the community's quality of life. Other external stakeholders may resist growth and, despite data demonstrating the positive results of growth, may view it as a net negative. For example, smaller communities may consider an institution setting a goal that is enrollment-growth oriented as a negative because this growth may be perceived to affect the charm or character of the community. In either case, building or sustaining effective working relationships with these external constituencies is an important condition for success (Anderson and Anderson, 2001). Within a campus, all institutional community members should be considered internal stakeholders, even though not everyone will be involved in implementing all parts of the enrollment plan.

Internal and external stakeholders should be included in the strategic planning process, especially if the planning team expects to link academic and/or co-curricular program demands and trends with institutional or employer needs, or if campus planning includes a significant growth in residential facilities. External stakeholders may play a significant role in shaping the quality of the local community, engaging students through internships, and providing a welcoming environment for campus visitors. Internal stakeholders are essential for coordinating and implementing the elements of the plan—they are the ones who will be turning the plan's vision into action.

However, this inclusion does not mean all stakeholders are equal. At the start of the planning process, institutional leaders should determine which stakeholders must be active participants and which merely require updates as the plan progresses. See Chapter 4 for a list of typical stakeholders to include.

Alignment with basic funnel management

Over the years, numerous theorists have talked about the need to move away from a "funnel" and move into more sophisticated enrollment management practices. Others have said the future is less like a funnel (i.e., lots of students on the top and fewer students on the bottom) and more like a "pipeline," as demonstrated in Figure 3-2.

Figure 3-2: The Enrollment Funnel

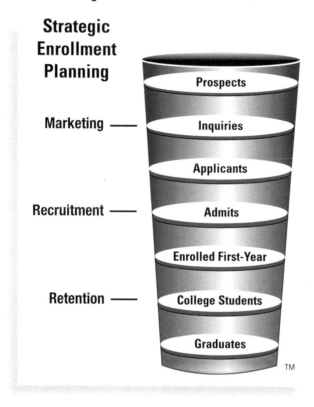

No matter how an institution frames its data analysis, a key step in effective enrollment management is consistently measuring the number and percentage of students from pre-enrollment through graduation. This funnel measures stages in the progression from initial interest through completion, identifies where gaps occur, and provides insights about where to focus efforts to increase new student enrollment and/or completion strategies.

New funnel approaches must also include separate or sophisticated funnel metrics that measure yield, persistence, and completion rates at different points in the funnel, because prospective students no longer enter the funnel in the traditional, linear prospect/inquiry/applicant fashion. For example, we know an increasing number of prospective students first contact an institution through an application. Institutions must redesign their admissions communication process to build a relationship with students once they have applied, using specific communications that connect prospective students with the institution and their major or other areas of interest they identified on the application. The communication and recruitment process can no longer be generic. Prospective students are providing information and preferences. Campuses must use that information to create customized communications to improve yield among students who enter at the applicant stage of the funnel. Consider Figure 3-3.

Figure 3-3: Enrollment Funnel Depicting Students Exploring College Choices Anonymously

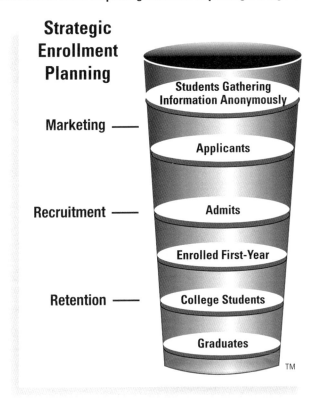

Strategic
Enrollment
Planning

Students Gathering
Information Anonymously

Marketing ——

Applicants

Recruitment ——

Admits

Enrolled First-Year

Retention ——

College Students

Graduates

TM

While this still resembles a funnel, notice how the top may be filled with students who remain anonymous before applying. Yet the goal for campuses—generating the same number of high-quality applicants—remains. This requires a strategic shift in marketing, perhaps one that emphasizes good outcomes (i.e., graduates prepared for graduate school or employment) rather than first-year experience programs or the value of attending an institution that provides small class sizes. Other than acceptance and financial aid, the sophisticated applicant of the future may be looking to the end of the funnel (graduation) and not worried much about what happens at the top of the funnel.

As we consider the rest of the SEP process, it is essential to consider how each variable discussed affects some stage of this funnel. Regardless of whether you describe this model as a funnel, pipeline, or some other term, remember that the goal is to enroll the optimal mix of students, provide them with the necessary support and connections to achieve their goals, and graduate them with degrees that prepare them for their future endeavors.

What makes excellent enrollment plans and outcomes?

Bernard Ginsberg (2011) emphasized the importance of the process. "Occasionally a college or university does, in fact, present a grand design for the next decade…. Such a plan typically presents concrete objectives, a timetable for their realization, an outline of the tactics that will be employed, a precise assignment of staff responsibilities, and a budget." He states, "The 2007 strategic plan of the University of Illinois, for example, put forward explicit objectives, benchmarks, timetables, and budgets." Obviously, *it was the process* that resulted in producing these explicit objectives, benchmarks, timetables, and budgets.

Since 2008, Noel-Levitz consultants have studied a large number of institutional strategic plans and strategic enrollment plans. In addition, they have engaged in an extensive review of strategic planning literature and conducted numerous dialogues with college/university campuses regarding SEP. Based on these contacts, literature reviews, and observations, one maxim has become perfectly clear: Excellent, long-range, strategic enrollment plans are the result of a collaborative, data-informed process.

What goes into that process? We have identified the most common characteristics of successful strategic enrollment plans, which generally include most, if not all, of the following:

- **Clearly defined strategic planning phases,** where strategies, tactics, and return-on-investment prioritization lead to goal setting, rather than the traditional approach of setting goals first and then planning strategies and steps;

- **A comprehensive and integrated scope** that considers multiple types of student enrollments and programs, as well as the interaction of these components;

- **An academic- and co-curricular-oriented process,** rather than a primary focus on marketing, recruitment, and retention tactics;

- **Data-informed** strategies, tactics, and enrollment goals;

- **Fiscally minded** strategies, tactics, and goals;

- **High participation and buy-in** across the institution;

- **High-quality implementation of the plan** with clear timelines, responsibilities, and accountability;

- **A continuous process** that develops, implements, evaluates, and refreshes the plans; and

- **An experienced and strong leader of the strategic process,** one with a track record of successful outcomes.

> " *Excellent, long-range, strategic enrollment plans are the result of a collaborative, data-informed process.*"

These essentials not only agree with the principles and trends that have been identified for a number of years as components of successful planning processes, but also address the most common reasons plans fail. In addition, the essentials are aligned with the significant factors cited in respected strategic planning literature (Bryson, 1995 and 2004; Steiner, Miner, and Gray, 1992; Haines, 2000; and Lake, 2006) and higher education strategic planning literature (Bean, 1990; Rowley, Lujan, and Dolence, 1997; Cope, 1981; Sevier, 2000; and Norris and Poulton, 2008).

As an institution seeks to create an SEP, the planning process is a great opportunity to change campus culture, encourage a greater understanding of the fundamentals of planning, and demonstrate that planning is more than an exercise. The goal of the planning process is to create a vibrant, living plan that is an ongoing and continuous process aligning strategy implementation with resource allocation to create a stronger future state. By actively managing and implementing the plan, institutional leadership has an enormous opportunity to demonstrate the value and meaningfulness of SEP to the campus community.

Aligning organizational strategic plans with strategic enrollment plans

Strategic planning is the disciplined effort to produce fundamental decisions and actions that shape and guide an organization's identity as well as its mission, purpose, and why it offers the programs and services it provides (Bryson, 1995). Most campuses have a strategic plan—some are used well and some sit on the proverbial shelf. The most effective strategic enrollment plans draw from the overall institutional strategic plan to set direction for the SEP process. If, when created, the strategic planning process was data informed, the enrollment planning process should roll seamlessly into the institutional strategic plan. However, the strategic planning process at campuses is often *not* data informed. In that case, the SEP process, if done correctly, will confirm or deny the assumptions, perceptions, and other non-qualitative measures that were used to establish enrollment and fiscal goals in the strategic plan. For example, many strategic plans call for an enrollment goal of XX by YY year, but often no data have been used to inform these enrollment goals. The SEP process can determine specific strategies, tactics, and anticipated costs to reach the stated enrollment goals or will provide evidence that the campus should realign expectations.

In its purest form, the strategic plan should establish mission, vision, and ways to ensure institutional effectiveness. The strategic *enrollment* plan should determine key performance indicators (KPI) related to enrollment (Chapter 9), key strategies (Chapter 7), and enrollment goals (Chapter 8) to be reached through implementation of the plan. Annual plans take the operational items identified through the planning process and move these tactics to action. The effective organizational model ensures that the institutional strategic plan blends with the strategic enrollment plan and that key operational staff use both of these plans to pursue priorities through annual planning and implementation efforts.

Figure 3-4: The Strategic *Enrollment* Plan as a Part of the Overall Strategic Plan

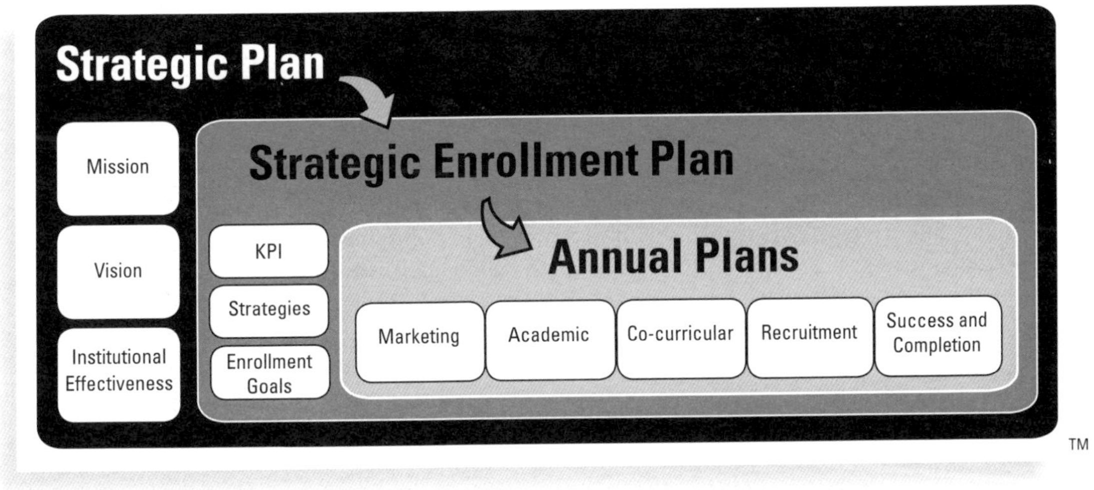

Strategic enrollment planning and strategic enrollment management

Today, institutional leaders face two competing demands. They must execute immediate actions in order to meet today's enrollment challenges, and they must adapt the ways they execute and achieve enrollment efficiencies in order to thrive in tomorrow's world. They must develop next practices while excelling at today's best practices (Heifetz, Grashow, and Linsky, 2009).

It is not uncommon for mature enterprises to become increasingly risk-averse, complacent, and perhaps unduly expensive, and not make the advancements necessary to compete in a future marketplace (Christensen and Eyring, 2011). SEP can rectify this organizational inertia by challenging a passive approach with data. Institutions may use the SEP process to devise a plan coupling best practices with emerging practices, relying on external data, imagination, and dynamic conversation to envision a future state unimaginable by some. This requires conducting a careful review of competitors and recommended best practices to understand how to become an innovative college/university, rather than simply a survivor, in the next five to seven years.

In order for the SEP process to be successful, it requires strategic enrollment *management* (SEM). SEM is an ongoing effort focused on ensuring that strategies and tactics are implemented; setting and monitoring key performance indicators; and reviewing data to ensure responsiveness to changes in competition, market share, or demand (if the market demand aligns with the institution's vision, mission, goals, values, and available institutional resources).

SEM is monitored through an oversight body such as an enrollment management council and not delegated exclusively to a vice president for enrollment management or dean/director of admissions. The goal of the council and the institutional leadership is keeping the institution focused on the future state described in the plan that aligns with the institutional strategic plan and other identified institutional priorities. In Chapter 9, we will define the role and purpose of the council in greater detail.

There are three fundamental components of the SEM process:

1. **Creation of the plan**, which serves to prioritize activities/programs/initiatives to ensure future success. The plan is based on an understanding of how the institution is characterized, differentiated, and competitively positioned.

2. **Implementation of the plan**, which employs the best methods/procedures to accomplish enrollment goals and institutional outcomes. This is based on an understanding of how the institution functions as a coordinated system with maximum campus involvement, shared leadership, and commitment to educational excellence and institutional effectiveness.

3. **Institutionalization and systemic integration of the SEM process**, which focuses on integrating SEP into the university's routine planning structures and is based on a commitment to the continuous improvement process.

SEM systems include institutional databases, external data sources, data reports, and analytical tools that allow institutions to continuously develop, manage, evaluate, and modify well-conceived enrollment strategies and activities.

Taking a more realistic approach to setting goals

In creating a strategic enrollment planning process for campuses, we at Noel-Levitz have identified two underlying principles. The first is that leadership matters. While this seems like common knowledge throughout higher education, our analysis of highly effective organizations shows that, due to a lack of leadership, few campuses live by their strategic enrollment plans—if they exist at all. Campus leaders play a crucial role in creating the plan and monitoring progress toward it.

" Campus leaders play a crucial role in creating the plan and monitoring progress toward it."

Second, the strategic enrollment plan must be led by a change agent. This person may be an academic dean, vice president, or someone who has a campus reputation to make sustainable change and the ability to lead the process, with a commitment to doing what is good for the overall organization and using the plan as a tool to transform the institution to its desired future state (Anderson and Anderson, 2001).

The planning model described in subsequent chapters advises campuses to review their data first; align their data with a situation analysis that informs the development of strategies, tactics, cost, and return-on-investment projections; and then develop enrollment goals linking academic and co-curricular priorities that have been determined through assessment of demand and capacity. Based on our analysis of realistic goal setting, the Noel-Levitz approach diverges from most planning models by asserting that institutions must identify key strategies, tactics, costs (human, technological, and actual dollars), and expected return-on-investments *before* setting goals. Without a clear understanding of the action plan to implement strategies and the resources needed to implement the strategies, goals are meaningless. Goals must be realistic and achievable based on campus readiness and resource allocation (or re-allocation) to support the activities needed to drive the institution to its desired future state.

Common characteristics of a strategic enrollment plan

Each institutional plan should have its own character and style. However, we strongly recommend that a plan be contained within 25 to 30 pages, include a two- to three-page abstract that provides a global or overarching summary of the plan, and have a robust appendix filled with plan details and data gathered to support the planning initiative. In general, plans should also be:

- **Futuristic**—The plan uses external, competitor, and state/regional data to identify how an institution's current offerings match the future external environment. The plan should direct the institutional community to a future state that is realistic, but also requires a shift from current practices to a combination of best and emerging practices to attract, retain, and graduate students who have had a strong and engaging experience.

- **Comprehensive and integrated**—The plan is focused on the entire institution, not enrollment per se, with a lens toward enrollment functions that will meet market demand and interest and advance the institution's market penetration within the programs it offers or new programs it will add. The enrollment functions ***support*** the academic and co-curricular programs, with the interconnections between these areas apparent in all enrollment and marketing efforts. In turn, strong, engaging, outcomes-oriented academic and co-curricular experiences advance the enrollment and marketing efforts of the institution. The ultimate outcome of the plan is the integration of the academic and co-curricular programs with marketing, recruitment, retention, and finance/financial aid strategies.

- **Data informed**—The process is data informed, not data driven (see Chapter 5 for a more detailed explanation of the difference between the two). There is both an art and a science to enrollment planning, and the planning team must spend time delving into multiple sources of data to gain a broad and deep understanding of the data and its relationship to a future desired state for the institution.

- **Academic-oriented**—Academic programs form the heart of the institution. Therefore, an evaluation and possible redirection of academic program offerings should be an essential part of the strategic enrollment plan.

- **Technologically current**—In a rapidly changing technological world, the integration of technology has shifted from a value-added feature to an expectation. As technology advances, institutions must incorporate an understanding of the costs and skill sets needed to provide a standard of operation now expected from students of all ages. The enrollment planning process must determine tactics or action items that build and/or enhance operational system efficiencies, technology enhancements, and services or activities to serve students.

Fundamental approaches

As the planning process progresses, an institution must evaluate whether current demand and market penetration strategies are working effectively to lead the campus to its desired future state. Dickeson (2010) identifies five fundamental challenges that institutions confront as they incorporate this type of analysis into their planning activities:

1. The power of legacy;

2. The realities of the marketplace, which will force differentiation;

3. Wrestling with the true quest for excellence;

4. Local reconciliation of higher education's function (teaching, research, and service); and

5. The specific ways to fulfill their most essential purpose.

A comprehensive planning process will address these fundamental issues.

As campuses consider academic and co-curricular demand and market penetration, they must set internal and external benchmarks to track programs and activities in their current and evolving future state. For example, there are several national benchmarks related to limiting classroom size; yet numerous studies have shown the effectiveness of instruction for class sizes in the hundreds when technology, lab experiences, and teaching assistants supplement the course lectures. While best practices provide a solid strategic foundation, a campus must set its own internal benchmarks and align them with expected outcomes in order to be truly strategic.

Institutions must also look at the financial viability of each program, future program demand, employment trends, and other factors (described in Chapter 5) when examining program demand and areas of future focus. Figure 3-5 shows an approach focused on aligning programs with a variety of internal and external factors. This process may lead to the elimination or restructuring of certain programs to align with future student demand and employment/graduate school needs.

Figure 3-5: Connecting Academic and Co-curricular Programs

Mission vision goals

Future knowledge and skills

Student outcomes

SEP Alignment

Fiscal health

Market penetration

Student success

Market share

Cost per degree completion

TM

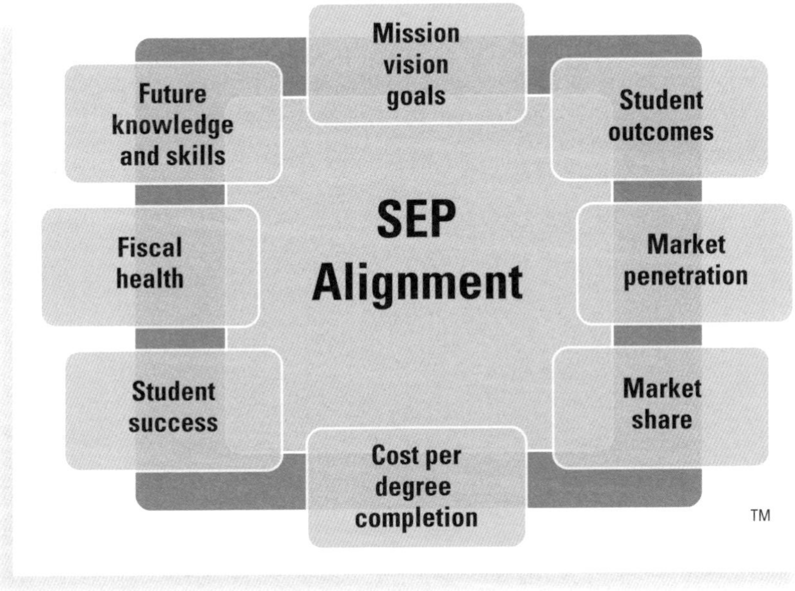

Conclusion

If completed with diligence and strong leadership, the planning process can build a culture of SEM within which the resulting plan is used as a tool to guide the institution toward a desired future state. As noted above, few campuses report having a strategic enrollment plan or effectively using their current plan to guide their institution's efforts in this manner. The goal of this planning process, and indeed of this book, is to help institutions think through the importance of planning, the process of planning, and the value of moving from a planning mode to a management mode. Ultimately, successful institutions will adopt a data-informed management model using a process that is continuously refreshed in order to ensure the campus reaches its desired future state.

Dialogue

As campus leaders consider embarking on an SEP process, they should consider the following:

First, discuss at the cabinet or senior-staff level, whether this is the right time to pursue such an initiative. If yes, the team should:

- Discuss the expected outcomes of the plan;
- Review data sources that might be available;
- Discuss the availability of institutional research to support the planning process; and
- Identify key stakeholders to engage in the planning process.

Of particular note, the leadership should determine whether this planning exercise should include a review of academic and co-curricular programs, trends, demands, and capacities. If it does not seek to link these programs, the process shifts from an SEP process to a long-range enrollment planning process. While all the elements of the planning process (as described in Chapter 4) remain valid, the planning team assumes there will be no changes in current program offerings and/or integrates pre-planned new program or program reduction activities into its process.

As leaders discuss the potential of the planning process, they should consider who else to engage in a discussion of the value and benefits of the planning process.

Lastly, institutional leaders should discuss the value of the planning process, the reason for planning, and the need to establish a long-term plan with deans, directors, and department chairs, ensuring them of the institution's commitment to moving from planning to an active institutional management process after the plan is completed.

Strategic Enrollment Planning:

A Dynamic Collaboration

Section Two: Key Elements of a Strategic Enrollment Plan

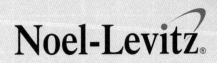

CHAPTER 4

The Planning Process

By James Mager

What makes for excellence in a strategic enrollment plan (SEP) and the strategic enrollment planning process? While the question may be answered in many ways by individuals at different institutions, most would agree that the plan and the process should lead to enrollment outcomes and student success metrics that meet or exceed the goals developed during the planning process. In addition, an excellent plan is one that pushes the institution to increase performance or advance levels of practice and also has enough detail to ensure the plan will be implemented.

However, it is unwise to tie planning excellence and success exclusively with the achievement of enrollment goals. If an institution exceeds its enrollment goals, but the goals were conservative ones set in an external environment that provided ample enrollment growth opportunities, achievement of those goals may simply be the result of demographic factors rather than a comprehensive enrollment plan that encouraged innovative actions and sophisticated practices.

> **Chapter highlights**
>
> - **Planning phases define the process**
>
> - **SEP scope is determined early**
>
> - **Six Ps outline the planning topics**
>
> - **Dialogue links the process with the plan**

Many higher education institutions (and other organizations) call their planning process strategic when they are, in fact, conducting traditional planning under the trendy guise of "strategic planning." Traditional planning typically involves setting goals, either short- or long-term, and then developing steps to achieve those goals (Bean, 1990, and Rowley, Lujan, and Dolence, 1997). This type of planning can succeed in some circumstances, but is fraught with risks, including the example of conservative goal achievement cited above. Others risk setting enrollment goals that are unrealistic or arbitrary; creating a plan that is not aligned with demographic realities, the competition, or the institution's strengths and weaknesses; and having a plan with a narrow scope, to name but a few.

Strategic planning primarily aligns an institution with its external and internal environment (Rowley et al., 1997; and Steiner, Miner, and Gray, 1992). Unlike traditional planning, goals are set toward the end of the process, after analyzing the environment, strategy development, and business investment decisions, rather than at the beginning.

Recommended process phases and steps

Strategic planning phases, as opposed to traditional planning phases, are critical to a successful SEP process. These phases align with fundamental planning elements that ensure successful SEP processes are integrated into planning. They also align with best practices identified in strategic planning literature (Bryson, 1995 and 2004; Lake, 2006; Haines, 2000; and Steiner et al., 1992) and higher education strategic planning literature (Bean 1990; Rowley et al., 1997; Massey, 2001; Dickeson, 1999; Dolence and Norris, 1994; and Sevier, 2000).

The scope or details of the plan may be aligned with strategies defined within six categories—the Six Ps—that link other plans (academic, technology, fundraising) and are framed within a concept of: 1) the product (academic and/or co-curricular programs); 2) place and delivery (site and delivery method); 3) price (gross or net costs); 4) promotion (marketing and recruitment); 5) purpose and identity (mission and brand); and 6) process (how things are accomplished and linked to fiscal planning and management). These will be addressed in more detail later in the chapter.

The following phases and steps provide a recommended starting point for SEP process design. The four interactive phases have inherent feedback loops. See Figure 4-1.

Phase one: Preparation and data analysis

In phase one, the institution completes a thorough data analysis (which includes an intensive review of internal and external data), determines key performance indicators, and creates a new or updated situation analysis framed from an enrollment perspective. This situation analysis sets the stage and reason for the institution to commit to a strategic enrollment planning process.

This phase may include:

- Reviewing the Institutional Strategic Plan (if one exists);
- Defining the scope of the planning process;
- Organizing the leaders and participants for a successful process, as demanded by its scope;
- Defining the key performance indicators (KPIs) for the planning process;
- Collecting and reviewing data related to the current and future state; and
- Conducting a data-informed situation or SWOT (strengths, weaknesses, opportunities, and threats) analysis related to the identified KPIs.

Phase two: Strategy development

Phase two is an output of the situation analysis. Strategy development should maximize institutional effectiveness across the defined strategic areas as well as the overall realization of institutional mission and vision.

During phase two, the planning process includes:

- Brainstorming strategies to optimize the KPIs;
- Identifying the major tactics for each possible strategy (Note: Strategies are larger initiatives while tactics are specific action items or activities needed to complete or accomplish a strategy);
- Determining estimated costs, impacts, and return on investment (ROI) for each of the possible major tactics;
- Identifying additional data for collection in order to refine the possible strategies, major tactics, costs, and ROI; and
- Prioritizing the strategies and major tactics based on attractive ROIs and other considerations.

Phase three: Enrollment goal setting and plan finalization

Goals are established during phase three. Goal setting includes two key items: 1) a thorough review of the anticipated ROI based on each strategy implemented, and 2) enrollment projections to determine specific enrollment goals.

Additional action items during this phase include:

- Conducting enrollment and fiscal projection scenarios;
- Determining multiyear KPI goals based on the most attractive scenario;
- Finalizing a written plan; and
- Conducting the appropriate approval process for the plan.

Phase four: Plan implementation and modification

During phase four, the planning team implements and monitors the plan. In addition, the campus creates a strategic enrollment management council that monitors KPIs and requests quarterly progress reports on strategy implementation.

Action items for this phase include:

- Forming a strategic enrollment management council and committees;
- Thoroughly implementing the plan at every level;
- Monitoring and evaluating the plan's outcomes;
- Continuing the planning process to align with new data or environmental changes that were unanticipated when the initial plan was created; and
- Updating the plan based on monitoring and continuous planning process.

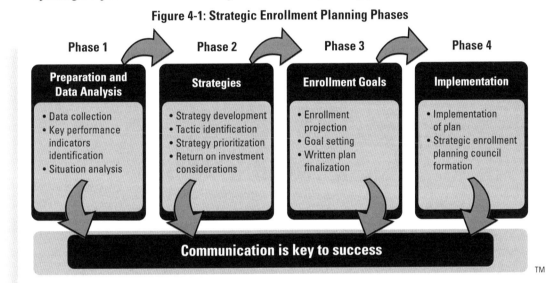

Figure 4-1: Strategic Enrollment Planning Phases

The importance of communication

It is essential that campuses communicate with stakeholders throughout these four phases. Primary stakeholders will need to be actively involved; secondary stakeholders should be informed as planning and implementation progress. While the steps may be tweaked and modified to meet the needs of particular institutions, planners should keep these fundamental phases and components in mind as they design their own processes.

Points of emphasis for planning process success

The process phases and activities described within this chapter are based on sound fundamentals, but merely following the recommended process will not ensure success. There are a number of other important factors that affect the outcome of the process.

Process leaders and the planning participants are critical to the ultimate success of the planning process. The process leader is an institutional expert in the specific area of strategy or tactic development and implementation. The planner-participants (those involved in implementing the strategy or tactic) bring not only their particular expertise to the planning process, but also contribute analytic, innovative, and big-picture skills. The process should not be seen as a means of garnering buy-in from naysayers; rather, it should bring together the best campus minds, those who understand the larger view and the value and importance of the planning process. Therefore, these personnel decisions should be made with extreme care at the beginning of phase one.

Decisions regarding the respective roles and organization of these leaders and planning participants are also important to the ultimate success of the process. Having dynamic leaders and planning participants without clear roles and responsibilities can lead to unsatisfactory results or even to a collapse of the process. Dynamic leaders and planners working as a coordinated team can result in tremendous success with the planning process, implementation, and ultimately enrollment. (A section dedicated to the important topic of "organizing for a successful planning process" is covered later in this chapter.)

These personnel and organization decisions must be preceded by a preliminary decision regarding the scope of the process, because this scope determines the kind of expertise and representation that will be required throughout the planning process. The scope also determines *what long-range enrollment issues will be addressed in a strategic, integrated manner* for the next three to five years and which issues will not be addressed. Therefore, in making decisions regarding scope, the benefits of addressing certain issues and types of student enrollments must be weighed against the risks of choosing not to address certain issues in an integrated, strategic manner. The topic of determining process scope is addressed more fully below.

Planning timetable and outcomes

The strategic enrollment planning process that leads to the initial plan document should take 9 to 12 months. Completing this process in a thorough, high-quality manner requires time. Taking less time will almost certainly result in a plan that is not fully data informed, is deficient in participation and buy-in, and has not fully analyzed cost/ROI. As a result, the plan will not lead to the desired enrollment outcomes with minimal or even reasonable risks.

However, the intensity and involvement of this process also requires it to be finished in a reasonable amount of time. If the planning process produces nothing tangible to affect an institution's enrollment future within 12 months, the negatives quickly begin to outweigh the benefits of prolonging the process to produce a more perfect plan. In this case, the planning process is vulnerable to being bogged down and moving from an action-oriented group focused on creating a plan to one that becomes paralyzed. The plan is unable to move forward with strategies or tactics because it is waiting for more data than is necessary. In addition, those not central to the process (trustees, academic leaders, faculty, and staff) may become impatient and/or lose confidence in the process when nothing tangible is produced.

Keep in mind that the goal of the data analysis is to understand trends, patterns, and behaviors, and should spur creative thinking and action. While more data can always be collected, it is essential that the planning leaders remain focused on established priorities and understand that the plan is a living document.

The best initial strategic enrollment plans are dynamic efforts, produced and approved within 9 to 12 months, and consist of the following:

- Strategies and tactics prioritized by target years for implementation. Each of these strategies and tactics includes timetables, resource needs (fiscal and human), and individuals responsible for high-quality implementation.
- Expected ROIs and multiyear KPI goals related to the implementation of these strategies and tactics.

- Planning topics that are still in the process of analysis, strategy development, or evaluation, including timetables, resources, and individual responsibilities.

- Enrollment projections based on institutional readiness and the realities of the current state versus the desired state.

- Regular updates to the campus community regarding the planning process, with relevant data sent to appropriate units to help jumpstart activities or gain further unit buy-in by explaining the implications of data.

- Steps for monitoring, evaluating, and updating the plan—it should be a living document supported by an ongoing strategic enrollment management process.

After the first edition of the plan has been produced and approved for implementation, the SEP council should be created and the composition of the committees refreshed. There will be committee members and leaders who want to stay involved in the process (or at least are willing to stay engaged) and others who wish to be relieved. However, senior leaders must remain actively involved in managing implementation.

The enrollment successes that come from the planning process are more dependent on high-quality implementation than on the plan itself. These enrollment successes start with decisions about who will lead the implementation of each strategy and each tactic. They continue with detailed quality-control systems that are implemented not only by the leader of the each tactic, but also by those with other levels of involvement.

Leaders and doers who are successful at meeting high-quality implementation standards need to be recognized, rewarded, and retained. Those who are not meeting these standards need to be counseled, mentored, and possibly relieved of their planning responsibilities. Sometimes the actions that must be taken are not pleasant; however, too much valuable time and money has been invested in the planning to allow the enrollment and fiscal success to break down at the implementation phase. For these reasons, decisions regarding the leadership and monitoring of the implementation processes are extremely important to the plan's ultimate success.

> *" Two dimensions to planning process scope: 1) the types of student enrollment the process will address; and 2) the topics the process will address for each type of enrollment."*

In summary, long-term enrollment and fiscal success require strong institutional leaders to provide *detailed attention* to the planning process, essentials, and points of emphasis listed above. Failure to do so can result in an SEP process that does not produce results or is never completed.

SEP scope defines the boundaries of the process

Before the strategic planning process begins, institutional leaders must have thoughtful discussions about its scope, because these discussions will determine who should be involved in the planning process. Decisions about scope will also determine which long-range enrollment issues will be addressed in a strategic, integrated manner for the next three to five years, and which issues will not. Although there may be valid reasons to modify the scope later in the process, this creates significant inefficiencies that are best avoided if possible.

There are two dimensions to the scope of the planning process: 1) the types of student enrollment the process will address; and 2) the topics the process will address for each type of enrollment.

Enrollment types included in planning scope

What types of enrollment will the planning process address? Will it target only traditional undergraduate enrollment or include other populations such as nontraditional undergraduate, non-degree enrollments, graduate students and/or professional school students? Will the process only address traditional, on-campus enrollment, or will it also address enrollments in online and hybrid courses and programs? Will the process include enrollments at remote sites and branch campuses? Finally, will it address how these enrollments interact with each other?

Taking a comprehensive approach by answering "yes" to all or most of these questions is recommended unless this would make the planning process too large and unwieldy. Be aware that data collection for all subpopulations can bog down the process, so institutional priorities must be set to ensure that data for each population can be collected in a timely manner.

Why take such a comprehensive approach? Colleges and universities are comprised mostly of departments and programs: academic, student life, student support, and administrative. Each of these departments and programs has its own physical facilities, utilities, and technology applications. It is important for each department to have clear strategic enrollment plans and expectations for every type of student it serves, not just for certain types of students. Not having clear plans and expectations for other students who use these same departmental resources will likely lead to costly inefficiencies in the future at the departmental level and, in turn, for the institution as a whole.

For example, assume there is a strategic plan and an expectation that business undergraduate students will grow significantly in the next five years. What kind of physical facility will the College of Business need to serve not only these students but MBA students (not addressed by the strategic plan) who will be using the same facility? Moreover, what implications might this have for an adjacent academic department that is competing for the same expansion space?

The hazards of not planning comprehensively are many and multiply quickly when considering the interactions among departments and programs. Having a plan for each department and program, as well as a comprehensive plan that addresses the interactions of these departments and programs, will help avoid these types of inefficiencies.

On the other hand, taking a comprehensive approach to strategic enrollment planning can be very challenging to manage because of all the distinct parts and the interactions among these parts. This is especially true at larger institutions with hundreds of moving parts that need to be addressed both as separate components and as interactive components. All of these interactions will need to be addressed by planning subcommittees that represent clusters of these parts, and, in turn, these subcommittees must be efficiently and effectively coordinated by the planning process leaders.

As a result of these planning challenges, some institutions might be better off initially focusing on certain types of enrollments and programs, such as traditional undergraduates, then addressing the enrollments of other student populations later. This sequential approach worked for The Ohio State University in the 1990s, when the focus of the enrollment planning process was first on traditional undergraduate enrollments at the main campus. Later, processes were developed to address graduate student and branch campus enrollments.

The bottom line for making decisions about the scope of the process for different types of students is that there is no right or wrong decision for a comprehensive approach versus a more concentrated approach. The advantages and risks must be carefully weighed before determining the scope. It is best to change the scope of this continuous planning process as few times as possible and only after carefully weighing the advantages, challenges, and risks of changing scope as the project progresses. During the initial planning process, data collection and review may help senior leaders determine the plan's scope.

Enrollment topics included in planning scope

The second dimension of scope entails determining the topics that the planning process will address for each type of enrollment that is selected. These are known as the Six Ps:

1. **Product strategies** related to academic programs and courses; student life; co-curricular and extracurricular programs; and student success, retention, and graduation programs.

2. **Place and delivery strategies** related to program and course delivery innovations/options (e.g., off-site, online, and executive format strategies) and the integration of enrollment planning with physical facility and technology planning.

3. **Price strategies** related to tuition and fees and discounts such as scholarships, assistantships, as well as need-based financial aid.

4. **Promotion strategies** related to institutional and program marketing, student recruitment, and prospective student influencers such as parents, guidance counselors, advisers, and teachers.

5. **Purpose and identity strategies** related to effective realization and illumination of mission, distinctiveness, and brand of the institution.

6. **Process strategies** related to fiscal planning and management, data and information systems, institutional effectiveness assessment systems, institutionwide engagement, organizational strength of the campus community, and systemic coordination of planning, including determination of priorities and strategic direction.

One of the most common mistakes that institutions make is conducting an enrollment planning process that primarily or exclusively addresses marketing, recruiting, student persistence and success, and scholarships/financial aid. The foundation of each higher education institution—and, therefore, the foundation of institutional strategic enrollment planning—is the viability and effectiveness of its product, including its academic programs and courses, co-curricular and extracurricular programs, student life opportunities, and support for student success. The content and quality of this product either meets or does not meet the wants and needs of its students. The reputation and content of the product are the main influencers for prospective students choosing to enroll.

The strategic enrollment planning process should address the following questions for each academic, student life, and student support program:

- Has the program been effective in attracting, satisfying, and retaining students in the past and present? Why or why not?

- In the future, can the program be effective in attracting, satisfying, retaining, and graduating students, given recent and projected external demographic trends, competition, opportunities, and threats and in light of the institution's internal strengths and weaknesses?

Even though the institutional product is the foundation of enrollment success and therefore the basis for a successful enrollment planning process, it is often the most elusive area for an enrollment manager to control (Lesick, 2009). Therefore, developing product-related strategies needs to be at the forefront of the SEP process and must involve the product leaders in academics. Institutions must have effective product plans and strategies before they can effectively and efficiently complete the development of pricing and promotion strategies.

Where and how these courses are delivered is also an important topic in the strategic enrollment planning process. Will each program and course be delivered in convenient and attractive ways to its students? What are the costs and advantages to making them more convenient and attractive in the future? Does the institution offer an attractive mix of program and course delivery options such as on-campus, remote sites, online, hybrid, and executive format delivery modes? If so, what is the cost and return on investment?

During the planning process, the greater the emphasis on the development of high-quality and attractive products, places, and modes of delivery, the more likely it is to produce enrollment success. Promotion and pricing are secondary. The planning process should shift the emphasis from promotion and pricing strategies to effective programming and strong outcomes. This, of course, is the whole point: providing first-rate, highly sought-after programs at convenient places for a chosen subset of the market. That is why the institution exists and why successful strategic enrollment planning is largely about aligning an institution with its external and internal environment.

Strategic pricing of the institution's products, places, and modes of delivery is another important part of strategic enrollment planning. The pricing (and net tuition) approach includes the development of data-informed strategies for discounting prices for certain student populations. However, it is crucial that an institution have the best possible understanding not only of its current and future products, places, and modes of delivery, but also how attractive these are in comparison to competing institutions' products, places, and modes of delivery before developing its pricing strategies.

Once strategies for products, places, and price are in place, promotion strategies can be addressed. These typically take the form of both institutional and individual program marketing strategies as well as more targeted prospective student recruitment strategies. The process of developing promotion strategies also takes into account the role of prospective student influencers such as parents, guidance counselors, advisers, and teachers.

As the strategic enrollment planning process continues, the planning team should be constantly confirming or modifying the institution's purpose or institutional identity, aiming for more effective realization and illumination of the mission, distinctiveness, and brand of the institution. Keep in mind that there may be external opportunities and threats or emerging internal strengths and weaknesses that make a case for using the planning process to modify the institution's purpose, identity, or even its mission. The institutional mission, distinctiveness, and brand will coincide with the institution's strengths, keeping the process aligned with those characteristics.

Finally, the scope of the planning process should address the institution's ongoing, internal process strategies in the areas of fiscal planning and management, data and information systems, systems for assessing institutional effectiveness, institutionwide engagement, campuswide organizational strengths, planning priorities, and strategic direction. These ongoing processes must provide for the continuous integration of strategic planning, enrollment planning, physical facility planning, technology planning, fundraising planning, budget planning, and assessment. A strategic enrollment planning process can be a major force in ensuring this integration. Without this integration across all of these processes, the institution is vulnerable to enormous enrollment planning inefficiencies that can cost millions of dollars in facility and technology costs alone.

Organizing for a successful planning process

Once the scope of the process has been established, institutional leaders will be ready to determine the best leaders, planner-participants, and the organization of the SEP process. The SEP process can be organized in many different ways; however, there are a number of principles to keep in mind. The following observations and recommendations have emerged through Noel-Levitz's formal consultations and informal conversations with higher education professionals regarding the most effective ways to organize the planning process.

The president plays a critical role in setting the tone regarding the importance of this process for the institution's future. True strategic enrollment planning requires a significant investment of time on the part of participants, institutional leaders, and departmental leaders. The president must leave no doubt that this process is so critical to the institution's future that the planner-participants and the process leaders must be fully engaged in it. (See the dialogue section of this chapter for more on how the president can set this tone.)

At least one of the leaders of the process should have experience in successful strategic planning, not just traditional planning. If the institution does not have one or more leaders who have strategic planning success in their background, an outside facilitator who has this experience should be identified to partner with the appropriate institutional leaders in managing the SEP process.

It is human nature for people to support what they build. Theretofore, institutional leaders must design a planning organization with a wide net to include as many people as possible. It will include those who are not on one of the process-planning committees, with special attention to ways and means of communicating and involving deans, faculty, administrators, and staff. One way to accomplish this is for the planning council and the committees (described in the next section) to include planning participants who not only bring their own expertise to the planning process, but also can communicate outside of the formal planning meetings with their colleagues and/or constituents and then contribute their feedback to the process. Another way is to continuously provide updates and ask for feedback at different venues such as departmental staff meetings, deans' meetings, faculty councils, student affairs councils, and trustees meetings. Other means for spreading the net include developing and maintaining a high-quality, up-to-date SEP Web site and a high-quality, consistent SEP newsletter.

> *" Institutional leaders must design a planning organization with a wide net to include as many people as possible."*

The planning process includes topic-specific subcommittees. An effective process not only explores large concepts and directions, but also analyzes numerous external and internal factors, trends, and issues in order to develop effective, reality-based strategies. Topic-specific subcommittees might be formed to address areas such as academic program planning and delivery modes, graduate student enrollment, international student enrollment, nontraditional enrollment, pricing strategies, and marketing strategies. Detailed expertise is needed to inform each topic and guide the work of these subcommittees.

With an array of planning committees and broad, institutionwide representation, a small coordinating/action/steering committee is needed to lead and manage the process. This committee ensures that the process embraces the essentials outlined in this chapter and in this book. This committee is the hub that connects all the working subcommittees/groups, the SEP council, the president, and the president's cabinet.

The process and its participants must have an academic and co-curricular orientation, be fiscal-minded, and be data-informed. It is important to have high-level, fully engaged participants from academic affairs, academic colleges and departments, student affairs, fiscal affairs, and the appropriate data analysts, typically from institutional affairs and enrollment services. If these leaders indicate they are too busy to be fully engaged, then their availability should be addressed with the president, because either the message that this process is extremely important to the institution's health has not been received, or the president must authorize alternative topic-specific leaders who can fully engage in the process. The planning process requires leaders with high-level authority to speak for a particular administrative or academic division, college, or department.

Responsibility and accountability are the centerpieces of this process. Typically, each planner-participant serves one or more of the following roles:

- Provides expertise on a given topic;
- Communicates with constituents and brings feedback to the process;
- Is seen as a campus leader and someone who seeks to improve the entire institution, not just his or her own department;
- Serves as chair of a working group determined through the planning process; and
- Has the authority to speak and/or make decisions for a department, college, division, or institutional governing body.

Figure 4-2: Example of SEP Organization

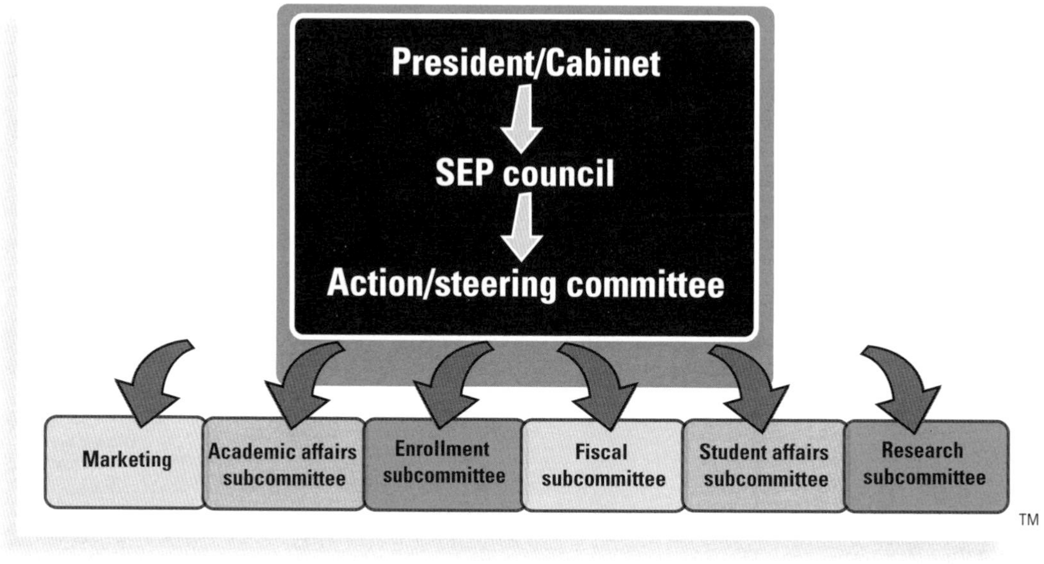

The following outline provides an overview of a recommended structure for a successful SEP process that has worked for numerous campuses.

Focus on oversight: The SEP council

The SEP council composed mainly of campus leaders, in conjunction with its action/steering subcommittee, directs the process and ensures institutionwide processes for communication, participation, endorsements, and approvals. It should have representatives from the following:

- Academic affairs and selected deans (one of these chairs or co-chairs the council);
- Enrollment (facilitates and possibly co-chairs the council);
- Fiscal services;
- Institutional research/planning;
- Student affairs;
- Selected faculty (typically from faculty-governing bodies such as the faculty council and the curriculum committee);
- Specialists (e.g., graduate, adult learner, campus technology); and
- Others based on the institution's culture (e.g., president, chief of staff, student, etc.).

Focus on planning details: The action/steering committee

An action/steering group coordinates the planning process and ensures that the details of the planning process are followed. This team keeps the process moving forward in a timely manner, reports to the SEP council, and ensures that each action subcommittee is supported during the planning process.

The steering group will address a variety of topics. Topics might include academic program planning, student life, student retention, distance learning, pricing, and promotion. Institutions may need to consider subpopulations when determining work process (e.g., traditional undergraduate, nontraditional, graduate, and international).

The steering group directs the process, coordinates the subcommittees, determines the agenda items for the council, and keeps the president/chancellor or other senior-level leaders highly involved in the SEP process. It is important that the action committee have high-level representation from academics, enrollment, business or financial affairs, student affairs, and institutional research. In addition, the committee should continue to link activities back to ROI considerations and have the systems in place to measure and monitor results.

The president/chancellor typically provides direction for the SEP council and the action/steering committee or is an active member of one or both of these groups.

Governing bodies that endorse or approve the plan

The faculty senate, council of deans, and others, depending on institutional culture, coordinate their agenda with this process and provide appropriate direction, feedback, endorsements, and/or approvals.

The board of trustees should provide vision, feedback, and appropriate approvals throughout the planning process.

Summary

Successful strategic enrollment planning is a complex, intensive process that is not intuitive for institutions. This is why the great majority of enrollment professionals report that their respective institutions do not have an excellent strategic enrollment plan in this very challenging higher education environment (Noel-Levitz, 2011).

Successful strategic enrollment planning and long-range enrollment and fiscal success rely on a chain of events that guide the process and lead to success. To ensure enrollment and fiscal success, institutions should rigorously implement an excellent, multiyear, strategic enrollment plan. Institutions must also develop and continuously apply a successful SEP process to produce an excellent, multiyear, strategic enrollment plan. Finally, to develop and implement a successful process, institutions must execute the process essentials that are outlined in this chapter, with emphasis on choosing the right process leaders and organizing them effectively, while also conducting continuous high-quality dialogue, both formally and informally, among process participants and throughout the institution.

For institutions to remain viable and successful in a dramatically changing environment, leaders should acknowledge that the journey to enrollment and fiscal success is long and complex and must be truly strategic.

Dialogue

This chapter has made the case that it is the process that determines whether an institution produces a successful strategic enrollment plan with excellent outcomes or an ineffective plan that may be nothing more than a tremendous waste of time. Along with this, it is important to emphasize what makes the process and its essentials work: dialogue. As noted in Chapter 2, this dialogue best occurs in an environment of trust.

Figure 4-3: Dialogue Links the SEP Process With the Plan

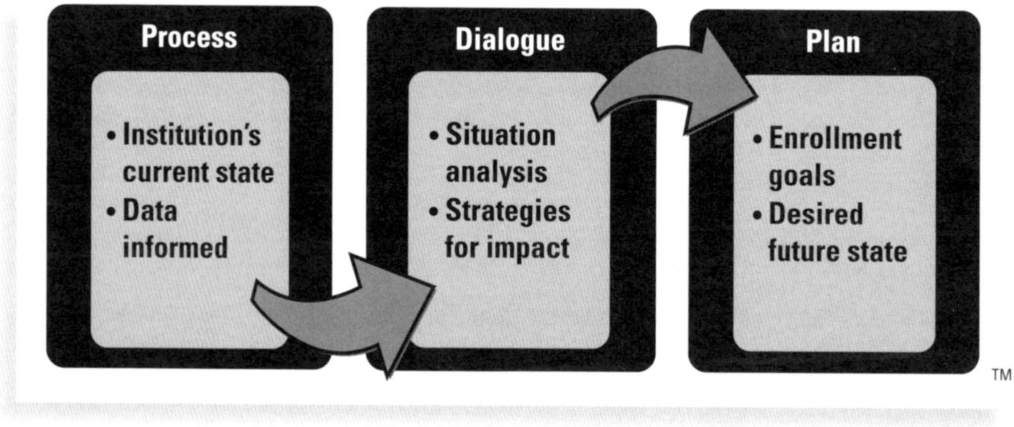

Process	Dialogue	Plan
• Institution's current state • Data informed	• Situation analysis • Strategies for impact	• Enrollment goals • Desired future state

TM

Specifically, the dialogue occurs among many different parties: 1) the president and the president's cabinet, the deans, the institutional community, and the board; 2) the chief academic officer, the chief enrollment officer, and the chief fiscal officer; and 3) academic affairs and the deans, academic department chairs, and faculty. Moreover, it is dialogue that the SEP process leaders have with other key department heads and staff who support students. Throughout this experience, the informal conversations among all these parties may have as much impact as the formal dialogue process.

Both formal meetings and informal dialogues between colleagues are so important to the success of the process that they need to be continuously nurtured and even orchestrated by the process leaders as part of the SEP process design and implementation. In fact, each week, process leaders should be asking themselves, "What have we done this past week to encourage critical informal and formal dialogue?" "What are we coordinating for the next week and the next month to nurture dialogue about the SEP process?" It should be a topic of discussion at many deans' council meetings, faculty council meetings, staff meetings at all levels, president and provost speeches, and numerous day-to-day informal conversations.

The following approaches will ensure a high level of dialogue regarding the SEP process. Their implementation must be planned and monitored—they are too important to the success of the process to be left to chance.

President/Chancellor communication: Just as the SEP council and its action committee are at the center of the SEP process, the president/chancellor plays the key role in setting the tone for institutionwide dialogue about the process and the expected outcomes from the process. The president creates the buzz that this SEP process will make significant impacts on the enrollment and fiscal health of the institution, as well as its culture and image. The president talks about these topics continuously in individual conversations with board members, vice presidents, deans, faculty members, and staff. The president also speaks about these topics in speeches and written communications. However, care must be taken that the expected outcomes are discussed in general terms, not in terms of precise numbers, until the SEP process produces quantifiable goals that are supported by strategies, tactics, and fiscal and human resources.

Academic dialogue: Because the SEP process should be academic oriented, the dialogue among process leaders and deans, academic department chairs, and faculty is paramount. At most institutions, deans and faculty members are more likely to buy into an SEP process that is being led by an academic leader (i.e., the provost, an associate provost, or a respected dean) than one that is led by another administrator. It is important for the SEP council to be chaired or at least co-chaired by an academic leader. For example, at The Ohio State University, the SEP council (under a different name) was chaired by a respected dean who spoke frequently about the SEP process at council of deans' meetings, faculty senate meetings, and academic department chair meetings, as well as in informal conversations with deans, department chairs, and faculty. This continuous dialogue with the academic community not only reset the priorities and the culture for undergraduate students and their enrollment trends, but also created buy-in for investments in key enrollment strategies and tactics—investments that may have been redirected away from other important academic initiatives. This academic leader must be highly knowledgeable about external and internal trends that affect enrollment in order to be a credible communicator with the academic community. Therefore, dialogue between the academic leader and the chief enrollment officer is also a key component to the planning process.

Co-curricular dialogue: Because the planning process should have an orientation that covers co-curricular issues, student life, and student success, the SEP process leaders should be in constant dialogue with department heads in student affairs, student advising, and student success centers. To ensure this happens, have key individuals from these departments on the SEP council and action committee. These individuals not only serve as the dialogue links between the SEP process leaders and the student support departments, they bring valuable insights and expertise to the development of the strategies, tactics, estimated costs, and estimated returns on investment. Again, these leaders can interact in two ways: 1) through formal contacts with the institution's student support departments; and 2) informal day-to-day contacts through individual conversations and staff meeting discussions.

Fiscal dialogue: The fiscal aspect of the SEP process requires frequent dialogue with the chief fiscal officer, as well as communication with other fiscal officers (e.g., associate vice presidents; budget directors; and fiscal officers in departments such as academic affairs, student affairs, and academic colleges). The full engagement of these fiscal officers is critical because the SEP plan will not be successful without innovative resource planning that is supported by institutional and departmental fiscal officers.

Data/research dialogue: To ensure the process is data informed, there must be continuous dialogue with the individuals who provide the data that drive the SEP process. At many institutions, the primary individual responsible for providing this data is the director of institutional research. At some institutions, there are data analysts within the office of enrollment services who also contribute valuable data and analysis to the process. No matter how the institution is organized to retrieve and analyze enrollment and environmental data, formal and informal dialogue on a daily basis is a must for the success of the process. See Chapter 5 for more on ensuring a data-informed SEP.

Data-informed Versus Data-driven Planning

By Gary Fretwell

"The future is embedded in the present." – **John Naisbitt**

A data-driven institution collects both internal and external data. While there are plenty of data available for campuses to use, most institutions lack the systems needed to collect, analyze, and make informed decisions based on data indicators. Since a rigorous assessment of the institution and its environment is at the heart of strategic enrollment planning (SEP), an effective SEP process requires developing strong systems to collect, analyze, and effectively interpret data.

Chapter highlights

- **What data-informed institutions ask**

- **Linking mission to future state**

- **How to determine institutional distinctiveness**

Two roads to setting and achieving goals

Imagine a college that wants to boost enrollment by increasing the number of students in its business program. Sensing an upswing of interest in this area, the college creates a beautiful brochure focused on its business program and its various majors, enhances that section on its Web site, sets a target number for new students expressing an interest in business, and urges its recruitment staff to go forth and enroll more students with an interest in business. If this effort is successful, the institution may find itself forced to react by increasing class sizes, hiring adjunct faculty, and even reconfiguring facilities. In the interim, student satisfaction may suffer as decisions are made hastily, instead of through a systemic enrollment planning effort, which includes monitoring strategy implementation to measure how actions are influencing outcomes.

Alternatively, the college might begin by gathering and reviewing pertinent data: What percentage of inquiries in recent recruitment cycles expressed an interest in business majors, and what were the eventual numbers of students enrolling in those programs? What are external perceptions of the institution's current business program? What are the job prospects for graduates with this major in the college's state or region? Who are its public, private, and for-profit competitors in this program area? How well are those competitors known compared to the knowledge of this college? What is the capacity for growth in the business department? Is the internship office prepared to facilitate more placements among area companies? Moreover, and perhaps most importantly, how would a heftier focus on business programs align with the institution's mission and vision?

All of this information can be used to shape a plan that establishes targets for inquiries, applicants, and matriculants; sets benchmarks for stages of growth; and triggers the appropriate deployment of resources in the areas of recruitment and departmental expansion. These steps help ensure that the institution is able to deliver on its promises to prospective business students and enable them to graduate with the skills and experiences needed to achieve future success.

The right path in this scenario seems obvious, yet it remains the one less traveled.

Unfortunately, in the current environment, many institutions have a wealth of internal and external data at their disposal, but do not use this data in any meaningful way that drives actions or interconnects numerous data collected to make impactful decisions. They are unable or unwilling to make appropriate use of the considerable resources that could help them effectively navigate their challenges to ensure long-term growth and stability. They are *data-driven* rather than *data-informed*. There is a critical difference between the two, as the latter approach means data informs the development of strategies with related tactics or action items to accomplish the strategies.

Data-driven often means that data is viewed singularly and not collectively to make decisions. For example, students may rate their level of satisfaction lower than other questions asked related to campus recreation. The same students may also rate their level of importance related to campus recreation as low. Without looking at multiple data sources (to be data-informed), a campus may act on low satisfaction ratings without considering other variables. The SEP process is designed to look at multiple variables before drawing conclusions. In addition, the review of data helps create specific performance indicators (PIs) linked to key performance indicators (KPIs). This data-informed approach is the heart of the SEP process.

" The SEP process is designed to look at multiple variables before drawing conclusions."

Creating a data-informed campus culture

Most institutions collect data. However, few institutions use that data to understand trends or patterns that should be monitored and instead use data to establish annual enrollment strategy. Leaders may look at a particular data element and set a goal to change it, deciding, for instance, to set a goal of increasing the number of inquiries or applicants. Meanwhile, many campus leaders fail to consider aligning both internal and external data with trend data to determine the real issues the institution faces. For example, few institutions are prepared for the 10-year prediction that enrollments will decrease.

A data-informed institution, on the other hand, takes the all-important next step of analyzing its data and drawing a more informed awareness of its situation and environment. The institution uses that awareness to make decisions that align with its mission while allowing it to adapt intentionally to the future instead of simply reacting to it. A data-informed institution asks, "Does our data allow us to understand our context and draw implications about how we will need to change in order to fulfill our mission and vision in the future? Does our current state align with the future needs, demands, and trends? If not, can our institution sustain itself?" Such institutions are, in effect, developing a kind of data wisdom that provides an impetus to move forward and drives the SEP process.

As challenging as this might seem, there is nothing magical about data. It is simply a resource that can be neglected, exploited, or understood. Frequently, a campus will have reams and reams of data with no one purposefully assessing it, considering its implications, or suggesting ways to change institutional behavior based on what it indicates. A campus must charge key personnel with taking the data and drawing conclusions from it, as illustrated in Figure 5-1.

Figure 5-1: Using Data to Inform Decisions

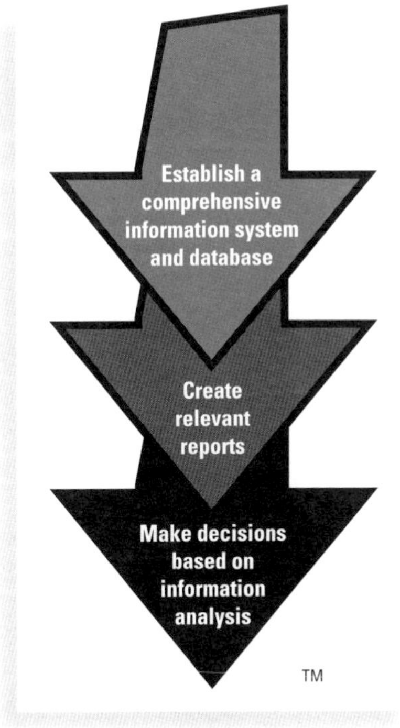

It begins with the establishment of a comprehensive database of internal and external information that an institution can use to better understand its current situation and the context within which it operates. From these sources, the institution must extract relevant reports that inform campus leaders about its context, trends, strengths, and challenges. Finally, the institution takes that information and uses it to make decisions that will guide its operation on both strategic and tactical levels.

Within this framework, it becomes plain that it is not enough to simply collect data. It is essential to understand what data reveal about an institution's state and environment, and then use that data sagely and with integrity.

The foundation for strategic enrollment planning

In Noel-Levitz's SEP work with all types of institutions, one immutable conviction has been proven over the years: A campus cannot effect enrollment change until it has a clear understanding about its current situation. SEP is not about guessing or assuming, but understanding an institution's enrollment experience across all market types and across the stages of recruitment, enrollment, matriculation, and graduation of students.

With this background information defined, campus leaders have additional questions to answer. Where do we want to go from our current state? What does the kind of institution we wish to become look like? Do we have absolute clarity in terms of new student enrollment, returning student enrollment, persistence and graduation rates, market demand, market penetration, the mix of students, pricing, and revenue objectives?

Once an institution understands where it is and where it wants to be, it can begin exploring the existing elements that will allow it to plan for change. Based on data and expectations, the institution can then develop a set of strategies that will facilitate movement toward its desired future. Again, it all begins with a solid grounding in the institution's current situation and external context.

Lacking context, institutions often make decisions based on incorrect or incomplete perceptions. The use of anecdotal comments and unproven assumptions frequently become catalysts for enrollment decisions. For example, a college may decide to confront its financial pressures by increasing its price in a non-incremental fashion. Before making this decision, the institution fails to analyze whether the market will bear that level of increase or whether there is sufficient demand for its product to warrant the increase. Alternatively, perhaps an institution wants to grow its first-year enrollment. Has it studied relevant internal data to determine if and where there is a capacity to grow in terms of its current programs and facilities? Has it analyzed external data to assess demand for its programs in its market area and the level of existing competition?

> *" It all begins with a solid grounding in the institution's current situation and external context."*

As institutions develop a data-informed mind-set, they are frequently confronted with three challenges. The first is the failure to collect essential data on a consistent basis. Second is an inability to access data in the form of relevant reports. The third is the need to create an institutional culture that relies on data to inform future decisions with leaders who practice data-informed decision making and provide staff resources to collect data for assessment. Therefore, it is essential that a campus invest in the creation of a comprehensive institutional database and dashboards with an eye toward consistent data collection and data accessibility, ensuring that staff will be able to input data with relative ease and extract knowledge as well as numbers from the resulting database.

The path from mission to strategy

"The key to success in the 21st century is alignment—staying in alignment with a world that will be characterized by complexity, diversity, and pace of change." – **Ed Barlow**

Enrollment plans are best devised in the context of institutional mission and intended strategic direction. This process leads an institution to affirm its mission and identify elements of the strategic plan that will be realized through effective enrollment management. The process also aligns the institution with its guiding vision and takes into account the external realities the institution will face as it works toward achieving its future state. As an example, an institution might desire to add a study-abroad requirement for all students. With the broader institutional mission and vision as a backdrop, campus leaders might ask questions such as: What will it mean for net tuition if students study at international locations that do not provide tuition exchange with our institution? How will this impact our enrollment or type of students? What systems will we need to put in place to re-engage students once they return from abroad? What are the cost implications for students who may not have the ability to afford a study-abroad option? What are the implications for student athletes?

As an institution frames its vision in terms of its goals for the number and type of students it wishes to recruit and the necessary investment in attracting and retaining them, it must consider external factors, institutional capacity by academic program, other facility constraints, and net tuition revenue needs that will affect that optimal enrollment. The data help clarify the internal and external challenges. With this knowledge in hand, the institution can begin to create the strategic plan, resulting in a set of clearly defined goals.

This approach turns the more common route to devising a strategic plan on its head. A traditional process presents goals and outlines what the institution will do to achieve them. Instead, the data-informed approach stresses that a campus begins by clarifying what is important in terms of institutional mission and vision. Next, it examines the internal and external context within which it operates. Finally, based on that data, it asks what resources it can reasonably apply to those strategies in order to move forward. Once the institution understands and interconnects its data, it is possible to make choices and set goals accordingly. Otherwise, a college may have 100 strategies but no way to resource them—a pointless exercise that leads to frustration and futility.

Choosing data that matter

On any college campus, the list of items that could be tracked and analyzed is daunting. For that reason, it's helpful to think in terms of themes or categories that will encourage an institution to divide, prioritize, and conquer. An obvious place to start is by making a distinction between internal and external data.

Internally, campuses should be tracking the makeup of their undergraduate and graduate students by type, academic program, entry point, and conversion rates at each stage of the recruitment process, as well as retention and graduation data. Campus administrators should have good data about recent enrollment patterns and trends at their institution. Campuses must also have the means to track information such as the quality of the academic experience, student expectations, and the level of student engagement and satisfaction. Financial indicators comprise another critical field of data with campuses tracking their net tuition revenues, auxiliary income, and costs and revenues by student group, as well as developing an understanding of the price sensitivity of prospective students in various income subgroups. This will allow the institution to create financial aid awarding strategies that are grounded in data and aligned with a desired future state.

In terms of external data, institutions can examine a number of factors, including demand for programs the campus offers, overall perceptions, and perceptions of specific program areas. Institutions can also study competitors and points of differentiation, shifting demographics and changing needs of students in the institution's marketplace, and how changes to state funding could impact the institution going forward.

Helpful resources for making comparisons among institutions include the Integrated Postsecondary Education Data System (IPEDS) from the National Center for Education Statistics (NCES), and College Results Online provided by The Education Trust. State and regional data can yield information on occupational trends, projected numbers of high school graduates, and shifting state and regional demographics. Other readily available sources of information include the Cooperative Institutional Research Program (CIRP) American Freshman Survey, along with state and association reports that summarize relevant data for their constituent institutions. Colleges should mine these data to develop an understanding of trends in student demographics, attitudes, and other information. Although the data may not be institution-specific, it can provide valuable groundwork for long-term institutional planning.

Organizing data around the "Big Three"

Data organization and analysis can be considered within the context of the "Big Three": What does the institution do well? What do students demand? What does the competition offer? Institutions seeking to increase their profile or national ranking should also consider institutional rankings of aspirant institutions (i.e., those the institution aspires to be more like).

The institution

Even if an institution intuitively knows what it does well and what changes need to be made, it can best effect change when informed by data that address:

- Student satisfaction and engagement;
- Faculty/staff satisfaction and alignment with student expectations;
- Alumni satisfaction/outcomes; and
- Student attrition.

The prospective student market

Understanding the student market may demand the most wide-ranging research. An institution may need both primary research and secondary data to examine areas such as:

- Demographic trends;
- Projected demand for academic programs;
- Price sensitivity;
- Lost inquiries and applicants;
- Brand/image; and
- Delivery format preferences.

The competition

A campus needs to understand current or new programs offered by competitor institutions that are drawing a larger share of the market. Comprehensive analysis should address:

- Competitor enrollment trends, including degree production by program;
- Competitor marketing messages and communication strategies;
- Competitor academic program offerings; and
- Institutional image vis-à-vis competition.

As an institution surveys the broad data landscape, it must zero in on the questions of *authenticity, relevance, and differentiation*. Using a data-informed process, what can the institution authentically claim about the type of campus it is and its offerings, what is *relevant* to the students the institution wishes to reach, and what are its points of *differentiation* in respect to other options considered by students?

Figure 5-2: Convergence of Authenticity, Relevance, and Differentiation

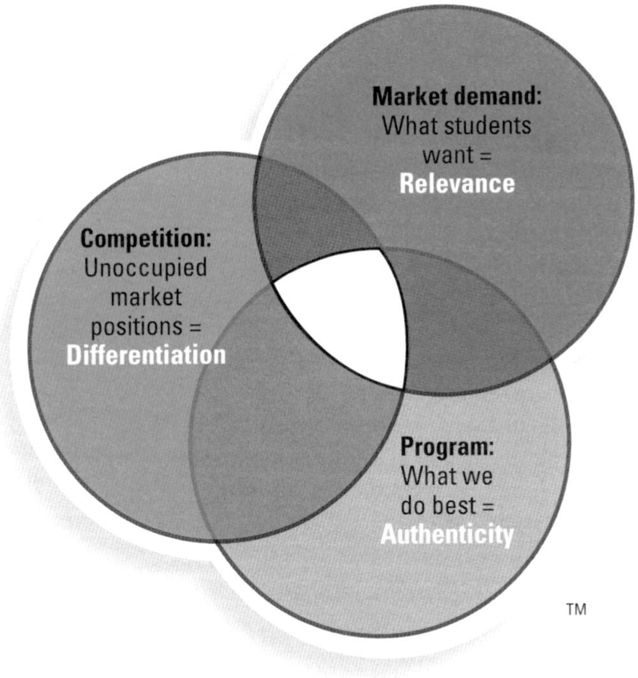

Figure 5-2 illustrates the campus "sweet spot" or interconnection between authenticity, relevance, and differentiation. An institution likely has its strongest potential to gain market share, to provide curricular or co-curricular programs that meet needs, and to increase its reputation where these three converge.

Analysis of the data

Data assessments should identify gaps, strengths, opportunities, and/or threats to the institution. These themes frame the analysis and help inform strategy development and the selection of key performance indicators.

As the institution reviews data, it needs to maintain a broad view and consider the interactions among multiple data points. Looking at only one or two reports may offer a partial frame of reference, but the data must be triangulated or cross-examined in light of other reports to yield broader themes. Reviewing multiple data sources that lead to similar conclusions can build confidence in the results and allow the planning team to use these conclusions to drive strategy development.

Key performance indicators

With this broad backdrop of an institutional knowledge base, and with the tools and procedures in place to refresh that knowledge on an ongoing basis, a campus is prepared to create a data-informed strategic enrollment plan. In our approach to creating a strategic enrollment plan, the components of that plan are most clearly described as *key performance indicators* and *performances indicators*.

A key performance indicator (KPI) relates to a major area of focus such as enrollment mix, external awareness, or revenue. KPIs are specific to each institution and based on its mission and vision. They may, in effect, form a kind of wish list for the institution. For example, having determined that it has the capacity to accommodate more students, an institution may set a KPI of increasing its enrollment in a certain area. Given that objective, it will need to determine a subset of indicators, or performance indicators (PIs), that are steps on the road to achieving the KPI. Those might include increasing the number of first-year or transfer students, improving retention, enrolling more online students, and/or opening satellite locations. Each PI included in the plan will include targets and a timeline, allowing the institution to benchmark its progress with clearly identified data points.

> *" The idea is to start with the institutional vision, determine the priorities for accomplishing it, and identify the appropriate KPIs and PIs to build a working strategic plan."*

Depending on an institution's mission and vision, other KPIs might relate to increasing diversity, becoming more selective, or increasing net revenue. The idea is to start with the institutional vision, determine the priorities for accomplishing it, and identify the appropriate KPIs and PIs to build a working strategic plan. Some KPIs might be more difficult to achieve or may require a sequencing of resources. Again, in a data-informed environment, institutional leaders will be able to anticipate these challenges and launch or incorporate stages of the strategic plan at appropriate times. In addition, institutional leaders will be measuring progress on PIs that will influence KPIs and understand that initiatives may take up to three years to meet target projections.

Because institutions can access volumes of data, both internally and externally from the marketplace, KPIs are critically important. As an institution establishes a vision that supports its institutional mission, KPIs will allow the institution to align its efforts with institutional objectives and choose the data points needed to create and monitor the strategic plan.

The following are types of top-level KPIs, along with the PIs that might support each KPI:

KPI: Enrollment
Potential PIs

1. Undergraduate enrollment

2. New freshman enrollment

3. Transfer enrollment

4. Undergraduate second- to third-year retention rate, third- to fourth-year retention rate, and beyond fourth-year graduation rate

5. Graduate enrollment

6. Graduate retention rate

7. Graduation rate

KPI: Enrollment profile changes (diversity, academic)
Potential PIs

1. Inquiry profiles

2. Applicant profiles

3. ACT and SAT market share profiles

KPI: Retention and graduation
Potential PIs

1. Student satisfaction indicators

2. Student engagement indicators

3. First- to second-term persistence

4. Grade-point distributions by student cohort and course

5. Number and percentage of students unable to enroll in desired major

6. Number and percentage of students unable to enroll in desired courses

7. Student debt burden and profile

8. Award gaps between student need and actual financial aid awards

KPI: Fiscal health
Potential PIs

1. Net tuition revenues

2. Auxiliary (housing, dining, bookstore) total revenues and net revenues

3. Education and general costs by student subgroups (program and ability level)

4. Net tuition revenue and scholarship costs by student subgroups (ability level and resident/ nonresident)

5. Net tuition revenue and financial aid cost by needy student subgroup

> " An effective strategic enrollment plan will delineate both clear objectives and a set of data points to track their progress."

This is hardly an exhaustive list of KPIs or PIs, but it makes the point that an effective strategic enrollment plan will delineate both clear objectives and a set of data points to track their progress. Without these elements, an institution cannot create its future because it won't know what it should look like when it achieves its desired state. Chapters 8 and 9 will provide additional insights into KPIs and fiscal health.

Creating a data-informed situation analysis

One of the most important prerequisites to developing enrollment strategies is a SWOT analysis: identifying current *strengths*, current *weaknesses*, projected *opportunities*, and projected *threats*. Institutions will want to develop strategies that take full advantage of identified strengths and opportunities, manage weaknesses and threats, and turn one or more of the weaknesses into opportunities for improvement. Below are common definitions for each SWOT element:

Strengths: Existing characteristics (programmatic, physical, and financial) that clearly contribute to institutional success and the achievement of enrollment goals.

Opportunities: External factors that have the *potential* to be developed into strengths.

Weaknesses: *Existing* characteristics that detract from institutional success and the achievement of enrollment goals.

Threats: *Potential* external conditions that could become obstacles to institutional success and achievement of enrollment goals.

Figure 5-3: SWOT Analysis

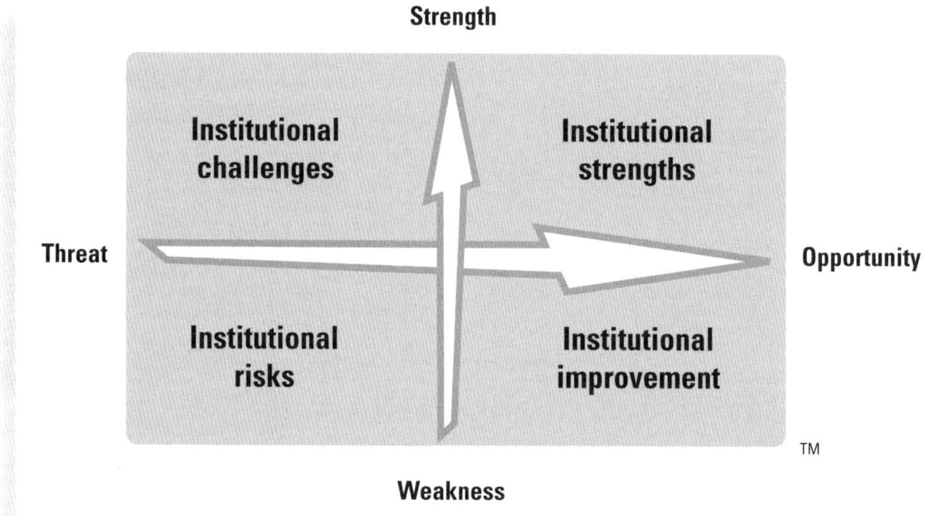

As part of the discussion connecting data with the institution's current state, the institution should compare its strengths and weaknesses to those of competing institutions.

Next, the management council should review the SWOT analysis and collectively pull themes from the data to create a current situation analysis. For SEP, the situation analysis should become a narrative that communicates the current state and the challenges to reach the desired future state, thereby illuminating the need for change, priorities for action, and current activities to be continued or further enhanced. The situation analysis also uses data to make statements of fact and sway the campus away from unsupported opinions.

Dialogue: Next steps in becoming a data-informed champion

- Take a thorough inventory of data you have and gaps that exist;
- Establish reports that clearly capture key data findings;
- Share the results of initial data findings; and
- Explain why the plan is data-informed, not data-driven, and help the campus understand the difference.

Themes drawn from the data review might include changes in communications and resources, including staffing and budget, as well as implications for the amount of time required to respond and proactively move forward.

The SEP process can also demonstrate how data can be used throughout the campus, regardless of its connection to enrollment, to inform priorities and prompt action. Data collected through the planning process should be stored and shared in open sites (either during or after the planning process) to ensure transparency.

When identifying data elements and to ensure that the review of data becomes an ongoing process, institutional leaders should consider the following:

- Who will be responsible for collecting and collating the data as well as monitoring the data on a quarterly basis?
- What types of data are needed to support the planning process and foster a better understanding of opportunities or threats in meeting institutional strategic plan goals?
- How will these measures be linked to the long-term planning and plan monitoring process?
- How widely are data currently shared among important campus units? How will data need to be shared in the future?
- Does the current SEP planning team understand the importance and value of KPI collection, monitoring, and annual/biannual updates?
- How will KPIs link to academic programs as they are evaluated and reviewed?
- Who will be responsible for an ongoing review of external data that will affect KPIs?
- How will the KPI review and the work of the strategic enrollment management (SEM) council be linked to the institution's financial condition?
- How will the review and the work of the SEM council be linked to the institution's marketing efforts to showcase campus bragging points?

" The SEP process can also demonstrate how data can be used throughout the campus, regardless of its connection to enrollment, to inform priorities and prompt action."

This is hardly a comprehensive list of discussion points, but it is meant to spur campus dialogue about the importance of data usage and its use in the SEP process. For example, an institution may not be at a point where academic program evaluation and restructuring can be incorporated into the planning process; however, the campus can use internal and external data to understand program trends and expected future demand. If a campus has a distinctive computer information program that is small but expected to see increased demand due to increased employment opportunities, the planning process might identify this and result in the designation of specific marketing or recruitment efforts to expand interest and increase enrollment. In this same example, if the data show a large gap in the interests of entering students and degree completion, strategies can be developed to help support program outcomes and increase completion rates. These strategies would support the academic program, but not necessarily move into a depth of analysis that would be considered a detailed program review. Regardless of current academic program offerings, it is essential that the data provide information and insight about student interest (by subpopulation) and current or potential market share.

To be truly strategic, campuses must use data to inform SEP strategies and goals. Failure to incorporate relevant data throughout the process can limit success.

CHAPTER 6

Aligning Academic and Co-curricular Programs

By Evelyn (Bonnie) Lynch

In studies conducted by Noel-Levitz, OmniUpdate®, CollegeWeekLive, and NRCCUA®, a majority of prospective students indicated that they looked at Web pages related to an academic program offering before any other information. While there certainly are many factors leading to a student's selection of a college or university, student satisfaction data also indicates that the quality of academic instruction (instructional effectiveness) is most important when comparing other institutional factors (Noel-Levitz, 2011, 2012). Therefore, the need for institutions to connect and align academic and co-curricular programs with their new enrollment efforts is paramount. From a broader perspective, connecting students (even undeclared majors) with academic programs, and deepening that connection through co-curricular and support services, is critical to strong enrollment management outcomes.

Chapter highlights

- **Academic and co-curricular programs are at the forefront of SEP**

- **The process examines internal and external variables**

- **Planning analysis includes ROI of program offerings**

Unfortunately, few institutions build an enrollment management program that connects academic and/or co-curricular programs with enrollment management practices to yield optimal enrollment and fiscal results. Instead, enrollment managers are often pushed to enroll more students in popular majors or in co-curricular programs such as a particular athletic sport. This approach is inefficient and does not consider what the institution should be doing to maximize its enrollment and revenue.

The strategic enrollment planning (SEP) process seeks to implement a balanced approach to planning that ensures quality and capacity are maintained or grown in thoughtful ways to ensure the student experience has strong outcomes and is completion/graduation oriented. Chapters 1 through 3 defined SEP and identified the significance, characteristics, and desired outcomes for guiding institutions to a desired future. Chapter 4 described the phases and key elements of the process. Chapter 5 discussed the data-informed SEP process and identified key performance indicators (KPIs) and performance indicators (PIs) as the foundation for data collection, analysis, and goal determination and evaluation.

This chapter explores important considerations in aligning the SEP process with academic programs and co-curricular programs. Here, the term program refers to an academic major, minor, graduate degree, long-term certificate, or student service, and is not synonymous with the department in which it is housed. This chapter builds on the framework and concepts of the previous chapters to describe the alignment with and inter-relationships among academic programs, co-curricular services, and the strategic enrollment plan.

Academic programs, priorities, and planning

Despite the historical success of the American K-12 and postsecondary education systems, they are no longer keeping pace with the rapid changes and innovations that are driving domestic and foreign economies. College and university presidents must now provide and demonstrate improved educational quality for diverse student groups using varied instructional delivery approaches while maintaining mission integrity, institutional quality, and fiscal accountability in an uncertain future (Bobbitt, 2011; Cullinan, 2009; Gee, 2009). A strong SEP process is mindful of this and uses data to understand market demand. Numerous articles and studies from leading higher education organizations stress the imperative for institutions to become more nimble in their ability to change and modify curricula or enhance technological practices to reach a broader potential student population and/or meet the emerging employment demands predicted for the near future.

Beset by economic, social, and technological/digital changes, along with questions posed by funders, alumni, and legislators about curricular relevance, access, and student learning outcomes, American higher education is now at a major turning point (Brown, 2011). As tuition increases continue to outpace inflation and student debt continues to rise, parents question the return on their investment in their children's college educations (Bassis, 2009; Guskin, 1996). Institutional responses or the seeming lack of effective responses to current economic challenges contribute to the perception that colleges and universities have lost touch with society (Brown, 2011).

> *" As the SEP process moves forward, it must be linked with the realities of student preparedness and needs to set the stage for improved college completion rates."*

There is evidence of radical changes to come in professional roles, occupations, and employment needs, as well as employer expectations of knowledge, skills, and personal attributes needed for the new global markets. *A Better Measure of Skills Gaps* described the "new reality" of inadequate preparation across major employment sectors for workforce developers and educational providers (ACT, 2011). Although not conclusive, these preliminary results suggest that the gap in foundational skills widens as the level of education increases.

Concurrently, the Lumina Foundation (2010) reported that U.S. attainment of higher education degrees or credentials must increase by 60 percent by 2025 to keep pace with the growth of better-educated workforces around the world. To attain this goal, Lumina estimated an increase of 23 million additional college graduates over the number predicted by the present graduation rate.

As institutions develop their plans to educate a larger and more diverse student population, they must align their efforts with the realities of these learners. Students will likely have skill deficiencies in one or more content areas and need additional engagement or support strategies (human or technological) to succeed at a majority of institutions. As the SEP process moves forward, it must be linked with the realities of student preparedness and needs to set the stage for improved college completion rates.

Academic and co-curricular planning

The academic enterprise is both the heart of an institution and its major cost center (Leslie and Fretwell, 1996). Yet academic programs have seen little additional investment as fiscal resources have been directed toward institutional recruitment/marketing strategies, better-quality service (more staff), advanced athletic or recreational facilities, and/or dynamic and diversified student centers (Astin, 2003). In order to compete in today's markets, institutions have allocated resources for purposes that foster advancement of all programs. Fewer resources have been focused on ways to improve faculty performance in the classroom or provide them with the professional development needed to integrate technology as a supplemental tool to further engage students and improve course outcomes.

While academic programs and departments have seen few boosts in funding, they have also been insulated from short-term cost cutting during times of financial turbulence. Reductions are often made in nonacademic areas, particularly in student affairs, marketing, and physical plant/operations, as these areas are sometimes considered discretionary and their work viewed as peripheral to the mission of the institution (Ehernberg and Webber, 2010). If academic programs are included in an across-the-board cut, funding is usually returned to its prior level once the situation has stabilized. Moreover, on many campuses, the annual budgeting process does not include academic program/department revenues or academic productivity measures (e.g., credit hour production, degrees/certificates awarded) as part of the process. The direct and indirect costs to operate academic programs are assumed as baseline expenses in each budget cycle.

At the outset of most institutional strategic planning processes, academic programs are considered to be equally aligned, integral to the mission, and therefore beyond re-allocation or termination considerations (Leslie and Fretwell, 1996). Dickeson (2010) suggested that institutional planning efforts were usually additive, resulting in new resources, new faculty in existing programs, and new programs, with little consideration of future employment or graduate school opportunities or of initial start-up recruitment and marketing costs to generate students for new academic programs.

The SEP process seeks to create a future state where a process is established to study all of the aforementioned considerations (and likely additional ones) before announcing or approving a new academic or co-curricular program. In a similar concept to program review, the SEP process ensures that the campus has done research to explore market demand and the ability to penetrate existing markets to determine if program offerings are minimally sustainable, ultimately financially profitable, and aligned with a desired future institutional state.

As noted, planning for student affairs generally occurs within the broad context of institutional planning, with mixed fiscal and resource outcomes. Such planning efforts may result in internal personnel efficiencies and/or changes to existing in-house programs or activities, but most often, these actions are not aligned with the institution's overall vision for the future or with academic affairs (Atkins, 2010). Recently, student affairs leaders have advocated for the use of traditional planning models as a strategy to position co-curricular units and demonstrate relevance to mission, student outcomes, and the external and internal future (Ellis, 2010). In his discussion of academic and student affairs collaboration in strategic planning, Whitney (2010) noted that, "Student affairs and the faculty have a stake in working together," and identified retention and persistence as areas for collaborative planning. Yet too few institutions plan collaboratively, and, when they do, it is generally at the department level rather than campuswide.

Along with academic reputation, students are also attracted to institutions because of the range and types of co-curricular programs available. Such co-curricular experiences take many forms, depending upon the types of students, institutional mission, personnel, and fiscal resources allocated to them. For student-centric institutions, co-curricular experiences are no longer viewed as ancillary or peripheral but are seen as integral to student success.

Data suggest that well-planned, large-impact experiences, in and outside of the classroom, contribute to retention, persistence, and graduation (Kuh, 2008; Newton and Smith, 2008; Terenzini, Pascarella, and Blimling, 1996; Zlotkowski, 1998). Collaborative, high-impact practices shown to correlate with student success include, but are not limited to:

- Living-learning communities;
- First-year seminar/course linking;
- Early-alert systems;
- Supplemental instruction;
- Athletics/Intramurals; and
- Service learning.

In his discussion of faculty perspectives on undergraduate education and curriculum, Bok (2006) stated that the "extra curriculum" was most often overlooked as a valuable component of a student's educational experience. While acknowledging that the overall impact varied based on the type of student and the nature of the institution, he suggested that such experiences may have a more lasting impression than classroom experiences. He concluded that what students study in class often affects the value of their extracurricular experience, which, in turn, can enhance what they learn in class.

Collaborative endeavors between the academic and student affairs spheres may result in conflicts over turf, resources, and expertise. Schroeder (1999) identified obstacles and constraints that contributed to the separation of the formal and informal curriculum and how such impediments differed by institution type. Whitney (2010) compared the faculty and student affairs divide to a clash of cultures based largely on a lack of understanding about how each unit contributes to the mission and vision. He concluded that collaboration between academic and student affairs is now essential, and institutions must deliver on the promises and information given to students in the recruitment process.

Figure 6-1 contrasts the prevailing silo perspective of segmented academic and co-curricular programs with the desired alignment of these two areas.

Figure 6-1: Strategic Enrollment Planning Academic and Co-curricular Alignment

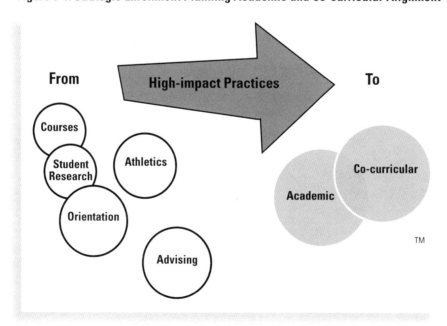

©2012, Noel-Levitz, Inc.

Considerations in strategic enrollment planning

SEP is a complex and organized effort to connect mission, current state, and changing environment to long-term enrollment and fiscal health.

SEP aligns and integrates academic and co-curricular programs with marketing, recruitment, retention/completion, and finance/financial aid strategies, with an eye toward future demands and trends. SEP begins with data collection and the alignment of that data with a situation analysis. Figure 6-2 depicts examples of significant variables in the external and internal environments that must be considered in academic and co-curricular data collection.

Figure 6-2: External and Internal Influences

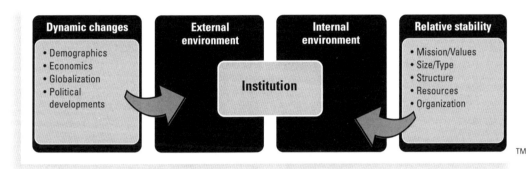

External environment

As we have discussed in this and previous chapters, external pressures on higher education are dynamic and influence institutional decision makers both directly and indirectly. It is important for decision makers to examine externally focused information, such as employment trends, SAT/ACT state data trends, Western Interstate Commission for Higher Education (WICHE) data, and workforce readiness data, and compare these data to institutional offerings, adult learner trends, and regional accreditation information. However, decisions based primarily or solely on external information may ultimately be deleterious to institutional soundness. National databases, public policy documents, and large-scale research and evaluation reports are of limited value when considered in isolation from institutional data. For example, demographic trends and occupational projections may influence an institutional leadership council to urge the initiation of a new program in response to reported enrollment increases at competitor institutions. External influences must be taken into account, but successful SEP is also integrated and comprehensive.

Internal environment

In traditional academic planning, the primary focus is internal review, program prioritization, and possible re-allocation of resources. There is minimal focus on external forces/conditions (e.g., competition analysis, demographic projections, occupational trends) and the implications for current and future states.

Decision making occurs at all levels and across all units of an institution, often in isolation from other units and departments within the organizational sphere. Although it is obvious that the larger and more complex an institution, the greater the challenges of sharing information and collaboration, even smaller institutions are not immune to silo-style decision making.

Senior leadership, deans, department heads, and academic and student affairs program coordinators generally do not stop to question how each decision impacts the institution's overall budget, effectiveness, or efficiency. The longer-term effects of repeated independent decision making across all units may not be evident in conventional planning, self-studies, or academic reviews. However, the cumulative effect of this uncoordinated decision making becomes evident in the SEP process and begins with linking KPI/PI identification to fiscal management (see Chapter 9).

KPIs provide accountability and direction. The initial step in the process is identification of campuswide academic and co-curricular program-level KPIs (e.g., quality and outcome measures) and supporting PIs. One approach to thinking about KPIs is to categorize campuswide and program-level KPIs and PIs as *input, process, and output measures*. Inputs focus on entering variable characteristics. Processes focus on the activities and levels of engagement that occur through the student experience. Outputs focus on progression (return from one term or one year to the next) and degree/certificate completion.

Table 6-1: Examples of Internal Key Performance Indicators (KPI)

KPI	Institutional Input	Institutional Process	Institutional Output	Program-level Input	Program-level Process	Program-level Output
Enrollment	X					
Student quality	X					X
Retention			X		X	X
Graduation			X			X
Faculty/Staff satisfaction		X			X	
Finance		X		X		
Financial aid	X			X		
Institution visit	X					X
Capacity and demand for academic programs		X		X	X	X
Expenses/Revenues by program					X	X
Quality of faculty	X					
Quality of educational experiences*	X	X	X	X	X	X
Student satisfaction	X	X	X		X	X

* Includes academic and co-curricular programs (e.g., athletics, service learning)

Although Table 6-1 presents KPIs in a linear format, they are multi-faceted and interactive variables, with campuswide data reflecting the highest level of the institution and the program-level information as a subset of the institutional data (Rowley, Lujan, and Dolence, 1997). For example, the institutional enrollment KPI is the sum of all program enrollments over a given time period. Changes in program-level KPIs (e.g., student satisfaction, demand and capacity, retention) will influence the institutional enrollment and other institutional KPIs (e.g., student quality, finance). Data should be multiyear, providing a three-year profile/pattern at a minimum (a five-year span is preferable), as this allows for a one-year extreme swing in either direction. KPI identification must include agreement on definitions (e.g., cohort, major, graduate, FTE enrollment), and be used consistently by all offices and in enrollment communications.

Strategic enrollment planning: Strategy development and prioritization

The situation analysis, derived from the KPI/PI analysis, provides the foundation for determining and prioritizing the key strategies that are the precondition for realistic and attainable enrollment goals. This sets the stage for academic program and co-curricular strategy development. Ultimately, the planning process should seek to align curricular, co-curricular, and support services with new student and enrollment processes that connect through each stage of the enrollment experience (prospect/inquiry through completion). This happens through an intentional process that uses data to define future need and market potential of programs.

For illustrative purposes, let's summarize the situation analysis from a hypothetical institution, Unchanging College (UC). This mid-size private college, which is becoming increasingly tuition-dependent, is recognized for its liberal arts focus (36 majors, 18 minors) and small class sizes. Nursing, international business, and graphic design/arts have been added over the past 20 years, and these professional programs provide the largest revenue stream, but there is increasing competition from Behemoth University (BU), 60 miles away, with its seamless new bachelor's-to-master's programs. Moreover, a competitive private college is considering the addition of weekend and online bachelor's degree and master's programs at locations near UC. The UC faculty, 80 percent of whom are tenured, are concerned about the competition but equally opposed to online, hybrid, or weekend courses, believing that such programs would dilute the college's legacy and reputation.

> *" Academic programs need to be closely examined for mission congruity, productivity, and continued relevance and student demand."*

State and national reports project a decline in the number of high school seniors in UC's primary market areas, but a growing adult-learner segment. Its residential population is declining; tuition is increasing an average of 5 percent each year; the discount rate has edged close to 48 percent each of the past five years; and student exit data reflect greater dissatisfaction than satisfaction with the college experience. Faculty are concerned admissions is lowering standards to "bring in the class." Although enrollment is flat, numbers were up in all phases of the funnel for the past four years. The five-year retention rate averaged 80 percent, with significant increases (7 percent) over the past two years, corresponding to the addition of a first-year seminar, early-alert pilots, and the expansion of intramural offerings. Despite its improved retention, reputation, and alumni support, there is an increasing recognition by key faculty and new academic administrators that "something has to change."

In traditional planning, attention will likely be focused solely on enrollment instead of the entire institution. Academic programs will not be closely examined for mission congruity, productivity, and continued relevance and student demand. Strategies considering purpose, programs, price, place, process, and promotion will not provide the foundation for comprehensive planning. Most likely, the planning will result in short-term and short-sighted responses, such as across-the-board cuts. At best, the institution may survive, but neither it nor its students will flourish.

Whether the overarching enrollment goals are focused on increasing, maintaining, or decreasing enrollments, understanding how product (programs), current and projected demand, student success, and ROI intersect is essential. The following discussion illustrates the use of the SEP process in three key enrollment strategy areas:

1. Program, institutional effectiveness, and student success.

2. Purpose and identity.

3. Place and program delivery.

Although Chapter 8 provides a thorough discussion of fiscal considerations, the costs of educational capacity and demand are discussed here as well.

Program, institutional effectiveness, and student success

In the case of Unchanging College, as with all institutions, the strategic enrollment council and/or senior leadership (strategy groups will vary by institution) may initiate the academic and co-curricular strategy discussion by asking fundamental questions such as:

- How does each program align with institutional mission, vision, and goals?

- How does the program align with future-oriented knowledge and skills?

- How does the program contribute to the fiscal health of the institution?

- How does the program document student success outcomes?

- What is the current market penetration of program offerings compared to the expected level of interest?

- What is the percentage of market share among students enrolling in the state/county/region?

- What are the costs of the program per student-to-degree completion?

Responses to these questions will position specific academic and co-curricular programs in relation to the current institutional environment and the needs/requirements of the external environment (i.e., KPI/PIs, situation analysis). As will become evident, these responses will also guide short- and long-term SEP priority determination.

At UC, these fundamental questions involve a program demand and capacity analysis. Figure 6-3 depicts program options as a function of current and projected demand (capacity) and net operating income. As an institution considers cost versus mission versus future state, it can pursue one of the following seven options for academic program planning:

1. Do nothing.

2. Modify/enhance what already exists.

3. Create multidisciplinary programs out of the existing curriculum.

4. Create entirely new programs.

5. Adopt alternative delivery formats for nontraditional markets or within traditional markets if there is growing demand for these formats.

6. Connect undergraduate majors to complementary graduate offerings.

7. Close/Downsize underperforming programs or programs that data suggest will no longer align with future market interests.

Figure 6-3: Evaluation Programs–Strategic Options Instead of Strategic Response

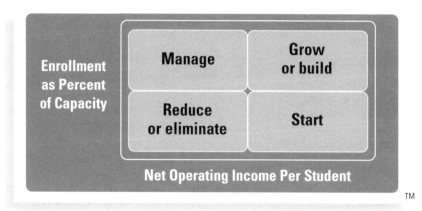

UC must determine:

- Academic courses/programs that are over capacity or under capacity;

- High-cost and/or low-completion academic programs;

- High completion and high-cost academic programs;

- Co-curricular program costs and outcomes (e.g., living-learning wing of residence hall); and

- Progression and completion rates linked to each program.

Moreover, the revenue versus cost-per-student to deliver these programs must be analyzed.

Although this analysis is time consuming, it will yield valuable information (e.g., highly discounted students in the most in-demand or costliest programs). Capacity and demand may be influenced by days and times of course offerings, scheduling of co-requisites, time between classes and distance between buildings, and ease of scheduling. These are obvious but frequently overlooked variables that may indirectly influence retention, progression, and course and program decisions.

For example, suppose there is a high entry-level demand for chemistry. The institution needs to determine whether the program is cost effective if only 10 of the 60 students who enter UC considering chemistry graduate with a major in chemistry and the other 50 leave the institution. If the reverse is true and 60 students enter the program but 80 graduate, what are the strategies being employed to retain and attract new students from other majors (or undecided students) to succeed in the program? Without this analysis, institutional behavior patterns over time lead to an attitude of "this is how we do it" without regard to the potential negative consequences or the connections among recruitment, program delivery, interconnection with campus experiences/services, and completion.

Dickeson (2010) listed 10 criteria and related applications to prioritize academic programs:

1. History, development, and expectations for the program.

2. External demand for the program.

3. Internal demand for the program.

4. Quality of program inputs and processes.

5. Quality of program outcomes.

6. Size, scope, and productivity of the program.

7. Revenue and other resources generated by the program.

8. Costs and other expenses associated with the program.

9. Impact, justification, and overall significance of the program.

10. Opportunity analysis of the program.

Since Dickeson's focus was on academic programs and services, nonacademic programs were not considered, but the same criteria could apply to these areas. For example, some campuses have a rich and robust Greek tradition. Over the years, these programs may have evolved into strong positive organizations that provide significant community service to the local area, generate more graduates, and/or develop major alumni contributors. The size, scope, and productivity of Greek programs may justify the needed staffing and other resources to further enhance these programs, while the reverse may justify a decrease in support for these programs.

Purpose and identity

As UC reviews its curricular and co-curricular programs to ensure it has a quality product and is producing graduates well prepared for careers or the achievement of higher credentials, it must also consider whether its current mission aligns with a future state of higher education. The College Board Trends in Higher Education Series has reported numerous positive outcomes linked to degree completion, particularly at the bachelor's level. UC has generally adhered to this line of thinking as it considered any radical changes. However, they must continue to review their true market niche and market potential, connecting their current mission with a vision for a future that understands market demand, competition, and program strengths. In considering what it does best, UC must also understand the market demand for or relevance of its program offerings (both curricular and co-curricular).

Place and program delivery

As UC considers the relationship between demographic strategies (e.g., increase adult learners) and program growth options, an analysis of the competition might prove useful in gaining acceptance for alternative delivery formats. Although it's often difficult to implement new approaches in traditional higher education cultures, the positive revenue implications of executing low-overhead, low-cost, high-demand programs may be considerable.

Co-curricular programs

As an emerging component of SEP, co-curricular programs are subject to analysis by cost, program areas, and student populations (e.g., undecideds, transfers, athletes). However, students do not segment their college experiences or choices by cost centers or organizational structures. Institutional leaders who understand students' perspectives and the value of academic and co-curricular collaboration will reap the benefits in retention, progression, and graduation. Although difficult to determine, the cost-per-student of these success initiatives will prove to be an investment in long-term institutional success.

Conclusion and dialogue

"The future ain't what it used to be." Yogi Berra's words serve to remind institutional leaders of their responsibilities in guiding colleges and universities toward the future. At its most basic level, SEP invites institutions to envision their future and determine the scope and magnitude of change required to spur progress toward the desired state. As an institutionwide process, SEP includes all facets of the institution, including academic programs, and presents an opportunity to align academic and co-curricular programs with institutional mission. Equally important, it provides a pathway to foster links between academic and co-curricular initiatives.

Some questions the campus community should consider include:

1. How does the campus integrate curricular, co-curricular, and support service functions to yield a dynamic and seamless learning experience with positive outcomes?

2. Based on current employment trends, what are the top five to ten academic programs that will help meet the greatest employment needs?

3. What are the resources needed to ensure that these majors (linked to employment demand) are being delivered in contemporary ways that teach the skills needed for future professionals in these areas?

4. How do co-curricular and support programs help to engage students, make them more well-rounded, and prepare them for the future (i.e., employment or graduate school)?

5. How many students graduate from each major? What is the five-year average of the number of students who graduate from each major? For programs with low or no student graduation rates, is this due to lack of student interest, lack of targeted new student enrollment efforts, or lack of up-to-date curricula that engage the students and link the degrees to skills for the 21st century?

6. How many students complete gateway or prerequisite courses successfully (i.e., with the thorough understanding of course outcomes) to prepare them for advanced-level courses?

Remember that exploration of change and opportunity in the academic arena is not for the faint of heart, and communication and transparency are essential to successful planning. For those who persist, however, the long-term institutional benefits are well worth the investment of time and resources.

CHAPTER 7

Strategy Identification

By Brian Ralph

The process of strategy identification and development is arguably the most pivotal component of strategic enrollment planning (SEP). This stage connects the current state to the desired state. The migration from current state to desired state requires strategic thinking and strategic behavior, both of which flow out of critical analysis of the environment to develop and implement creative, impactful strategies.

It is helpful to think of SEP as a continuum that resembles a teeter-totter. The early stages all sit to the left of the fulcrum. Climbing up that ramp is hard work; it requires tenacity, focus, and courage to keep asking questions and seeking data to answer those questions. However, as an institution identifies and develops strategies, actions, and tactics, the teeter-totter begins to tip to the right, moving the campus to action. Most campuses find this part of the process, tipping to the right, to be an exciting time, as all of the knowledge and research begins to bear fruit and provide direction.

Chapter highlights

- **Why develop strategies before goals**

- **Situation analysis drives strategy development**

- **Working groups set a plan for action**

Figure 7-1: Migration From Current to Desired State

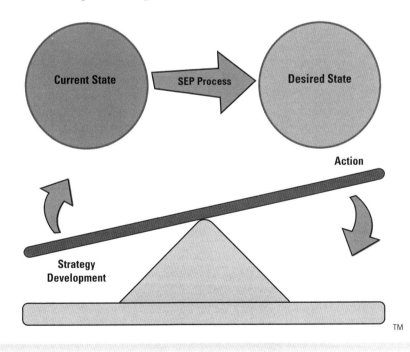

The beauty of SEP is that the desired state evolves from research and a clear (or perhaps slightly less foggy) view of the direction an institution can head, taking into account the current and anticipated future environment in which it will have to operate. As we learned in Chapter 5, the current state is most accurately understood through a thorough and robust assessment of an institution's strengths and weaknesses as well as a close look at what is going on in the external environment. The opportunities and threats that are all around an institution must be monitored. According to Kotler and Fox (1985), "The first step in strategic planning is to analyze the environment, because changes in the environment usually call for new institutional strategies." The quality of strategy development to create a stronger future state will correlate directly with the quality of the environmental assessment and the depth of understanding of the current state.

SEP enables a campus to develop a plan that is grounded in information and research, not in anecdotes and hope. Connecting the data and information from the environmental assessment to strategy development is critical to the success of the process. As we all know, too often planning starts with setting arbitrary and uninformed measurable goals with little or no understanding of an institution's strengths and weaknesses, the external environment, or what steps may be needed to achieve those goals. We have all been part of (and probably contributed to) discussions in which stories of a single student from six years ago drove the development of six strategies about how to improve the ventilation on the sixth floor of the residence hall because the student called six times to complain that the air was stagnant. Of course, we learn later that there wasn't a ventilation issue but rather the student forgot to breathe. In all seriousness, way too many strategies and goals are developed and executed based on anecdotes, legends, and opinions with no reference to research and information collected through an exhaustive environmental assessment.

We will discuss strategy development in detail throughout this chapter with the topic of goal setting addressed more fully in Chapter 8. True goal development comes from an understanding of the likely enrollment impact of each strategy and which strategies are ultimately selected and funded in the SEP.

Using the situation analysis

As participants in the SEP process dig deeply into the results of the situational analysis, the entire group will gain clarity about the areas that need work as well as the opportunities for success. An important component of strategy development is a clear understanding of the need for two distinct levels of strategic thought: top level and second level. Top-level strategies are broad statements about what we are going to do. Second-level strategies bring focus and accountability to our needed actions.

Top-level strategies are general statements relating to the categories outlined in Chapter 4 (the Six Ps) that highlight what the institution will do to move toward its desired state. For example, a top-level strategy statement could be, "Noel-Levitz University will provide co-curricular programs that will attract new students to the university and increase the retention of currently enrolled students." Top-level strategies are an outflow of the Six Ps and are generally crafted by the leadership group of the SEP process.

Second-level strategies are specific actions that will enable the institution to fulfill the top-level strategies. A corresponding follow-up example would be, "Develop weekend programming and events that engage students." The quality of second-level strategies is directly related to the level of engagement by faculty and staff in the strategy development process. The strategies and commensurate action plans not only identify a specific tactic, but who is responsible, when it will be executed, how much it will cost, and a measurement tool that will make it possible to know when a plan has been successfully completed.

The best way to start developing strategies based on the situational analysis is to form working groups aligned with key areas of focus. Examples include external environment, competition, enrollment, selectivity, capacity and demand, quality of the educational experience, marketing, student engagement/satisfaction and outcomes, quality of faculty and staff, persistence and graduation, diversity, finances, and financial aid, as well as specific subgroups in areas where data indicate a large gap between institutional practice and the desired reality. It should be noted that few campuses will have this many working groups. The situation analysis should determine the areas of priority and the working groups needed to address them.

The working group process is extremely important to the success of SEP. For perhaps the first time, these groups will be "confronting the brutal facts" that Collins so powerfully addresses in Chapter 4 of his book *Good to Great* (2001). In particular, the working groups will "lead with questions, not answers." The answers come much later in the process.

One of the most compelling aspects of the working group process is that it often leads to strategies that diverge from an institution's current path. Strategies evolve in this manner for two reasons. First, the SEP process pulls people together who, in many cases, have not worked together before. This alone creates an exciting dynamic of new ideas and approaches to the development of strategies based on the data collected in the situational analysis phase. Secondly, the data itself often bring to life a completely different approach or way of thinking because it is either new data or data that contradict the current world view held by some (or many) on campus. It is critically important that the working groups embrace the challenge of grappling with different points of view and conflicting data so that the institution will be in the most knowledgeable position possible when it considers strategic next steps. There is an opportunity here for faculty and staff to emulate the very heartbeat of an academic institution by engaging in its defining discipline—critical analysis.

> *" There is an opportunity here for faculty and staff to emulate the very heartbeat of an academic institution by engaging in its defining discipline— critical analysis."*

Working groups diverge, converge, and act

The working groups will develop such divergent paths at times that they may, in fact, leave old thinking behind to follow a completely new path that is sprinkled with breadcrumbs from fresh data and the environmental assessment. The divergent thoughts will eventually converge through analysis of the information, and with that comes clarity and the development of potential strategies that would not have evolved without insightful critical thinking by members of diverse working groups. The journey also equips the group to be thoroughly informed and prepared to prioritize strategies at the appropriate time. Lastly, this approach enables the institution to move incrementally toward what Peters and Waterman call a "bias for action" and willingness to experiment (1982). The participants naturally challenge the status quo because they are immersed in an environment that forces them to ask deeper questions.

The working groups should thoroughly review the research and data from the situational analysis and develop an executive summary of the information that pertains to their group. This step is critical, as it represents the first interaction between the data and the members of the SEP working groups. These groups are typically composed of faculty and staff from across the campus with experience and/or expertise in the themed areas. It cannot be stressed enough that the broader the representation, the more powerful the outcomes. The temptation will be to pick the usual people from a small group of departments that seem to be the "logical" participants in the process. This attitude will short-circuit the power of the SEP process.

Getting diverse input isn't the only benefit of broad campus representation in the process. The working groups will form relationships that will be essential for establishing partnerships on strategies and initiatives that evolve through the process. Some members of the working groups may be part of the SEP council and many others may contribute to the SEP process exclusively through the working group structure. The role of the SEP council is to ensure the various strategies converge into a comprehensive and realistic plan.

Potential working group tasks and responsibilities

As stated above, working groups are formed around key areas of focus. Below is a sample of potential working groups and their foci. (Note: No campus should have this many working groups. The institution will determine which working groups are needed based on data review, institutional priorities, and the identification of possible strategies.) In order to remain strategic, there must be a central focus on the interconnections between the academic and co-curricular areas, i.e., the product.

> *" The role of the SEP council is to ensure the various strategies converge into a comprehensive and realistic plan."*

- The **external group** will evaluate data and information that is outside of the institution, such as demographics, population trends, and employment statistics. This is a very important task, as many institutions are painfully insular and unaware of the environment in which they operate. The results of this group's work will likely be highly instructional for the rest of the campus community.

- The **competition group** will evaluate the competitive landscape. They will assess the different types of competition in their market and how the institution will need to address and adapt to a changing environment. Developing the definition of competitors is always an entertaining exercise. It will be important for the group to develop agreed-upon assumptions regarding competition so that the work conducted is valuable to all. Typically, a discussion of competition focuses on topics such as cross-admits, geographic proximity, athletics, peer institutions, aspirant institutions, and program offerings.

- The **enrollment group** will take an intensive look at enrollment-related data and trends, addressing questions about the composition and behavior of enrolled students, including demographic trends, performance, and persistence.

- The **marketing group** can take on a variety of tasks depending upon the institution's level of maturity related to marketing functions. Some working groups will focus on social media, sophisticated marketing and communication messages, and strategies guiding students to specific next steps in the enrollment process.

- The **selectivity group** will tackle data and issues related to admissions rates, academic profile, institutional profile, etc. Selectivity is a complex issue because of the number of variables that must be taken into consideration. It is important to designate members of this group who are well-versed in the intricacies of admissions stages and processes, such as admission requirements, actionable application information, GPA calculation variations, and test score utilization.

- **Capacity and demand** is a multifaceted topic that a group will address by assessing such matters as classroom space, faculty load, program demand, and curricular requirements. It will be important to have academic leadership in this group as capacity incorporates issues such as classroom size, faculty-to-student ratios, pedagogical approaches (e.g., hybrid courses), course demand, and related areas.

- Another working group will assess the **quality of the educational experience** through the analysis of learning outcomes and quality of instruction data. Academic leadership is also critical for this group, as concepts of learning outcomes and instructional quality are highly complex, often contested, and not easily measured. Furthermore, regional accreditation bodies have been placing more and more emphasis on these issues, with a resulting need for substantial expertise.

- The **student engagement/satisfaction group** will focus on data related to student surveys (e.g., National Survey for Student Engagement [NSSE] and Student Satisfaction Inventory™ [SSI]) along with other measurement tools utilized by the institution to identify potential ways to bring about improvement. Understanding the level of student engagement and satisfaction is important to predicting student success and building institutional awareness of issues that impact a student's journey (Kuh, Kinzie, Schuh, and Whitt, 2005).

- The **quality of faculty and staff** has a significant impact on enrollment success. Therefore, another working group will wrestle with data ranging from customer service to adjunct faculty counts. This group may need to grapple with the definition of quality; I encourage you to explore the best ways to measure it on your campus, comparing your tools with the wide range of indicators that are utilized by other colleges and universities.

- The **persistence and graduation group** will use data to develop strategies that address student success. Issues can range from admissions practices and course scheduling to academic support and student life. This group needs to have broad representation from numerous areas of campus because of the breadth and depth of persistence issues.

- The **diversity group** will focus on matters relating to the ethnicity, religious backgrounds, and other characteristics of enrolled and prospective students, as well as faculty and staff diversity, and how these issues impact the institution as a whole. It will be important for this group to develop a working definition of diversity so that the analysis and strategies are aligned and the group's work will be supported. Clarity and agreement about the definition of diversity is essential to success, as each institution may define it differently.

- The **financial group** will evaluate resource utilization and allocation and develop strategies to enhance the financial health of the institution. This group may navigate some delicate questions, as the costs of programs and services are assessed in order to help prioritize work. "The inescapable truth is that not all programs are equal," as Dickeson points out (2010). Dickeson's book, *Prioritizing Academic Programs and Services*, provides methodology and considerations for campuses to rethink their academic offerings and align those offerings with enrollment-related strategies.

- Obviously, the **financial aid group** (sometimes a part of the previously mentioned financial group) will review the research to determine appropriate strategies for policies regarding scholarships, grants, discounting, etc. As financial aid and pricing continue their ascent as key policy issues in higher education, this group will need to understand both the internal and external questions at play.

Working group responsibilities

Once these groups have been formed and the scope of their work defined, the participants will begin to develop second-level strategies that the institution might undertake to build on its strengths, address weaknesses, take advantage of opportunities, or prepare for threats. As mentioned earlier, these groups are charged with evaluating all available data relating to their area. "Strategies need to be detailed enough to provide direction, but they do not have to describe every step in the process" (Black, 2001).

Once the working groups have developed a list of potential strategies through a brainstorming process, they must estimate the cost of execution and the potential impact of implementation for each strategy. To keep from getting bogged down at this point, the group may use general ranges of cost (high, medium, and low) and impact (high, medium, and low) to create a matrix of potential strategies. Cost and impact will be relative for each institution ($25,000 may be a lot of money on some campuses, but the equivalent of a departmental supplies budget at another). It is important to set general parameters so that everyone is operating under the same assumptions. It may be best to use dollar ranges (e.g., low cost is $0 to $2,500).

Because SEP is a fluid process, often members of a group will look around the room at the end of a brainstorming session and say, "Why in the world would we wait to execute X strategy? We can do it with existing resources, it is high impact, and we can do it now"; and off that strategy goes into implementation without waiting for the creation of the SEP plan. While some might argue that the plan should be completed and approved before starting implementation, this example suggests that some action items may be so easily implemented and demonstrate such a high return on investment that waiting is a mistake. Needless to say, the credibility of the process and those involved will be substantially undermined if the vast majority of strategies and action plans require significant financial resources. Every campus should be able to identify numerous low- or no-cost strategy and action plan options. Failure to do so demonstrates a lack of creativity and authenticity in the assessment of the research and current practices.

Regarding the fluid nature of SEP, some planning processes have a pour-lather-rinse-repeat cycle to them, a tidy start and finish. However, this is not the case with SEP. The SEP process requires flexibility, adaptability, and willingness to try things midstream while keeping an eye on the future state, the realities of the current state, and quickly changing economic or demographic variables that may affect the long-term plan.

Figure 7-2: Fluid Nature of SEP

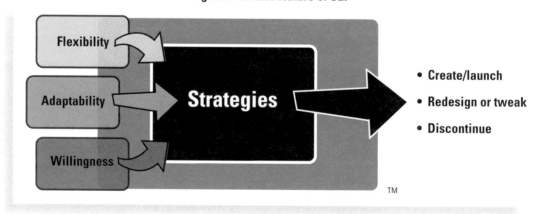

After the group has assessed costs and impact, they will identify which strategies should be at the top of the list and which ones should be at the bottom, thereby helping the council to determine priorities. There is an important point to consider here—prioritization allows the entire group to build consensus (most of the time) not only on what is important, but on which strategies will get the best results and which will require new or reallocated resources. The exercise of assembling preliminary strategies and prioritizing them allows the group to realize that not all great ideas cost a lot of money and, if they do, their priority indicates that the desired action has the potential to make a significant difference and is therefore worth the investment. Once the prioritization is complete, the group should create action plans for each strategy and finally move to a more detailed analysis of cost and enrollment impact, with estimated returns on investment (ROI). When this is done well, prioritization is relatively easy because the high ROI strategies quickly move to the top of the working group's list of recommended strategies for inclusion in the larger SEP plan. (We will look more closely at ROI in Chapter 8.)

Action plans are documents that outline each step/task required for the execution of a second-level strategy, the timeline to complete each task, the person(s) responsible for each step, other campus areas that need to be involved and/or are affected by the plan, the budget and/or resources needed, and an evaluation component that will guide the institution in determining the impact of the action plan and measuring its effectiveness. We will look at a specific example later in this chapter.

Strategies before goals

Once the group members have fleshed out the second-level strategies, they will explore setting quantifiable goals. Given the tendency to stumble around the concept of goal setting at this point, it is important to clarify what is meant by the goal-setting process. Many leaders and organizations set arbitrary quantitative goals prior to research and strategy development, an unwise practice that often misaligns an institution with the evolving environment as well as the institution's own strengths and weaknesses (Sevier, 2000).

It is critical that an institution understand its context and develop strategies in light of the environment first, and then set quantifiable goals that are realistic and in line with the institutional vision. For example, it is not unheard of for a campus to set an arbitrary goal to increase enrollment by 15 percent over the next two years. However, what if the situation in which the institution finds itself makes that fundamentally impossible? What if the institution's core market is going to decrease by 5 percent over that same time period? What if its budget is running a deficit and perhaps carrying an unhealthy, unfunded discount rate? And how does an institution even wager a guess at a goal if it doesn't know what strategies it is able to employ, taking into account talent, resources, and the like? Furthermore, what if increasing enrollment is not the most effective way for the institution to solve the revenue problem? Quantitative goal setting is obviously very important, but it must follow a comprehensive situational analysis, strategy identification and development process, and projections about return on investment in order for the goals to be based in reality. Goals developed after strategies are identified will be far more accurate, because organizational leaders will be able to envision the execution of a specific strategy and the potential impact on the campus.

> " Goals developed after strategies are identified will be far more accurate, because organizational leaders will be able to envision the execution of a specific strategy and the potential impact on the campus."

A final critical point to consider during the planning process is the need to make prioritization extend beyond potential new ideas to an honest review of current practices. As we have learned, successful implementation of the SEP process requires the prioritization of many possible new strategies in order for the institution to properly align its resources. However, the last time I checked, a day was still 24 hours long, and even the most enthusiastic SEP participants will not be able to change that. Therefore, the organization must review its current practices and strategies to decide what it should continue doing and what it should stop doing, especially in light of the creation of dozens of new strategies. Many of these will be started immediately and others will be scheduled over a two- to five-year period. During that period, it is essential that the various departments assess the effectiveness of existing strategies and eliminate ineffective practices, allowing them to deploy human and financial resources in a way that allows the institution to maximize its effectiveness. If the groups continue to do what they have already been doing by simply adding several new and vital strategies, they will fail to implement and execute any of them successfully; and, it goes without saying, the campus must engage in a disciplined approach to assessing strategies with a faithfully executed stop-start-continue evaluation loop.

Working group action planning development

To understand how this process comes to life, consider the example of a working group that was focused on the topic of student engagement and satisfaction. As you would expect, the group first considered the various forms of information available from the National Survey of Student Engagement (NSSE), the Student Satisfaction Inventory (SSI), and metrics collected by the office of student life listing the number of clubs and organizations, membership counts, number and types of student events, and so forth. Once the group reviewed all of the available information, they drafted a one-page executive summary of the key observations made by the group. This is an important step, because it forced the group to discuss the research in detail and agree on the most important components and issues.

" It is critical that an institution understand its context and develop strategies in light of the environment first, and then set quantifiable goals that are realistic and in line with the institutional vision."

After summarizing their findings, they moved to the strategy development phase in order to identify and create suggested steps to address the issues and opportunities presented by the research. They produced a list of potential strategies that addressed strengths, weaknesses, opportunities, and threats identified through the research process. At this stage of the process, it was critical that the group *not* be encumbered by historical or current constraints (real or perceived). In order for the group (and the institution) to move forward, it needed to think about the potential/desired state instead of being held back by current and past strategies. In other words, this stage enabled the group members to think big and creatively about how the institution could tackle the issues that had been identified.

The working group in this example developed numerous strategies, many of which, after being subjected to budget assessment and prioritization, were eliminated. Let's examine their second-level strategy to improve student engagement on weekends, as significant findings showed that students were feeling disconnected from the campus during weekends and going home.

Second-level strategy example

Develop weekend programming through the office of student life that will engage residential and commuter students.

What issue are we trying to solve?

The research shows that our students believe the quality and quantity of weekend programming is poor. Furthermore, students are not staying on campus over the weekend and tell us they leave because "there is nothing to do." Strategies aimed toward solving this issue will impact student satisfaction and improve our first- to second-year retention rate (Key Performance Indicator—Three for Noel-Levitz University).

Tasks

- Develop a Saturday Night Program Series providing a large-scale programming event (concert, comedian, coffee house, game show) every Saturday night for the fall and spring semesters.

- Develop a Weekend Spirit Program that links specialized giveaways or entertainment with home athletic events on Friday, Saturday, or Sunday. In the program, include special seating and t-shirts/sweatshirts for students who attend three or more athletic events each month.

- Upgrade Sunday brunch menu to more upscale and cook-on-demand selections such as waffle bar, omelet bar, etc.

- Require residence halls to provide one weekend activity per semester to engage residential students.

Budget

Reallocate student programming fee dollars—add $50,000 for additional programming and $2,500 for athletic spirit program. Additional programs can be absorbed into existing budgets.

Evaluation

Satisfaction scores and participation at events will be the metrics used to gauge the success of new programs.

The above action plan is obviously rather simple and makes certain assumptions, but it serves as a good example of how the situational analysis feeds strategy development. The action plan is a direct next step to accomplish a strategy that was created to address a weakness and hopefully improve student satisfaction and, therefore, retention.

Selecting strategy priorities

Usually, individual working groups each create 15 to 25 strategies and action items that are forwarded to the larger group. No campus can implement 100-plus strategies and action items effectively. One method to bring a large group to consensus on a list of potential ideas is to rank all of the items by impact, effort, and cost. Each item is brought before the group and evaluated on each criterion one at a time. Once each item is ranked, the entire list can be sorted with ease.

Ranking is done by assigning an A, B, or C to the three categories of impact, effort, and cost: A for the highest (or most), B for medium or moderate in each category, and C for lowest (least). For instance, moving from paper registration to online registration would be a long, complex process that would likely require expensive software. However, students would perceive this as having a high value. The ranking evaluation would look as follows:

- A-Impact
- A-Effort
- A-Cost

Therefore, online registration would be an AAA.

Another idea might include relandscaping the campus and creating a new front entrance. This might be one team member's favorite idea, but the rest of the team may feel that it would not make enough impact. The evaluation would look as follows:

- C-Impact
- A-Effort
- A-Cost

In this case, the landscaping project would be a CAA.

Once the entire list has been ranked, it is important to open the discussion to ensure that the group is confident with the rankings. Next, sort the items with all of the AAAs at the top, all of the CCCs at the bottom, and each of the combinations and permutations in between.

This exercise allows the SEP team to identify "low-hanging fruit" (i.e., ACC— high impact, easily implemented, low cost). Low-hanging fruit could be acted upon right away while the teams identify other high-impact, lower-cost ideas over the course of the planning process. In this manner, there can be some immediate "quick hits" during the actual strategic planning process.

Dialogue

We have learned that strategy development and identification involves a fluid process requiring faculty and staff to be courageous and bold in their thinking in order to bring about the best results. It starts with a high-quality environmental assessment and ends with detailed action plans. It is critical that the institution spend time developing the working groups and encouraging a climate of inquiry throughout the environmental assessment and strategy development process. A failure to be thoughtful about group composition will weaken the effectiveness of the process.

What can you do to ensure unencumbered and productive brainstorming and strategy identification on your campus?

- Take a minute to think about the organizational culture and institutional assumptions that might be keeping your campus from maximizing its potential. As I mentioned at the opening of the chapter, the quality of strategy development correlates to the quality of the situational analysis; do everything you can to make sure the analysis is thorough, honest, and as unencumbered as possible.

- Embrace the value of divergent thinking. Be sure to include faculty and staff from various parts of campus. Be intentional about including smart but independent-minded individuals who seem to elevate the level of thinking. The SEP planning process is not a time to try and convert the non-believer or less-motivated campus employee. This process should engage the most innovative, creative campus minds that, together, can create a stronger future state for the institution. Be a champion for facing the music regarding the dramatic changes occurring in higher education. The environment in which colleges and universities are operating is challenging and becoming increasingly scrutinized. Furthermore, demographic, economic, and social dynamics are changing in significant ways—ignoring those issues will place the future of the institution at risk.

> *" This process should engage the most innovative, creative campus minds that, together, can create a stronger future state for the institution."*

Infuse the process with patience and persistence. The analysis of data, creation of potential strategies, prioritization of strategies, and action plan development take time and focus. SEP can be exhilarating and exhausting. Be sure to tap working group leaders who are skilled facilitators and develop working assumptions that enable participants to be on the same page.

CHAPTER 8

Establishing Enrollment Goals and Identifying Return on Investments

By Marilyn Crone

This is where the rubber meets the road. A comprehensive situational analysis is complete, including agreement on the fundamental planning assumptions. The campus is engaged to identify, develop, and prioritize numerous long- and short-term enrollment-related strategies that support the mission, values, and overall goals of the institution. Action plans have been developed that reflect the tactical steps it will take to accomplish these strategies, the order of those steps, the "ring leader" to complete each step, how much time each will take, and additional resources (particularly budget dollars) that will be required.

External eyes on universities

An article in *The Chronicle of Higher Education* (Carlson, 2011) cited Moody's Investors Service's "2011 Outlook for U.S. Higher Education," noting, "The outlook for a relatively small number of well-managed diversified colleges looks stable in 2011, an upgrade from the negative forecasts that the credit-rating agency had given higher education over the past couple of years. In its latest report, however, Moody's maintains a negative outlook for the majority of higher education institutions, which it says are too dependent on tuition, auxiliary income, and state support." This is an uncomfortable report to read.

Moody's juxtaposes two types of institutions: "The strongest institutions are in top demand and have fingers in a number of business lines. Meanwhile, the weakest institutions, which draw students from a regional base and lack diversity in business lines, could still be endangered." Three "critical credit factors" drove the gloomy 2011 outlook: "weakened prospects for net tuition growth," "differing degrees of pressure on non-tuition revenues," and "the need for stronger management of operating costs, balance-sheet risks, and capital plans." If an institution has issued public bonds, the institution should be interested in the opinions of ratings agencies such as Moody's, as their opinions can impact the availability and cost of the institution's credit.

Make a mental note of "diversity in business lines," which we'll consider in this chapter. Newman, Couturier, and Scurry (2004) provide a helpful context for thinking about such diversification in *The Future of Higher Education: Rhetoric, Reality, and the Risks of the Market*. They write, "one goal of an entrepreneurial effort should be development of diversified funding sources as a means of creating greater stability and facilitating response to new opportunities in a time of volatility … It is, however, critical that the nature of any new funding stream be compatible with the institution's mission and values."

Chapter highlights

- **Enrollment goals need clearer agreement with strategic planning goals**

- **Strategies lead to clear goal setting**

- **Return-on-investment analysis is critical to plan success**

Linking enrollment goals to the institutional strategic plan

An institution's strategic enrollment planning (SEP) council is charged with discerning and establishing enrollment priorities and goals. Setting realistic, quantifiable goals is essential. Surely these must take into account campus readiness and the likelihood of attractive returns on investment (ROI). In this context, we are grateful to George T. Doran for coining the term "S.M.A.R.T. Goals." In an article written for *Management Review* in 1981, Doran explained that "S.M.A.R.T." describes goals that are specific, measurable, assignable, realistic, and time-related.

An institution that has created a long-term institutional strategic plan (ISP) with broad campus support has a clear advantage over those that have not because they have direction, intentionality, and, hopefully, even momentum. For those without an ISP in place, undertaking the creation of an SEP will serve (in part) to provide institutional direction focused on enrollment management that aligns with curricular and co-curricular programs as well as budget and fiscal planning and management. Regardless, the strategies selected must serve to accomplish the goals the institution wants to achieve, and these goals must be quantified and evaluated based on a host of criteria, not the least of which is the financial implications of these choices.

" Whether or not the term enrollment management is used, the work of recruiting and retaining students is essential to a university's success."

Goals and associated revenues and costs must be brought together in a coherent manner that allows the chief financial officer's team to build a multiyear financial model that will clarify and direct funding for the institution's operations and aspirations. Yes, we are talking about dollars and cents in addition to headcount. Whether or not the term enrollment management is used, the work of recruiting and retaining students is essential to a university's success. Like it or not, it is a business function that touches and is touched by every other part of the college/university. Moreover, the results are of interest to both internal stakeholders (administration, faculty, staff, and students) and external stakeholders (board members, government officials, accrediting agencies, financial institutions, rating agencies, and alumni).

How we implement enrollment management impacts:

- The cost to recruit *and* retain students, in the broadest sense, inclusive of institutional gift aid in addition to recruitment, student support, and other operational costs (not to be confused with the more narrowly focused "cost to recruit").

- Net revenue produced by those students with varying levels of academic ability/preparedness who study in programs of varying:

  – Interest/demand, e.g., business and health science programs are generally easier to sell because of the clarity of career options.

  – Profitability, e.g., cost of delivery (faculty, facilities, utilities, equipment, and special insurance) may be more expensive for some programs, and certain programs require lower student-to-faculty ratios. Some programs may be considered so mission-critical that an institution is willing to allow them to merely break even or perhaps even run at a deficit.

  Obviously, few institutions can afford many such financially challenging programs. As described in Chapter 4, the process of creating an SEP is as important as the plan itself because of the rich dialogue that occurs during the process that likely wouldn't occur otherwise. For universities that choose to run financially challenging programs, there is benefit in articulating such a choice and understanding the associated cost of resources to the institution.

- Requirements for flexibility, e.g., online courses, mixed modal delivery, evening and weekend offerings, multiple entry points, and services such as daycare.
- Persistence and graduation rates of different student segments, including student-athletes.
- Outcomes desired by students (job and graduate/professional school placement with corresponding average starting salaries and lifetime earnings), which lead to future giving capacity as alumni.

- Capacity in the system, e.g., requiring the addition of new course sections, instructors, technology infrastructure and support, student life personnel, clinical placement (or other internship) sites, as well as classroom, office, lab, housing, and dining facilities.

- Reputation (rankings) of the college/university related to desired class quality (student profile) objectives, student-to-faculty ratios, and other indicators of interest such as first-generation, race/ethnicity, gender, in-state/province, out-of-state/province, international, and enrollment at particular campuses in a system.

Prioritized strategies: An example

In conducting the situational analysis, an institution may have recognized that, in addition to being tuition-dependent, tuition revenues are largely generated by one or two principal populations. Let's assume undergraduate and graduate degree programs are offered by the institution but the majority of enrollment is centered in a relatively small percentage of academic programs (some of which only operate at a break-even because of the high cost of delivery), drawn from a narrow geographic region, and offered in a face-to-face classroom environment. The academic program analysis clarified demand trends, numbers of degrees granted annually, cost of delivery, and external endorsements of quality. Further, the institution has significant ISP aspirations and deferred maintenance obligations to fund; in other words, they need increased net operating revenues. This institution's strategy prioritization process bubbled up nine strategies:

1. Increase first-year enrollment in two specific business programs and hold enrollment constant in high-cost health science programs.

2. Increase enrollment in periods with high facility capacity, e.g., summer and intersession.

3. Increase enrollment of out-of-state and nonresident international students.

4. Increase enrollment in two graduate programs of distinction with interest from large regional employers.

5. Increase enrollment of transfer students with associate's degrees (or equivalent hours from a four-year university).

6. Increase retention of second- to third-year students.

7. Improve the student satisfaction and processes of the financial aid office.

8. Develop the capacity to offer some high-demand classes online.

9. Purchase and implement a constituent relationship management system for both recruitment and retention (and development) purposes.

Before setting goals

At the highest level of establishing enrollment goals, an institution must determine whether they want to increase, maintain, or shrink enrollment. Below are a few examples for choosing a particular direction:

- **Increase** enrollment: The institution is focused on growing net tuition revenues, has capacity to grow, and has academic programs with growing demand.

- **Maintain** enrollment: The institution has little or no capacity to grow but may have other enrollment goals, such as improving academic quality, shaping the enrollment in specific academic programs, or improving the geographic and/or socioeconomic diversity of the student body.

- **Shrink** enrollment, either by design (maybe they are focusing on higher student academic quality and a narrowed set of academic offerings) or by necessity (e.g., catchment area is regional with declining high school graduates; there is declining employer support for students pursuing master's programs; there is increasing competition from a lower-cost provider; there is declining demand for the academic programs historically offered).

> " At the highest level of establishing enrollment goals, an institution must determine whether they want to increase, maintain, or shrink enrollment."

An institution may offer courses at the undergraduate, master's, and doctoral levels, and is making decisions about increasing, sustaining, or shrinking enrollment at each of these levels and in various colleges/schools and programs within the levels.

Let's address "capacity to grow." Like beauty, this critical determination is often "in the eyes of the beholder." A dean may believe she can only grow enrollment in certain academic programs with four-year students; meanwhile, the enrollment staff sees significant demand for some of those programs and much of it is from transfer students. The residential housing staff may believe they are operating over the preferred capacity and encourage reducing housing occupancy. When faculty offices are severely limited, faculty may uniformly express the opinion that the college/university is operating at capacity, even if enrollment demand exists and classroom and lab utilization is not optimized. There may legitimately be little or no growth opportunity for traditional face-to-face instruction at the undergraduate level, but there may be opportunity at the master's level. There may be no opportunity for growth on the main campus, but there may be demand for academic offerings at satellite locations and/or delivered in multimodal ways.

As these examples illustrate, the issue of capacity is one that deserves a rigorous discussion and debate so that conventional assertions are not unintentionally accepted. For example, you may be at classroom capacity because (current) faculty members are unwilling to teach in the evenings or weekends when there is student demand for a particular program. Addressing this demand may mean that such courses are taught by new faculty members.

Setting goals

Let's resume our look at the prioritized nine strategies in our example. At long last, the SEP council is given permission to establish enrollment goals for which there are capacity, campus readiness, and hopefully even a sense of energy focused on strategy development.

Figure 8-1: Strategic Enrollment Growth Matrix

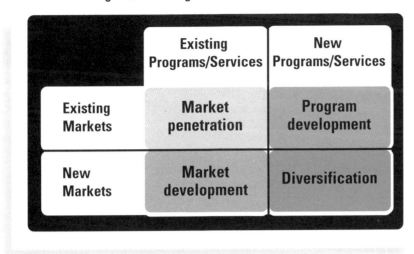

	Existing Programs/Services	New Programs/Services
Existing Markets	Market penetration	Program development
New Markets	Market development	Diversification

TM

Figure 8-1 provides a frame of reference for considering goal creation. After determining which strategies will be implemented based on a data-informed situational analysis, the following goals might emerge from this process:

1. Increase enrollment of first-year students majoring in accounting and finance by 100 while holding constant the enrollment of first-year students majoring in nursing (market penetration).

2. Increase the number (from 20 to 40) and average class size (from 10 to 25) of high-demand summer and intersession undergraduate courses and offer them at competitive pricing (less than that of regular terms) to current and non-university students (market development).

3. Increase undergraduate out-of-state enrollment from 20 to 30 percent and the international student enrollment from 3 to 10 percent over the next five years (market development).

4. Increase transfer enrollment by 125 students by actively recruiting students at community colleges and by developing partnerships with strong community college systems that recruit international students interested in transferring to a university upon completion of their associate's degrees (market development).

5. Increase graduate enrollment by 45 off site by developing a business model to offer an (existing) engineering master's degree at a large employer and an (existing) education master's degree at a regional educational center (diversification—remember the diversity in business lines mentioned by Moody's).

6. Increase the second- to third-year retention rate from 85 to 90 percent in five years by:

   – Increasing the number of living-learning communities so that every first- and second-year student participates (including commuters) in a pilot program in which junior faculty members, living in two of the residence halls, each host a living-learning community; and

   – Increasing the number of professional advisors by one each of the next three years to achieve National Academic Advising Association (NACADA) student-to-advisor ratios (program development).

7. Increase the financial aid office student satisfaction ratings from 4.8 to 5.3 (per the Student Satisfaction Inventory™) by improving the self-serve information on the financial aid Web site, creating a more welcoming environment in the financial aid office and implementing quality service training for all team members (program development).

8. Increase online course offerings to 15 in the next two years by recruiting a small group of faculty with interest in online course delivery to pilot courses, principally at the graduate level, and begin studying possible partner organizations to assist with the design and delivery of online courses, recognizing that revenue will be shared for these courses (diversification).

9. In collaboration with the university development office, develop a request for proposal (RFP) for a constituent relationship management (CRM) solution that will address the institution's recruitment and retention needs, as well as the communication/event management needs of the development office, and budget to purchase and implement the system in year two of the five-year SEP (program development and operational excellence initiative).

In their book, *Strategic Change in Colleges and Universities: Planning to Survive and Prosper* (1997), Rowley, Lujan, and Dolence provide an insightful perspective regarding the issue of quality versus quantity in strategic enrollment planning: "Partially because many academics may resent reducing their work to numbers, and partially because of the difficulty in measuring quality issues and outcomes, it is probable that a discussion may begin about how strategic planning appears to be more interested in numbers than in quality. In the final analysis, however, it truly is quality that strategic planning is designed to achieve while it seeks to manage quantity. As external pressures on higher education continue to mount, those pressures are directed more at producing high-quality outcomes for the resources provided."

Quantifying the impact of goals on enrollment and revenues

It is essential for an institution to have an enrollment projection tool that allows the campus to see the impact of specific goals on headcount (and type of headcount) and net revenues. An effective tool will provide the ability to:

- Increase/Decrease enrollment for targeted populations such as first-year, transfer, and graduate students;

- Increase/Decrease direct cost to students, e.g., tuition, fees, room, and board;

- Increase/Decrease residency by class, e.g., residency will increase as more out-of-state and international first-year students enroll;

- Increase/Decrease retention by class, e.g., specific interventions for the newest cohort of first-year and transfer students have been implemented, which will likely result in improved year-to-year persistence, impacting net revenues and graduation rates;

- Annualize revenue—while the focus tends to be on the widely reported fall enrollment, institutions enroll new students and existing students are lost to graduation and attrition by term, and the impact of these enrollment changes is critical to a good estimate of annual revenues for budget-planning purposes;

- Identify institutional aid, discount rate, and net revenue by class and across all classes at the undergraduate level (graduate financial aid is likely much less prevalent, so estimating it is less onerous); and

- Model the impact of changes in financial aid strategy across the timeline of the SEP and beyond.

Quantifying the cost of investments

At this point, the action plans take on particular significance. But let's be honest—the details within action plans should be considered more of a rough order of magnitude (ROM) than a return on investment (ROI). We just want them to be as good an ROM as time and expertise allow, because the timeline and costs articulated later in the action plans will allow constructing the cost-of-investment side of the ROI calculation to begin. Institutions must strongly consider the ROI and ROM when setting final strategies and action plans to meet established goals.

For example, a direct marketing campaign working with the purchase of 100,000 high school names involves a few assumptions. An institution may decide to purchase pre-qualified NRCCUA (National Research Center for College and University Admissions®) names in addition to College Board, ACT, and other name sources that are not pre-qualified. This decision will necessitate the purchase of SMART Approach® or another predictive modeling service that may not have been included in the budget. There will be a fulfillment item of some kind as a part of the direct marketing effort. Once the proposals of direct marketing vendors have been evaluated and a selection is made, a fulfillment item that is more costly than was estimated at the level of prioritizing may be pursued. Again, numbers will firm up in the process of implementing action steps, but they should fall within a reasonable confidence interval in order to build confidence in the work underlying the SEP.

> " Institutions must strongly consider the ROI and ROM when setting final strategies and action plans to meet established goals."

Let's look at the costs identified with the first four undergraduate enrollment-related goals noted in our example.

1. **Instructional costs** to increase the business course sections in response to the increase in first-year students will most likely begin in year two of the five-year SEP (when these students are sophomores). Realization of the incremental growth by 100 first-year students occurring over the five years of the SEP is estimated at 25 (year one), 50 (year two), 75 (year three), 100 (year four), and 100 (year five). Note that the enrollment projection tool will show an increase in first-year students in line with these estimates. With a student-to-faculty ratio of roughly 25:1, an additional faculty line can be added in years one and two for general education courses, then plan for the addition of a new faculty line in the business school in each of years three through five as the students recruited for business programs move into major courses in their junior and senior years. (Each institution may use larger or smaller student-to-faculty ratios for courses in the different class levels and for different academic programs, and may make greater or lesser use of part-time and adjunct faculty.) Be sure to add the fringe benefit amount to instructional costs.

2. To calculate **staff costs** to support the increase in undergraduate enrollment, a student-to-staff ratio, such as 50:1, can be used to account for the various support staff needs across the institution as enrollment grows.

3. In order to increase summer and intersession enrollments, consider hiring an existing faculty member known for creativity and active participation in achieving his/her department's enrollment goals. Costs are estimated to include an **administrative stipend, course replacement expenses, and marketing expenses** to promote these programs internally and externally.

4. To pursue out-of-state enrollment growth, estimate the cost of:

- **Name purchases** from multiple sources;
- **Predictive modeling software** to assist in rationalizing institutional resources appropriately, depending on the likelihood of a student enrolling based on certain characteristics such as distance from campus, high school, and academic interest;
- The selected **direct marketing vendor**, inclusive of printing and postage expenses; and
- **On- and off-campus events** designed specifically for the targeted market, inclusive of promotion, travel, space rental, technology, and food expenses.

5. The increase in transfer students may not necessitate a new staff member in the enrollment division but it may in student support services or transcript evaluators. This would likely include staff costs and expenses.

As the cost of investment in each of these areas is determined, note if the cost is:

- A base budget item, such as salary and fringe benefit costs;
- A one-time expense, such as market research and pricing research; or
- A capital expense, such as laptops, telecounselor equipment, and office furniture.

Account for costs in a manner consistent with the requirements of the institutional budgeting process.

Example of accounting for cost of investments for one year

To increase the market share of new students, the following costs may be incurred:

Table 8-1: Market Share Investment Example

Market share investments	Recurring	One-time
Enhanced telecounseling	$10,000	$10,000 (Capital)
Market research		$40,000
SMART Approach modeling	$11,500	
New faculty lines, including fringe benefits	$200,000	
New staff lines, including fringe benefits	$100,000	
Formalized predictive modeling	$25,000	
Constituent relationship module	$30,000	$150,000
Additional events and travel	$20,000	
Market share total	**$396,500**	**$200,000**

To increase the retention of first-year students to the second year and beyond, the following investments are indicated by the SEP:

Table 8-2: Retention Investment Example

Retention investments	Recurring	One-time
Academic advisor, including fringe benefits	$48,000	
Predictive attrition modeling program and supplemental support	$10,000	$30,000
Quality enhancement training	$5,000	$22,000
Other staffing, including fringe benefits ($50,000)*		
Other operating costs	$10,000	
Retention investment total	**$73,000**	**$52,000**

* Funded by reallocation of existing position—not included in total

Calculating the return on investment

We are principally using the concept of return on investment in the context of a financial investment. The calculation is relatively straightforward:

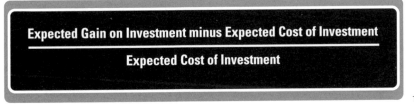

$$\frac{\text{Expected Gain on Investment minus Expected Cost of Investment}}{\text{Expected Cost of Investment}}$$

TM

However, the details of the calculations are important. While one does not need a finance background to calculate the ROI, it is handy to bring finance colleagues into this process to ensure everyone is on the same page. Below are a few comments that might prove valuable in this effort to determine the return on different investments.

1. SEP goals might prioritize a few investments that are discrete and best kept separate for calculating the ROI (for example, the ROI of different business lines, such as adult learners pursuing degree completion versus adding new graduate programs).

2. SEP goals might lead to a couple of growth scenarios. Examples might include: a growth scenario that is pursued only through improved retention (at capacity for housing, classrooms, labs, and offices) and one that includes both growth in new students *and* improved retention. Investments for these two different growth scenarios are likely quite different.

3. In considering growth scenarios, evaluate whether or not such growth will come at a greatly increased discount rate and require significant additions to fixed costs.

4. ROI will likely be calculated on the different scenarios or investments for each fiscal year and over the five-year horizon of the plan.

5. As important as it is to compare the ROI calculations, there are often valid reasons to prioritize investments with less glowing returns. For example, when developing a new business line, the ROI in the first few years may be negative, but this may be pursued with "eyes wide open" and with the expectation that it will not break even before year five but generate increasingly significant net revenue and net operating revenue streams after that. Further, *not* diversifying business lines may be considered a higher risk than continuing business as usual. Such decisions will be considered by the SEP council but, at the end of the day, fall into the purview of the senior administration and governing board of the institution.

6. The scenario of growth through improved retention may very well produce a much higher ROI than the scenario of growth in new students and improved retention. However, depending on the university's aspirations, need for greater net revenue, and apparent student demand, an institution may choose the scenario with the smaller ROI (maybe 5.2X as opposed to 15.0X) because it generates significantly greater net operating revenue. However, publicly traded institutions may bring different priorities to the planning exercise of comparing relative returns on investment. These stakeholders are different than shareholders.

7. Consider the difference in ROI between "do something" and "do nothing" scenarios. Since status quo is difficult to maintain, declining enrollment is most likely the result of a "do nothing" option, since competitors are not standing still. At best, this might mean maintaining the average enrollment picture from the past three to five years. Relatively few institutions have a brand or image effective enough to maintain strong enrollment demand regardless of changing economic times. The enduring excellence of these few institutions during a volatile economic era leads one to suspect that they have such a healthy brand because they regularly act to strengthen their offerings.

Concern about return on investment is not just the domain of the college/university chief financial officer; increasingly, this underlying concept is at the heart of the college decision process for many families. In her article, "When the Price Is Right," in *NACUBO Business Officer Magazine* (2010), Margo Vanover Porter quotes Martin Van Der Werf, former director of Chronicle Research Services in Washington, D.C.: "Higher education needs to realize that people are beginning to see higher education as a consumer transaction," he explains. "The days when families were willing to pay whatever without any assurance of what they were getting are coming to an end. More than ever before, people are really looking for a return on investment." This is also true with the SEP process. Resources are limited. The SEP must articulate clear goals achieved through specific strategies, leading to projected returns on investment, in order to appropriately influence key stakeholders to fund these strategies.

Dialogue

It is hard to overemphasize the value of waiting to set enrollment-related goals until the situational analysis is concluded; the demand and economics of academic and co-curricular (and even extracurricular) programs, in light of institutional aspirations and mission, are analyzed; planning assumptions are agreed upon; the otherwise unwieldy list of short- and long-term strategies is prioritized; and campus readiness to implement final strategies is achieved. Setting goals earlier would undermine the effectiveness of the SEP process.

Which goals are most worthy of pursuit over the next five years?

- Those that assist an institution in moving toward its preferred future, as opposed to the future that just happens;

- Those that represent the "sweet spot" among what is offered (or can be offered) in terms of a unique mix of academic and co-curricular programs, what is economically viable, and areas of strong student demand—all resulting in enrollment and related revenues that provide diversified revenue streams supporting institutional operations and aspirations;

- Those that have the concern for the success of students at their very core;

- Those that provide adequate returns on investment, even if goals with higher expected ROI are dismissed because the net revenues are deemed inadequate;

- Those associated with clear key performance indicators, drawn from the enrollment projection process, that will serve as indicators that an institution is on course or needs to adjust the course toward goal achievement; and

- Those that can realistically be accomplished during the planning horizon of the SEP.

> *" The SEP must articulate clear goals achieved through specific strategies, leading to projected returns on investment, in order to appropriately influence key stakeholders to fund these strategies."*

CHAPTER 9

Key Performance Indicators, Plan Evaluation, and Modification

By Joyce Kinkead

For enrollment managers, setting a pathway for an institution's future and putting the wheels in motion to achieve this future state can be an immensely rewarding experience. A strategic enrollment plan (SEP) determines a future state for the institution. An institution must use data to set this vision for the desired future state. The campus needs to know what it wishes to become, so that it can begin to move toward that desired state.

Reaching that overall objective requires achieving numerous goals along the way. However, the SEP process does not put goal setting first. Instead, as previous chapters have explained, SEP relies on a data-informed process that requires consistently analyzing important data points, using those points to guide planning, setting goals, measuring progress, and modifying behaviors and programs based on information gained through this feedback loop. After the plan is completed, an institution must establish a strategic enrollment *management* (SEM) council that shifts the institution from a planning mode to a management and action-oriented mode. The management council must continue to track and monitor the plan, updating it where needed based on current market or other changes.

Chapter highlights

- **Dashboards help institutions measure performance and track progress**

- **Diverse campus community involvement ensures success**

- **SEM council manages next steps**

The data-informed approach of SEP and SEM provides another benefit for campuses: it demonstrates accountability. In recent years, there has been a surge in calls to increase degree productivity and shift funding and performance models to focus on completion rather than entering enrollment. These calls for accountability and other external factors make the creation of this plan and oversight to implement it imperative to ensure that an institution remains viable for the long term. The productivity and completion agenda may force higher education to make dramatic reforms to current practices if funding models do indeed change.

Key performance indicators (KPIs) provide the means to set benchmarks, track progress, and fulfill demands for accountability and transparency. Chapter 5 introduced KPIs as an essential part of the planning process. This chapter discusses the importance of key performance indicators in further detail, how data dashboards can provide at-a-glance feedback, and ways to monitor and evaluate the plan. This chapter will also look at campus structures necessary to support the implementation of the strategic enrollment plan.

Key Performance Indicators (KPIs)

KPIs are commonly acknowledged measurements critical to the mission and fiscal health of the institution. As a rule, they:

- Are institution-specific, data-derived measurements that provide the foundation for determining the current state of the institution and, when matched with historical comparisons, are relevant for the creation of a situational strengths, weaknesses, opportunities, and threats (SWOT) analysis and overall strategic planning;

- Reflect the effectiveness of broad, cross-departmental cooperation;

- Provide points of differentiation when compared to KPIs of similar, competing, and/or aspirant institutions;

- Are often complex and expected to improve over a long period of time, as action items may take three to five years before delivering return on investment; and

- Are supported by and dependent on multiple performance indicators—see the following section for more details.

Top-level KPIs allow campus leadership to measure the health of the institution's mission and vision fulfillment. These KPIs must be connected with academic and co-curricular programs and services to ensure the mission is fulfilled and outcomes are enhanced over time (as explained in Chapter 6).

Typical KPIs include the following:

1. Enrollment

2. Student quality

3. Student progress

4. Market position

5. Program quality

6. Diversity or subpopulation enrollments and successes

7. Fiscal health (total revenues and net revenues)

Performance indicators

Under each KPI is a series of performance indicators (PIs), important measurements indirectly related to the mission and supportive of the KPIs. It takes improvement in multiple PIs to impact any one or more KPIs. Often, PIs can be addressed more readily than KPIs, although nearly all PIs are a part of the work done among two or more functional areas. Through the planning process, institutions can create a list of PIs to support KPI development.

These examples illustrate the relationship between common KPIs and PIs. Note that these are not exhaustive lists, but campuses engaged in SEP track many of these KPIs and PIs.

- **KPI: Enrollment**
  PIs: Headcount; full-time equivalent (FTE); off-site enrollment; online enrollment; transfer students; undergraduate and graduate enrollments separated by full-time and part-time status at census date; number of in-state students; number of out-of-state or international students.

- **KPI: Student quality**
  PIs: Average ACT score; 25th and 75th percentile SAT/ACT scores; average high school GPA.

- **KPI: Student progress**
  PIs: Cohort first- to second-year retention rates by subpopulation; cohort progression and persistence rates; two-, three-, four-, five-, and six-year graduation rates.

- **KPI: Program quality**
  PIs: Student-faculty engagement results; student outcomes; capstone course results; placement or licensure exams; student-to-faculty ratio; class size profile; undergraduate research; and graduate research.

- **KPI: Market position**
  PIs: Program awareness, academic demand research, Web site hits, microsite metrics, institutional brand/image studies, alumni survey data, employer survey data.

- **KPI: Diversity or subpopulation enrollments and successes**
  PIs: Enrollment numbers by academic year; percentage of students from diverse backgrounds compared to the majority population; underrepresented groups demonstrating success.

- **KPI: Fiscal health**
  PIs: Net and gross tuitions; revenues earned from auxiliary sources (housing, dining, and bookstore); education and general costs; education and general costs by student subgroups where specialized programs are provided to populations such as undecided or at-risk students with funding provided by the institution; net tuition revenue and scholarship costs by student subgroups (ability level and resident/nonresident); net tuition revenue and financial aid cost by needy student subgroup.

Taken as a whole, these KPIs and PIs provide the institutional leadership and campus enrollment management council with a snapshot of data to show improvements or decreases in progress, productivity, and revenues. Improvements in KPIs and PIs should also be an integral part of any institution's strategic planning objectives, whether they are related to enrollment management or not.

> " **The dashboard is a living document; some items may remain on it forever, while others may be deemed non-essential and dropped after a period of time.**"

Creating a dashboard

"Measure what you value, and value what you measure."

This is a good motto for an essential part of the SEP process: creating a dashboard or scorecard that can track KPIs and PIs. This dashboard must be accessible, easy to read, and understandable so it can be used and discussed easily in important meetings by the SEM council and other stakeholders. Several authors have suggested approaches for constructing such a tracking system (Doerfel and Ruben, 2002; Stewart and Carpenter-Hubin, 2000).

The dashboard is a living document; some items may remain on it forever, while others may be deemed non-essential and dropped after a period of time. An institutional dashboard might resemble the example shown in Figure 9-1.

A data dashboard is an annual snapshot; much of the information may be taken from the census data provided to the Integrated Postsecondary Education Data System (IPEDS). The institution decides which items are important to its success and gathers information on them. It is also important to monitor trends, comparing data for a minimum of three years (preferably five).

Notice how the dashboard in Figure 9-1 records metrics but also uses a trend line to show whether the direction is positive, negative, or holding in the same pattern. This type of tracking allows the SEM council and institutional leadership to monitor these KPIs to ensure that changes are moving in the right direction. This is a data-*informed* gathering and review process.

Figure 9-1: Dashboard Example (USU, August 2010)

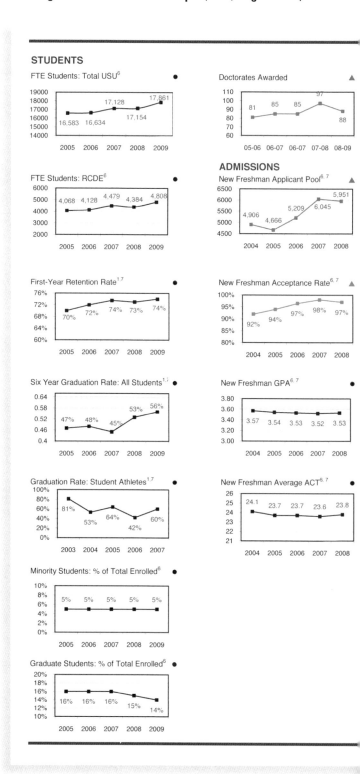

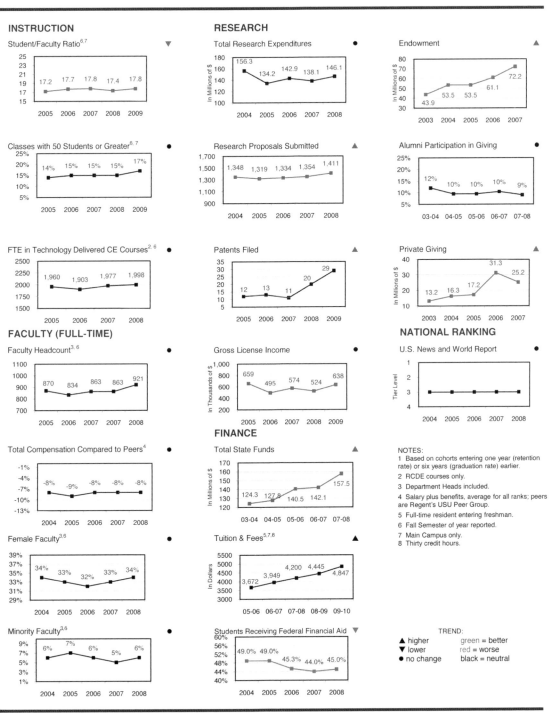

INSTRUCTION

Student/Faculty Ratio[6,7] ▼
- 2005: 17.2, 2006: 17.7, 2007: 17.8, 2008: 17.4, 2009: 17.8

Classes with 50 Students or Greater[6,7] ●
- 2005: 14%, 2006: 15%, 2007: 15%, 2008: 15%, 2009: 17%

FTE in Technology Delivered CE Courses[2,6] ●
- 2005: 1,960, 2006: 1,903, 2007: 1,977, 2008: 1,998

FACULTY (FULL-TIME)

Faculty Headcount[3,6] ●
- 2005: 870, 2006: 834, 2007: 863, 2007: 863, 2008: 921

Total Compensation Compared to Peers[4] ●
- 2004: -8%, 2005: -9%, 2006: -8%, 2007: -8%, 2008: -8%

Female Faculty[3,6] ●
- 2004: 34%, 2005: 33%, 2006: 32%, 2007: 33%, 2008: 34%

Minority Faculty[3,6] ●
- 2004: 6%, 2005: 7%, 2006: 6%, 2007: 5%, 2008: 6%

RESEARCH

Total Research Expenditures ●
- 2004: 156.3, 2005: 134.2, 2006: 142.9, 2007: 138.1, 2008: 146.1 (In Millions of $)

Research Proposals Submitted ▲
- 2004: 1,348, 2005: 1,319, 2006: 1,334, 2007: 1,354, 2008: 1,411

Patents Filed ▲
- 2005: 12, 2006: 13, 2007: 11, 2008: 20, 2009: 29

Gross License Income ●
- 2005: 659, 2006: 495, 2007: 574, 2008: 524, 2009: 638 (In Thousands of $)

FINANCE

Total State Funds ▲
- 03-04: 124.3, 04-05: 127.8, 05-06: 140.5, 06-07: 142.1, 07-08: 157.5 (In Millions of $)

Tuition & Fees[5,7,8] ▲
- 05-06: 3,672, 06-07: 3,949, 07-08: 4,200, 08-09: 4,445, 09-10: 4,847 (In Dollars)

Students Receiving Federal Financial Aid ▼
- 2004: 49.0%, 2005: 49.0%, 2006: 45.3%, 2007: 44.0%, 2008: 45.0%

Endowment ▲
- 2003: 43.9, 2004: 53.5, 2005: 53.5, 2006: 61.1, 2007: 72.2 (In Millions of $)

Alumni Participation in Giving ●
- 03-04: 12%, 04-05: 10%, 05-06: 10%, 06-07: 10%, 07-08: 9%

Private Giving ▲
- 2003: 13.2, 2004: 16.3, 2005: 17.2, 2006: 31.3, 2007: 25.2 (In Millions of $)

NATIONAL RANKING

U.S. News and World Report ●
- 2004: 3, 2005: 3, 2006: 3, 2007: 3, 2008: 3 (Tier Level)

NOTES:
1 Based on cohorts entering one year (retention rate) or six years (graduation rate) earlier.
2 RCDE courses only.
3 Department Heads included.
4 Salary plus benefits, average for all ranks; peers are Regent's USU Peer Group.
5 Full-time resident entering freshman.
6 Fall Semester of year reported.
7 Main Campus only.
8 Thirty credit hours.

TREND:
▲ higher   green = better
▼ lower   red = worse
● no change   black = neutral

Last Updated 8/2/2010

Note: Graphic reprinted with permission, from Utah State University.

When reviewing the data, the council should consider any extraordinary occurrences (e.g., economic situation, new state laws, significant state funding for financial aid, state appropriations, and changes in policy) that might affect the metrics.

Institutions just beginning the data collection process need to start somewhere. If the institution does not have three years worth of data, but the planning process revealed that certain data points are needed, an institution must start collecting and establishing the systems to collect those data to build a more robust dashboard over time. For some institutions, establishing a reliable and trusted dashboard may be a strategy or tactic identified as a part of the SEP process.

Another important aspect of a dashboard is comparing the institution to its peers, competitors, and aspirants. Figure 9-2 offers an example of a comparison dashboard that takes KPIs, such as retention and graduation rate, and quantifies them for the institution's peer group, as well as for its main competitors. In addition, environmental and political climate factors should be taken into consideration. Specifically, SEM councils should look at employment trends, enrollment patterns, and demographic shifts (e.g., Western Interstate Commission for Higher Education [WICHE] data), price sensitivity, and federal and state funding formulas. These factors can have a tremendous impact on an institution and influence strategy development for achieving institutional goals.

Figure 9-2: Dashboard Example (USU, April 2011)

	USU
STUDENTS[4]	
1st-Year Retention Rate (4-year avg. 2004-07)[1]	73%
6-Year Graduation Rate (4-year avg. 1999-02)[1]	53%
% Minority Students (Fall 2007)	5%
% Graduate Students (Fall 2007)	12%
Doctorates Awarded (2007-2008)	97
ADMISSIONS[4]	
New Freshman Acceptance Rate (Fall 2009)	98%
New Freshman Yield (Fall 2008) Enrolled/Admitted	48%
INSTRUCTION[4]	
Student/Faculty Ratio (Fall 2009)	18/1
% Classes with 1-19 Students (Fall 2009)	34%
% Classes with >= 50 Students (Fall 2009)	17%
FACULTY[4]	
Full-time	
Faculty Headcount (Fall 2008)	803
% Female Faculty (Fall 2008)	33%
% Minority Faculty (Fall 2008)	7%
Full-time Instructional	
Average Salary-In thousands (Fall 2009)[2]	
Assistant Professor	62.9
Associate Professor	69.1
Professor	89.1
All Ranks	70.8
Average Total Compensation-In thousands (Fall 2009)[2]	
Assistant Professor	87.4
Associate Professor	95.0
Professor	119.5
All Ranks	97.2
% of Instructional Faculty that are Full-Time (Fall 2008)	92%
% Faculty with Terminal Degree (Fall 2008)	70%
FINANCE	
% of Alumni Who Give (2-year avg. 2006-07, 2007-08)	10%
State Appropriations-In millions (FY 2007)	137.0
Undergraduate Resident Tuition & Fees-In dollars (2008-09)	4,445
Undergraduate Non-Resident Tuition & Fees-In dollars (2008-09)	12,951
Room and Board-In dollars (2008-09)	4,650
RESEARCH	
Total Research Expenditures-In millions (FY 2006)	139
Patent Applications (FY 2006)	13
Gross License Income-In millions (FY 2006)	0.49
NATIONAL RANKING	
U.S. News and World Reports (2008)	3rd Tier

NOTE 1: USU's numbers on the Comparative Data may be 1-2 years behind those reported on the Performance Dashboard because more recent comparative data for our peers are not available.

[1] Based on cohorts entering one year (retention rate) or six years (graduation rate) earlier.
[2] Total compensation is salary plus benefits, average for all ranks; peers are Regent's USU Peer Group.
[3] Non-LDS student tuition & fees at BYU
[4] Main Campus only

AVERAGE	Peer 1	Peer 2	Peer 3	Peer 4	Peer 5	Peer 6	Peer 7	Peer 8	Peer 9	Peer 10	Peer 11	Peer 12
86%	82%	85%	89%	76%	81%	93%	92%	90%	90%	83%	87%	81%
70%	63%	67%	70%	45%	62%	85%	78%	81%	78%	67%	79%	63%
21%	14%	8%	16%	47%	15%	12%	19%	50%	14%	14%	8%	11%
18%	19%	18%	23%	20%	15%	14%	19%	16%	22%	14%	8%	20%
333	206	308	328	72	173	620	594	500	341	189	76	397
73%	72%	85%	55%	96%	83%	52%	67%	N/A	N/A	76%	69%	80%
45%	41%	44%	49%	74%	45%	32%	55%	24%	40%	42%	78%	45%
18/1	17/1	16/1	18/1	20/1	20/1	17/1	19/1	N/A	N/A	15/1	21/1	15/1
34%	36%	33%	29%	45%	37%	30%	22%	N/A	N/A	39%	47%	43%
19%	18%	19%	20%	11%	21%	19%	22%	N/A	N/A	20%	11%	15%
2,001	1,184	2,186	1,768	703	1,562	3,137	2,648	2,723	2,146	1,952	1,326	N/A
35%	37%	35%	31%	38%	39%	35%	30%	35%	31%	42%	21%	N/A
14%	10%	14%	14%	16%	11%	13%	17%	25%	14%	9%	6%	N/A
69.6	70.1	71.4	70.2	52.8	70.5	72.0	73.6	77.0	70.4	68.3	N/A	73.1
80.1	80.6	81.8	84.2	65.7	77.1	86.7	82.5	83.9	82.9	75.2	N/A	79.9
110.0	108.6	111.6	115.1	79.1	93.9	130.4	120.3	123.4	115.9	101.8	N/A	115.7
84.0	89.1	84.8	88.1	63.1	72.7	86.7	87.9	103.4	87.4	76.8	N/A	83.6
89.9	87.6	93.1	88.7	67.4	97.6	90.7	88.2	106.0	92.8	87.3	N/A	90.2
103.0	100.9	105.2	105.5	84.1	107.8	109.5	98.8	114.7	107.5	96.4	N/A	98.3
138.4	135.9	139.3	141.3	100.5	127.4	159.9	142.2	164.3	145.7	127.7	N/A	137.6
107.5	111.4	108.4	109.7	80.5	101.6	108.4	104.9	139.2	112.5	98.1	N/A	101.6
94%	99%	95%	96%	88%	92%	95%	92%	94%	95%	89%	90%	85%
79%	99%	80%	85%	59%	74%	71%	88%	N/A	N/A	79%	72%	63%
15%	9%	17%	16%	7%	14%	20%	16%	11%	18%	18%	20%	9%
260.4	3.3	250.6	430.9	158.8	145.5	N/A	427.8	443.5	261.8	221.3	N/A	269.7
7,440	5,874	6,360	5,274	4,758	6,187	13,706	7,844	8,635	8,198	7,565	4,080	5,284
20,587	21,590	17,350	17,572	14,741	18,823	24,940	22,184	29,243	20,825	18,601	4,080	16,600
7,746	8,134	6,956	7,982	5,976	8,208	8,270	8,000	10,721	5,476	7,738	6,550	6,451
291	254	222	331	169	190	644	N/A	N/A	322	196	26	248
55	31	33	128	24	22	106	N/A	N/A	47	45	51	92
1.8	1.07	7.21	0.00	0.11	1.88	1.35	N/A	N/A	1.93	0.72	3.07	16.30
2nd Tier	2nd Tier	2nd Tier	2nd Tier	4th Tier	3rd Tier	1st Tier	2nd Tier	1st Tier	2nd Tier	2nd Tier	2nd Tier	2nd Tier

Note: Graphic reprinted with permission, from Utah State University.

While institutional dashboards provide an overarching view, they can be fed by unit- or program-specific dashboards. It is not uncommon for each institutional department or unit to establish a dashboard in order to measure its own valued metrics and evaluate its progress. This is a recommended outcome of the SEP process.

Figure 9-3 shows how a first-year experience and student success office might measure items of value: retention of students who participate in a pre-semester orientation program (in this case, the Connections program), parental involvement, and success of students re-admitted to the institution.

Drilling down into the information provided on these charts, note that students who received a grade of B- or lower in the pre-semester orientation program had a lower chance of being retained. Using this data, this group can be viewed as at-risk and the institution can create targeted efforts to address retention-related PIs and KPIs.

Dashboards must include the most essential metrics needed by the institutional leadership and SEM council to measure institutional progress towards achieving enrollment and other strategic goals. While all units within the institution play a role in achieving major institutional goals, some areas are particularly important to the overall effort. Recruitment, financial aid, and tuition pricing are keys to both short- and long-term enrollment projections. These data should have primacy in the overall data dashboard. Figure 9-3 also highlights another key area— retention and student success—which is universally important to all institutions.

Figure 9-3: Dashboard Example (USU, October 2009)

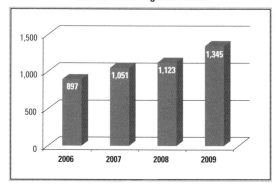

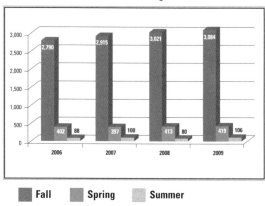

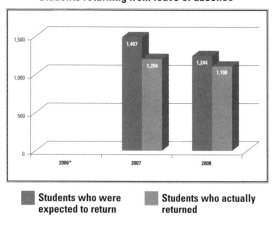

* Data not available

Total first-year students attending Connections

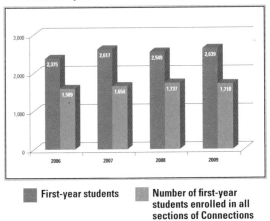

First-year students   **Number of first-year students enrolled in all sections of Connections**

Number of students suspended

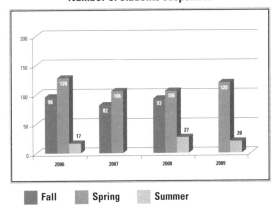

Fall   **Spring**   **Summer**

Retention rate for students who completed Connections

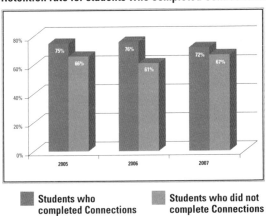

Students who completed Connections   **Students who did not complete Connections**

Number of students who appeal suspension

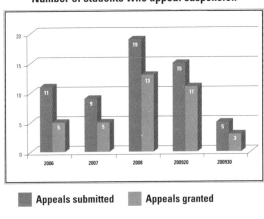

Appeals submitted   **Appeals granted**

Connections GPA retention rate

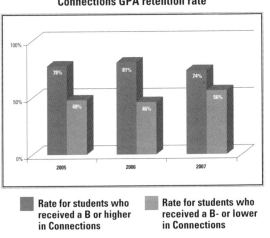

Rate for students who received a B or higher in Connections   **Rate for students who received a B- or lower in Connections**

Students readmitted with less than 2.00 GPA

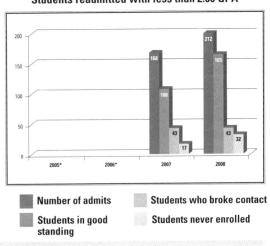

Number of admits   **Students who broke contact**

Students in good standing   **Students never enrolled**

An all-encompassing effort

What makes the SEP process all-encompassing is that *every* facet of the institution plays a key role. While recruitment, fiscal issues, and student retention will always be priorities, other areas are not only important on their own, but can impact those priority items. For instance, academic planning, the heart of any institution of higher education, determines who will enroll and why, factors that will directly impact any recruitment KPIs.

Student engagement is an important yet often overlooked area. Both Kuh (2008) and Light (2001) have addressed the issue of what matters to students in making the most out of college, particularly the aspects of engaged learning as measured by the National Survey of Student Engagement (NSSE). Learning communities, service learning, capstone experiences, and undergraduate research are some of the proven engagement activities that have an impact on students. Other studies (e.g., Nagda, Gregerman, von Hippel, Jonides, and Lerner, 1998) found that undergraduate research had a positive impact on the retention of under-represented students.

Certainly, the total student experience, including co-curricular planning and student programs, must be addressed. This is discussed in more detail in Chapter 6. This can go beyond traditional life and learning issues to include how important an institution's technology plan is to the socially networked student.

Marketing is another significant aspect of SEP and also one of the most controversial and misunderstood. For some in academia, the very idea of *marketing* suggests that an institution of higher learning has sold out to corporate values. Likewise, the notion of students as consumers or customers raises the hackles of some academics. On one hand, students truly are customers of departments such as the bookstore, housing, and food services. On the other hand, the relationship between students and faculty stems from the days of medieval learning when a sacred trust existed between novice and mentor. While not always voiced, many faculty members continue to believe in the innate dignity of their role. They may no longer dress in monk or dean robes (with the exception of commencement), but they continue to hold that sense of a revered relationship.

In this case, it is best not to engage in arguments about marketing and customers in the context of higher education. Instead, it may be more palatable for the academic community to refer to marketing as *strategic communications*, with an emphasis on communicating values, vision, ideals, and outcomes. As noted in previous chapters, the heart of the student experience is the academic program, supplemented by co-curricular and other learning experiences. The data metrics and dashboards in this area should inform opportunities for action and an understanding of which practices are or are not impacting student enrollment (from interest through completion).

While the creation of a strategic enrollment plan is grounded in data, there are several factors that make an institution a distinctive place of learning. While the SEM council cannot measure all aspects of the institution, it is important to note that the entire institutional experience, from marketing to engagement to alumni relationships, impacts new student enrollment and, more importantly, student persistence, progression, completion, and learning outcomes. (For academic officers, Baer and Stace [1997] offer a good primer on enrollment as does Barr [2002] on financial management. Kinkead [2011] provides information on marketing undergraduate research opportunities.)

Shifting to strategic enrollment management (SEM)

Once a strategic enrollment plan has been created, attention will shift from planning to management. The institution must ensure that the plan is overseen, monitored, evaluated, and revised as needed. For this, a high-level council is needed. Chapter 4 describes the key members of the SEP planning team. The SEM council's role is to ensure the resulting plan is implemented and to continue to scan the environment and SEP datasets for emerging opportunities that can be added to the plan in future years. Ideally, the council will exhibit exemplary collaboration with highly participatory decision making, engaged members, and representatives from across the campus. The council also serves the important function of educating the campus about the importance of the enrollment landscape as well as how institutional and national trends and data affect enrollment. Additionally, the council looks at big-picture issues, KPIs, and enrollment strategy recommendations for the institution.

Who sits on this council? The college/university SEM council is composed of individuals from major divisions of the college/university, including faculty, professional staff, and students, along with senior administrative staff from academic affairs, student affairs, business and finance, enrollment management, and institutional advancement. In addition to being representative of the campus community, the original SEP council members provide key functional assistance to the SEM council and expertise in areas relevant to SEP.

> " Once a strategic enrollment plan has been created, attention will shift from planning to management."

Defining the role of the SEM council

The typical responsibilities of the SEM council include:

- Monitoring implementation of the plan, including procedures to measure and track each benchmark indicator identified in the plan;

- Meeting quarterly as a committee to assess the overall progress of the plan and approve changes in the implementation of the plan for submission to the president, president's cabinet, and budget committee;

- Sharing periodic progress reports regarding the plan and its effectiveness with the campuswide community;

- Sponsoring special campuswide events related to SEM, such as providing opportunities to share best practices, organizing special meetings to discuss implications of student satisfaction research results for retention, or sponsoring professional development activities connected with new initiatives;

- Recognizing campus contributions and celebrating accomplishments; and

- Developing a revised strategic enrollment plan based on new information and the identification of desirable new strategies.

A subcommittee of the SEM council, the SEP action committee (or steering/working group), may be formed as the go-to people who direct the planning activities of the SEM council by setting meetings and agendas as well as preparing reports, documents, and recommendations for review and approval by the SEM council. Responsibilities of this *working* group—we use the term working to indicate the real work that they perform—include:

- Meeting at least monthly to evaluate the progress of the plan and identify actions that must take place during the next two months;
- Tracking KPIs identified in the plan;
- Tracking the measures of the effectiveness of each strategy and action plan identified in the plan;
- Tracking updated information related to new internal and external environmental assessments and projections; and
- Informing the SEM council of the progress of the plan, proposing changes or adjustments, and making recommendations regarding implementation of the plan.

" Ongoing assessments of benchmark indicators and external factors, as well as monitoring the progress of implementation, are critical to the plan's success."

Ongoing assessments of benchmark indicators and external factors, as well as monitoring the progress of implementation, are critical to the plan's success. Depending on institution size, another SEP subcommittee may be a budget group that meets twice each year following the tabulation of census data in the fall and spring terms. This information helps the budget committee understand implications of enrollment figures and, in turn, allows the committee to inform the SEM council about necessary changes in direction while providing updated enrollment projection reports.

Undoubtedly, units important to SEM will be working on their action plans concurrently. The results of these plans feed into the work of the larger committees and the council. Ideally, a consistent, robust assessment plan that measures KPIs and PIs will keep the campus focused on progress toward its goals.

Depending upon institutional priorities, council members may need to select a series of PIs to review on a biannual basis. For example, an institution seeking membership in the Association of American Universities (AAU) will review specific benchmark indicators aligned with best practices identified by AAU. A smaller institution seeking to grow enrollments may look closely at indicators aligned with enrollment growth or investigate new majors as dictated by market demand and employment trends. While there is no exact science for determining which performance indicators to use at a given institution, research unequivocally confirms that ongoing measurement is critical to long-term success (Rowley, Lujan, and Dolence, 1997).

Reporting to governing boards

As noted in Chapter 3, the planning process can support and further enhance relationships with external stakeholders. An institution's governing board cares deeply about the success of the campus and acts as its stewards, sharing its accumulated wisdom with campus leaders. Keeping these key individuals in the loop, even as members of the high-level SEM council, is advisable. SEM allows the state of the university to be considered and studied at several points during an academic year, not just during an annual address.

As demonstrated in Chapter 4, SEP requires a positive attitude and belief that the planning process will evolve into something action oriented and that will be implemented. The concept of shared governance dictates that progress and issues be widely communicated to keep all constituents informed and to educate the campus community. Governing boards can help sponsor campus events that celebrate successes, such as meeting benchmark goals (e.g., average GPA for entering students, graduation rates). A mutually supportive campus environment builds trust and contributes to a healthy campus in terms of faculty morale, student success, and fiscal security.

Reporting to the governing board may take the form of newsletters, agenda items, and events. In some cases, governing boards may not be solely institution-focused but may oversee an entire system. In fact, increasingly at the state level, systems of higher education are pursuing SEP as a way to improve system-level performance and achieve specific goals with respect to college participation and attainment. The belief that "a rising tide floats all boats" may be ambitious, as institutions' missions can vary widely, but it may indeed allow a state to become proactive in helping its citizens improve educational attainment. It can also contribute to economic success for such forward-thinking states.

Dialogue

Although there are many issues for campus leaders to consider in ensuring the success of SEP, below are some key questions to ask:

- What will the institution use as KPIs? In short, what is important to measure?
- What are the benchmark goals that the institution wishes to attain?
- How will academic, marketing, recruitment, curricular, co-curricular, and student success programs come together to inform a data-infused strategic enrollment plan?
- What will the institution's dashboard look like, and will all units sign on to create their own dashboards that feed into the larger institutional dashboard?
- An institution begins with enrollment projections based on current class assumptions, but then must update those based on new goals, demographic influences, and other trends. How will this be done?
- Who will be responsible for keeping tabs on important trends and updating the enrollment projection model every 36 months to ensure informed decision making?
- How will the campus deal with the often sensitive topic of academic program demand, trends, capacity, and future implications, in particular, how these relate to KPIs?
- How will the campus maintain momentum, retain key players in the planning process, and recruit new participants in order to monitor and implement the plan?
- How will the plan's actions and results be communicated to campus constituents, external stakeholders, and governing boards to ensure a sense that the entire campus community is in this together?

Strategic Enrollment Planning:

A Dynamic Collaboration

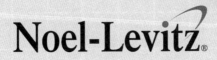

CHAPTER 10

Market Positioning

By Ruth Sims

Where are you heading?

As college and university leaders and marketers, we contend with an environment that is out of control. It is, at least, out of *our* control. Economic trends, social changes, and the prevailing political climate are powerful factors affecting our ability to recruit and retain students, yet we have little or no influence over these factors. This fundamental truth underscores the need for educational institutions to be flexible, nimble, and attentive to the winds of change.

Institutions that turn a blind eye to the environment and meander blithely wherever the road leads are likely to encounter unpleasant surprises. We navigate in an environment where maps are dynamic, and reliable institutional "global positioning systems" are simply unavailable. Chinese philosopher Lao Tzu offered this warning more than 2,000 years ago: "If you do not change direction, you may end up where you are headed."

Chapter highlights

- **Planning identifies gaps between reality and expectations**

- **Effective positioning employs a wide range of electronic venues**

- **Market research clarifies market changes**

How does an institution establish its identity in a changing environment? Fortunately, there are core marketing principles to help shape any strategic enrollment plan that remain unchanged from year to year, decade to decade. One example is integrated marketing, which is the unified and synergistic implementation of institutional messages and media in sharp contrast to sporadic, ad hoc marketing efforts. In addition, central for those involved in an institution's strategic enrollment planning (SEP) initiative is the concept of market positioning, the intentional selection of key features and benefits that define the institution's brand in a competitive context.

Positioning involves determining three things:

1. **Key strengths:** The distinct assets and capabilities of the institution in its delivery of the educational experience. These strengths must be documented through qualitative and quantitative research, not based simply on institutional mythology or unsupported aspirations.

2. **Market demand:** An understanding of which institutional strengths are most relevant to and desired by the marketplace, including unique segments within the market, such as traditional students, nontraditional students, and continuing education students. Some of an institution's salient strengths may be different from the factors that internal audiences value. For example, institutional history, longevity, and traditions are rarely of primary interest to prospective students, unless students have had some long-term attachment to the institution, such as following the success of an athletic team. (Note: Few institutions are one of these exceptions. Perhaps only 100 of the 4,500 American degree-granting institutions of higher learning can claim this kind of preferred status.)

3. **Competition:** Examination of competitors' strengths and weaknesses as perceived by the marketplace. Again, these must be documented through quantitative market research. Perceptions of competitors are not a substitute for primary research with target markets.

Figure 10-1 illustrates the process for determining which messages should drive an institution's marketing strategy.

Figure 10-1: Market Positioning in a Competitive Environment

Note that the institution is seeking to differentiate itself *within its primary competitive* set, not among all colleges and universities nationally. There are likely fewer than 50 institutions that have a true national reputation (and another 250 that believe they have a national reputation) but, as discussed in Chapters 3 and 5, it is essential to base any assessment of market position on data in linking enrollment planning with a desired future state. It is virtually impossible to find a niche that is unique, given the many similarities that exist among institutions' missions, programs, and target audiences. For that reason, it is far more important for marketing messages to be relevant and true than to be exclusive.

In his book *Selling Higher Education* (2008), Anctil points out that perceptions often drive differentiation more than reality: "Most people do not have the kind of access to colleges and universities that would allow them to make direct comparisons of the numerous characteristics that truly make institutions different from one another." This distinction is difficult for some to accept, but critical to understand as institutions consider their market position and future predicted market share aligned with market demands. Creating a "nationally recognized program" is difficult and costly. As institutions create strategic enrollment plans, they must carefully consider return on investment for specific goals in order to evaluate where they can realistically fit in the marketplace.

The role of strategic planning in market positioning

Whether or not to attempt to alter an institution's market position is a strategic decision that can be recommended as a strategy or tactic within a strategic enrollment plan. Ultimately, it is a choice that takes into account the institutional mission, market realities, and the potential return on investment for dollars allocated to shift market position, while keeping in mind the multiple priorities sent forward from the planning subcommittees.

How can an institution change its market position? Strategic planners evaluate and take action when gaps are found between what an institution offers and what the marketplace desires and expects. These actions may be relatively obvious, gap-closing strategies, such as adding new academic programs, or more comprehensive changes, such as improving the quality of classroom teaching institutionwide. Ignoring the gaps is not a viable option; if the key marketing messages that emerge from this process are not sufficiently relevant and substantial, they will not support meaningful and effective market positioning. In many if not most cases, closing these gaps and shifting perceptions will be a multiyear process that can be outlined through a series of tactics listed in the plan.

Human communication theory suggests that an individual's identity can be frozen through labeling or stereotyping in the absence of meaningful dialogue: "He is apathetic;" "She isn't good with numbers." The same is true of an institution. It is not uncommon for an outside consultant to hear comments such as, "Twenty years ago, we were a women's college, and we're still remembered that way," or "People think we're basically open admission, but that's no longer true."

For institutions, these frozen images are difficult to alter and can only be shifted through intentional branding strategies that facilitate an ongoing conversation with the marketplace—a conversation that best occurs through market research and interaction, not simply one-way marketing messages. Public relations efforts such as media interviews, story placements, social media initiatives, and strategically planned events can support the thawing of these frozen images, but it will take time to make a noticeable impact on market perceptions of the institution.

Market position strategies and data

As institutions consider SEP, there are a variety of data points and strategies that interconnect with marketing and recruitment efforts. These efforts cannot take place in silos; rather, they must occur throughout the SEP process. The goal should be to ensure that message and position are intricately linked to guarantee resources are purposed wisely and effectively.

It's an E-world, after all

Today's parents are sprinting to keep up with their children as the creative use of technology evolves from younger generations. In the same way, educational institutions must have their eyes and ears trained on Facebook, Twitter, Tumblr, and the Web to catch the next hot trend before the current trend fades.

How has this "e-era" changed college marketing? The upward trend line of admissions applications as the first point of contact shows that power has shifted from colleges and universities to their prospective students and those who influence them. Students can now learn almost everything they want to know about an institution and make a decision about enrollment without any human contact at the institution.

Most campuses have begun their foray into the world of e-marketing, some tentatively and some with great enthusiasm and creativity, and it has not taken higher education long to realize that e-marketing is not free. For most institutions to remain competitive in a growing multi-medium marketplace, institutions will either need to eliminate some print materials or travel recruitment activities to repurpose those funds to keep electronic tools and communication mediums updated or find new dollars to support these e-efforts.

The essential e-marketing tools checklist every campus should employ today includes:

☐ A formal Web site governance system that has defined roles and rules for managing the institution's site;

☐ A student-centered Web site for recruitment that has integrated:

   __ A content management system (CMS);

   __ User-tested navigation and content;

   __ A regularly updated search engine optimization (SEO) strategy for key pages;

   __ Site analytics that are used for ongoing site enhancement;

   __ A highly visible online inquiry form, campus visit form, and admissions application; and

   __ An online net price calculator.

☐ A mobile version of the institution's recruitment Web site pages;

☐ An e-communications strategy for recruitment;

☐ A purposeful and goal-oriented social media strategy;

☐ An admitted student Web site to support yield strategies; and

☐ Highly targeted search engine marketing campaigns to generate inquiries for appropriate programs.

Effective positioning demands that institutional marketing messages be intentionally and consistently woven through all of these electronic venues.

Build a Web site driven by student interests

A Web site is not a narcissistic mirror into which an institution can gaze lovingly upon its own reflection. Instead, it must be a living résumé submitted to the marketplace in the hope that the institution will be viewed as worthy of engagement.

The central concept of institutional democracy, that all people (and departments) have an equal say, does not work well for college and university Web sites. An institution yielding to this admittedly powerful cultural bias will find itself with a site that is a patchwork quilt of competing messages. A Web site must first serve the audiences that are most critical to the institution's future health and vitality. For the vast majority of tuition-dependent institutions, this will be prospective students.

Web sites can also serve current students, faculty, staff, and the local community, but the main driver for Web resources and functionality needs to focus on the way this tool recruits and engages students who are interested in enrolling at the institution.

The 2012 Noel-Levitz report, *The Mobile Browsing Behaviors and Expectations of College-Bound High School Students* found that the most-valued pages related to academic programs, followed by cost. Colleges and universities must understand that those pages are recruitment pages, not pages designed to serve their currently enrolled (or employed) students/staff.

Research is quite clear on what prospective students want. Despite marketers being enamored with graphic design, researchers Poock and LeFond (2001) reported the following ranking of college Web site characteristics indicating that Web site content is indeed king, closely followed by ease and intuitiveness of site navigation. These findings have also been verified by more recent studies.

Table 10-1: College-bound Prospects Preferences for College/ University Web Sites

College Web site characteristics		
Important/Very important	Percent	Rank
Content	97%	1
Organization/Architecture	95%	2
Download speed	88%	3
Organization by functional topic (admissions, athletics, etc.)	84%	4
Organization by target audience (applicants, alumni, etc.)	78%	5
Friendliness	73%	6
Distinctiveness	49%	7
Graphics (major emphasis)	49%	7
Graphics (minor emphasis)	40%	8

Source: Poock and LeFond, 2001

Since 2005-06, Noel-Levitz and its partners have been tracking the electronic college-search habits of students through the E-Expectations research series. In terms of content, these studies have shown that traditional students and parents pursue the topics outlined in Table 10-2 first when browsing an institution's Web site.

Table 10-2: Web Content Priorities for Prospective Students and Their Parents

What is the first link you'll look for on a school's Web site?		
Answer	Students	Parents
Academic programs	38%	42%
Enrollment and admissions information	24%	21%
Cost	8%	13%
Scholarships	7%	—
Other information	7%	5%
Student life information	7%	6%
Financial aid	5%	10%
Campus visit details	3%	—
Housing details	1%	—

Source: *E-Expectations Trend Report: The Online Expectations of Prospective College Students and Their Parents*, Noel-Levitz, Inc., 2011

Robust academic program descriptions, complete with faculty profiles, student quotations, and alumni success stories, will be significantly more effective than academic catalog-style copy that drones on about the "educational objectives of the business major." Each program description should be written to support the institution's central positioning messages, whether the primary focus is on faculty, practical experience, educational outcomes, or multiple themes.

To mitigate the political forces that often drive Web site content and design, smart campus managers leverage data from sources such as user-testing (feedback from actual prospective students who use Web or other e-tools) and Google Analytics to determine what's working and what's not.

As noted by Durkin (2010), "The ability of individuals to access information *in situ* – i.e., at the time, place, and in the context that is needed—may seem commonplace, but it is evidence of a fundamental shift in the structure of our way of life, our society, and our economy. It is the socio-economic equivalent of a massive tsunami sweeping across the globe. The surge keeps everything continuously on the move. Information asymmetry asserts that the advantage in any bargaining process (e.g., contracts, purchasing) is always with the party having the most or best information about the deal. In consumer products, the seller has historically held the advantage, while the consumer had to rely on confidence in a brand built by the seller to compensate for lack of information about the actual value. With digital media, the consumer's thumb can just as easily tilt the scale."

The accelerating E-Expectations of students

Ongoing E-Expectations research studies (a joint research effort of Noel-Levitz, NRCCUA [the National Center for College & University Admissions], and OmniUpdate) have documented significant changes in students' media habits over the last five years. For example, in the 2009 study, 50 percent of high school seniors reported using Facebook; in 2011, 80 percent of the surveyed high school seniors had a Facebook account. Use of e-mail as an effective communication resource during the recruitment process has remained fairly consistent for prospective students (86 percent in 2011) and parents (80 percent in 2011).

The 2011 *E-Expectations* study polled 1,089 high school seniors and 517 of their parents from across the United States. The parents were paired with half of the students who were surveyed.

Among the key findings:

- The majority of respondents said the college search and enrollment decision process is a collaborative effort between students and parents.

- One in five students said they removed an institution from consideration because of a bad experience on an institution's Web site.

- When first visiting an institution's Web site, a majority of students and parents click on links related to academics and programs of study.

- Among students who had Facebook accounts, 27 percent said that they had visited a college's Facebook page, compared with 12 percent of parents with Facebook accounts.

- Of the 86 percent of students who said they use e-mail, 93 percent stated they provided schools with an e-mail address, with nearly all adding that they submitted an e-mail address that they check at least once per week.

Interacting with the market through social media

Using social media is messy. It is difficult to manage and hard to measure. At the same time, it is imperative that colleges and universities be strategic in this arena. Social media provide powerful opportunities to connect authentically and transparently with important audiences.

An institutional social media plan should answer these questions:

- Which audiences will give us the best return on investment of our time (e.g., traditional students, adult students, parents)?

- In which outlets or forums will we be active?

- How do we intentionally and appropriately integrate key marketing messages and content into our social media plan?

- How will we staff the effort?

- What will be our institutional guidelines and governance process for social media activities?

- How will we measure the results (e.g., increase number of "fans")?

The management of social media is not a job for an untrained work-study student. It is best owned by an enrollment or marketing manager who has a clear sense of the goals and objectives of the effort. Professional enrollment staff should be engaged in:

1. Providing guidance and insight in the creation or removal of social media assets in concert with the institution's overarching marketing and communications goals;

2. Determining the methods for measurement and tracking activity;

3. Connecting with other campus constituents to respond to external queries; and

4. Defining the appropriate response to inappropriate behaviors on institutional outlets.

However, there is value in using student employees to assist with efforts to sustain a successful social media plan. They can be helpful in monitoring assets to alert professional staff to any problematic posts or technical problems. Their own posts regarding their experiences as students can provide valuable information to prospective students and parents. They can also alert professional staff to emerging social media trends or new resources. For this reason, some strategic enrollment planning teams include students, often on a subcommittee where they can help bring a student voice (and potentially their expertise) without the student voice dictating priorities within the larger plan.

For a market on the go: Mobile Web sites

Research studies tracking the use of electronic media show that mobile devices are being used increasingly as a primary way to access the internet.

Figure 10-2: Use of Mobile Web Sites by Prospective Students

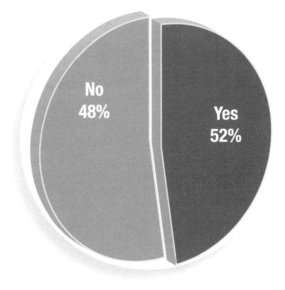

Source: E-Expectations Trend Report: *The Mobile Browsing Behaviors and Expectations of College-Bound High School Students*, Noel-Levitz, Inc., 2012

The number of prospective students using mobile sites for college search will almost certainly increase in the coming years. Therefore, colleges should stay ahead of the curve and allocate resources to mobile development, particularly for applications and interactive content that are suited for smartphones. At present, minimum content and functionality for a mobile Web site should include an institutional overview, contact information/inquiry form, degree/program offerings, faculty information, tuition and fees, campus map, and upcoming events.

Mobile technology differs from standard Web technology in a variety of ways, from accessibility to user expectations. Most campuses will need to outsource mobile site development to one of the many providers that specialize in this growing field. As Keller has observed, "Most colleges do not have the resources to build their own mobile applications from scratch. The environment is changing quickly, and developing new products for each new major device—iPhones, BlackBerrys, Android phones, iPads—can be prohibitively expensive" (*The Chronicle of Higher Education*, 2011).

In creating a mobile site, staff should not lose sight of the need to ensure the site is a true extension of the institution's market positioning rather than an entity of its own.

Contact-driven branding to raise awareness and motivate response

A common tug-of-war over marketing at colleges and universities is whether to focus on general advertising or direct marketing. Advertising uses mass media such as magazines, billboards, television, and newspapers, and is often considered attractive because it is highly visible to the campus community. General advertising is used to build name recognition and brand image, as well as to reach broad audiences for which target mailing lists do not exist, such as adult students interested in degree completion.

Direct marketing encourages students to respond and take action. As its name implies, it is targeted to the individual through tools such as direct mail, e-mail, and telecounseling. It almost always has a call to action. Direct marketing is a hardworking, productive tool for enrollment managers because it is targeted and measurable. However, it may be invisible to the campus community, leaving enrollment managers open to the criticism that "we aren't doing any marketing."

An evolving concept in strategic enrollment management and marketing is what might be called contact-driven branding, an approach that acknowledges the need for both measurability and the building of awareness. Contact-driven branding is a direct marketing approach with specific messages to specific potential students. Institutions that extensively use student search marketing (purchasing lists of names and then marketing to these prospects) recognize the value of this concept as they observe the many students who do not immediately respond to direct mail or e-mail marketing campaigns, but ultimately enroll because their interest in the institution was activated. In addition to talking with friends and family members about the institution, these students may have gone directly to the institution's Web site and Facebook pages. If the institution's market positioning is well-formed, the messages students receive will be consistent and reinforcing no matter what the marketing venue, general or direct. Institutions need to establish measurement systems to track this potential trend.

Market research is a dialogue

Since the days of patent medicines, marketing has been viewed as a one-way street. Speak loudly, make enough promises, use the right package colors, and the target will be sold. In college and university marketing, this often has translated into the senior administrator merely wanting a billboard on the nearby highway like that of institution X or the board members who are certain there must be more students in California or New York who want to attend their small Midwestern school.

In such situations, market research is the great equalizer and clarifier. All institutions, great and small, ultimately must bow to the market's expectations and perceptions. Market research lets the fresh air of the marketplace into the ivory tower.

According to author and educator Kotler (1999), "Companies often fail to recognize that their marketplace changes every few years," The same could be said of institutions of higher education. While higher education may seem slow-moving compared with fields such as business, science, and technology, a host of market factors are in constant flux, ranging from demand for various academic programs to tuition price sensitivity.

Although many colleges and universities are satisfied with the occasional market study, savvy institutions take the pulse of the marketplace regularly. Assessments can be conducted by collecting data elements readily available through national, state, and regional agencies. An ongoing market research plan, linked to performance indicators, ensures the institution is attuned to emerging trends and not taken by surprise by attitude shifts among key constituencies.

The list of possible research areas is extensive; however, the most valuable initiatives will support a strategic enrollment plan by:

1. Assessing the market:

- Image and perception studies: What is the institution's current market position and how does it compare with students' visions of their ideal institution?

- Academic program demand: How well does the curriculum align with developing market trends? Which programs are likely to encounter the greatest enrollment growth opportunities or declines? What are the preferred modes of program delivery (fully online, hybrid, campus-based), and what course scheduling is preferred (evening, weekend, etc.)?

- Price sensitivity analysis: What is the optimal tuition level for the institution's market, and how would changes to tuition and financial aid impact enrollment?

2. Assessing the institution:

- Student satisfaction and engagement: What areas are of greatest importance to current students, and what are their satisfaction levels with these items? How engaged are students in the educational experience at the institution?

- Employee satisfaction: How satisfied, productive, and mission-focused are campus employees as they interact with students?

- Alumni satisfaction: How do alumni feel about the quality and value of the education they received? What recommendations can they offer for institutional improvements? Will they recommend the institution to others?

3. Assessing competitors:

- Competition communications study: What marketing messages and media are competitors using to reach audiences that are also targeted by the institution?

- Market share analysis: What is the institution's share of the market, and where do its competitors rank in terms of market share and quality relative to price?

In the absence of market research, market positioning is reduced to a guessing game that will likely be driven by an incomplete understanding of the environment. In the classic *Harvard Business Review* article, "Backward Market Research," Andreasen emphasizes the need for highly actionable market research rather than research that simply results in "the reduction of the level of ignorance" (1985).

Linking market position with enrollment planning

Most strategic enrollment teams will be focused on some basic long-range enrollment management decisions (e.g., whether to expand market share in secondary/tertiary markets in anticipation of demographic declines in the primary market, whether to reduce or increase sticker price to expand enrollment or reduce the discount rate, and how to develop new programs to be delivered online to the nontraditional undergraduate market). Assuming every research event is driven by the need to answer explicit questions and make specific decisions, Table 10-3 presents a sample strategic enrollment research plan designed to survey multiple enrollment audiences over time.

Table 10-3: Sample Strategic Enrollment Research Plan

Timing	Audiences/market segments					
Year 1	Current students	Academic program demand study	High school guidance counselors	Parents of traditional prospects	Transfer students	Community college transfer counselors
Year 2	Prospective students	Competition study	Price sensitivity analysis	Graduate student prospects	Alumni	Employers of alumni
Year 3	Current students and their parents	Withdrawing student survey	Continuing education students	College employee satisfaction	Transfer students	Community college transfer counselors
Year 4	Prospective students	Alumni	High school guidance counselors	Parents of traditional prospects	Employers of alumni	Competition study
Year 5	Current students	Academic program demand study	Withdrawing student survey	Graduate student prospects	College employee satisfaction	Residence hall survey

Examples

A public university campus in a western U.S. state had plans to embark on a new branding campaign. As campus leaders evaluated the institution's strengths, they concluded that their racial and ethnic diversity, which extended to students, faculty, staff, and administrators, was their primary market positioning asset.

Just before launching the campaign, however, they sought market research to confirm their direction. The research showed that, of 25 college choice factors, diversity was ranked 24th in importance by their prospective students. Further qualitative investigation revealed that, because the institution's students came from homes, schools, communities, and workplaces that were highly diverse, diversity was a fundamental expectation, not a distinction. As a student buying motive, diversity would have been a barrier if absent, but its presence was not viewed as exceptional.

Although this was a large campus with an undergraduate enrollment of more than 10,000, the research suggested that students were seeking a high degree of faculty engagement in and outside the classroom as their primary institutional characteristic.

"I've been asked not to use the word 'marketing' and we don't call our educational experience a 'product,'" said the communications director at an Eastern institution. Meanwhile, faculty members insisted that the recent decline in incoming student ACT scores was due in part to the institution's invisibility in the face of aggressive advertising and recruiting by competing peer institutions.

Today's admissions counselor isn't disposable

A single admissions counselor at a small, private college or university easily could be held responsible for enrolling 50 to 200 students for a fall semester. If the institution averages $15,000 in net revenue per student, that recruiter is accountable for generating roughly $750,000 to $3,000,000 annually in institutional income. In the business world, that kind of salesperson would be highly valued and the target of vigorous employee retention efforts. In higher education, that recruiter often is at the bottom of the ladder in terms of compensation and prestige. A revolving door for the admissions counselor position is generally accepted at many institutions.

Where does this attitude come from? It may be a vestige of earlier eras when many campuses did not need to market themselves and could simply process applications, and frankly, at times it arises from the academy's assumption that the institution will just sell itself based on the superiority of its academic programs.

> *" An admissions counselor holds significant responsibility in his or her hands."*

An admissions counselor holds significant responsibility in his or her hands. In 2010, the average ratio of applications to admissions officers at colleges and universities in the U.S. was 527:1; representing 981:1 at public institutions and 402:1 at private institutions (College and University Professional Association for Human Resources, 2011).

Institutions that recognize the value of well-trained, professional admissions counselors are beginning to invest in developing the position into one that requires:

1. A broader focus on marketing, as counselors represent the brand image of the institution.
2. The ability to interact effectively with diverse populations from a variety of cultures and ethnicities.
3. Strengths in relationship-building and management, with a focus on determining fit between the institution and the student rather than simply on selling.
4. A firsthand knowledge of the use of technology in recruitment, from social media sites to text messaging.
5. An understanding of strategic marketing communications and the role of advertising, direct marketing, one-on-one interactions, and other tools.
6. Expertise in a variety of college financing solutions.
7. The ability to broadly and specifically articulate the institution's market positioning in a compelling way.

W. Kent Barnds—vice president for enrollment, communication, and planning at Augustana College in Illinois and a 20-year admissions veteran—observes, "The senior enrollment management role at institutions is becoming increasingly important. More and more enrollment officers are serving at the cabinet level, are engaging with boards of trustees, and are involved with institutional strategic planning. We've got to find a way to groom the next generation for this kind of role, and it starts with investing in our own counselors" (Personal communication).

Viewing admissions counselors as valued employees to be developed, rather than disposable assets to be recycled, requires an institution to:

1. Conduct succession planning for key positions and promote from within whenever possible.
2. Cross-train employees on multiple functions (e.g., financial aid), enabling counselors to build a robust skill set.
3. Offer a clear career path within the enrollment management function.
4. Improve compensation in relation to other institutional positions, offering internal recognition and financial rewards matching the importance of the role.

The 2011 National Association for College Admissions Counseling (NACAC) *State of College Admission Report* indicates a median salary for college admissions counselors at all levels of experience of $34,811. According to the College and University Professional Association for Human Resources, the entry-level annual giving officer earns an average of approximately $40,000, as does the entry-level alumni relations officer—a 15 percent difference in pay (2011).

Conclusion: Dull or differentiated?

Good market positioning is not pixie dust sprinkled over an institution in an attempt to make it more attractive to the marketplace or a coat of paint that disguises defects and deficiencies. It requires an investment in research, planning, and marketing strategies that both strengthen the institution by placing it in the intense spotlight of market expectations and allow it to move forward by highlighting its relevant strengths. For strategic enrollment planners, well-executed market positioning can help catapult an institution out of dull sameness into a place of distinctiveness that truly matters.

Dialogue

Use this discussion guide in your marketing and enrollment management teams to facilitate changes in attitudes and priorities:

- What key marketing messages is your institution using today with prospective students? Do these messages fit the criteria of being at the intersection of institutional strengths, market demand, and competitive opportunity?

- Is there a gap between the institution's current market position and its ideal position? How can strategic planning help to close that gap?

- What market research do you need to ensure that the strategic planning team has a comprehensive, data-informed understanding of the institution, the market, and the competitive context?

- How are you ensuring that your institution's Web site is driven by audience needs, not simply by institutional interests? Does the relative emphasis by audience on your institution's homepage match the importance of those audiences to your institution's future?

- Is your campus making a sufficient financial investment in e-marketing strategies, or are you acting as if tools, such as social networking, are free?

- How will you evaluate your current marketing practices that use social and/or electronic media to generate interest and help support the institutional brand?

- Is your institution intentional about providing a career path for admissions personnel? Are junior and mid-level admissions staff compensated at a level commensurate with institutional advancement staff and other comparable functions?

CHAPTER 11

Recruitment Strategies

By Sarah Coen

"The nicest thing about not planning is that failure comes as a complete surprise and is not preceded by a period of worry and depression."
– Sir John Harvey-Jones

Chapter highlights

- **The annual recruitment plan should support SEP goals**

- **Building relationships is key**

- **Subpopulations require differing approaches**

Student recruitment is a crucial component of a strategic enrollment plan (SEP). To reach a desired state, a campus must recruit the students who fit that planned state. This desired group may be traditional undergraduate, graduate, or nontraditional students. This chapter will mainly provide traditional undergraduate practices; however, most, if not all, of these practices could apply to other populations. An annual plan plays a pivotal role in the SEP process and, at most campuses, is separated by traditional, transfer, graduate, and nontraditional plans. It must not only be data-informed, but also in alignment with the overall goals contained in the SEP.

The quote above by Sir John Harvey-Jones sums up how many campuses feel about developing an annual recruitment plan. Often, recruitment plans are little more than a laundry list of recruitment activities or a calendar of admissions events—neither of which represent a plan. A well-conceived recruitment plan is an organized thought process and communication tool that describes what the institution wants to achieve and how it will accomplish it. In short, it is the roadmap to reaching new student recruitment goals.

A primary difference between an SEP and an annual marketing and recruitment plan is that the marketing/recruitment plan is typically developed—and accountability lies—within the office of admissions, while the SEP is developed with the involvement of a wide range of offices including faculty, staff, and administration throughout the campus. For example, if the SEP calls for an increase in academic profile, then the annual plan should include supporting strategies, such as purchasing high-ability student names for search and aggressively recruiting them to campus. The admissions team now needs to take this action item and determine which purchased names can best shape the desired profile. The plan drives the priorities of the admissions office and requires the leaders within admissions to determine the steps needed to reach the strategic priority.

Consider Table 11-1 from the *Marketing and Student Recruitment Practices at Four-Year and Two-Year Institutions* (Noel-Levitz, 2011), which shows the number of institutions that have an annual recruitment plan and the number that consider theirs to be of excellent quality.

Table 11-1: Prevalence of Recruitment Planning by Institution Type

My institution has a written annual recruitment plan		
	Percent of respondents in agreement	
Type of institution	**Yes**	**Yes, and it's of excellent quality**
Four-year private	83.7%	18.1%
Four-year public	81.5%	20.0%
Two-year public	70.5%	15.9%

Even though the majority of respondents reported having plans in place, a significant number failed to rate their plan as strong. Further, only about half reported that they had strong recruitment strategies in place. These data suggest a clear need for more campuses to focus on their recruitment strategies, as well as their planning.

Moreover, the recruitment of new students has become fiercely competitive and requires masterful planning and execution. Planning alone does not ensure results, but it does provide disciplined appraisal, goal setting, and strategizing that can minimize failure. Developing an annual recruitment plan that includes defining the current state, setting goals, identifying strategies, and writing the action plans can vastly improve the chances that new student recruitment and net tuition revenue goals will be met.

Defining the current state of recruitment

The purpose of this initial step in recruitment planning is to document the current state of enrollment through the use of historical data, market research, and an articulation of the internal and external environments in which the enrollment effort must be carried out. This step of the planning effort usually involves the following tasks aligned with the SEP process:

1. Reviewing the institutional mission statement that describes the basic reason for the existence of the organization.

2. Confirming the primary target markets and enrollment growth strategies your campus is pursuing and has outlined in the SEP.

3. Reviewing the SEP and mission statement, making sure they are consistent with each other.

4. Assessing current strengths, weaknesses, opportunities, and threats, or driving forces (combination of strengths and opportunities) and restraining forces (combination of weaknesses and threats). These driving and restraining forces should be included in the situation analysis and represent many of the forces that must be overcome—and exploited—in order to achieve enrollment goals.

Supporting data for recruitment planning

Chapter 5 discusses the importance of being data-informed rather than data-driven in the planning process. This holds true for the annual recruitment plan as well as the SEP. Unfortunately, what tends to drive most recruitment goals is the number of students needed to support the operating budget. A much better approach is to compile and review historical recruitment and admissions data, both overall and by specific program. Basic funnels (prospects, inquiries, applications, acceptances, deposits, and matriculants) should be included in the situation analysis, as well as any research pertinent to the planning process (e.g., source code analysis, territorial analysis, conversion and yield analysis, campus visit analysis, SAT analysis, and competition and market share analysis).

In addition to historical funnel data, it is also important to consider other data and research that can help drive the recruitment plan. The list of data below could be collected as campuses begin to write their SEP, as noted in chapters 5 and 9.

1. Review appropriate demographic trends and environmental data, such as:

   – In-state high school population and other important markets;

   – Graduation rates and projections;

   – Migration patterns (percent expected to stay in state/leave state for college);

   – Preferred majors by high school graduates;

   – SAT/ACT test score analysis;

   – Education attainment patterns of adults in the primary market; and

   – Job/Industry trends in the primary market.

> *" In addition to historical funnel data, it is also important to consider other data and research that can help drive the recruitment plan."*

2. Evaluate any information from recent competition studies to include:

   – Five-year enrollment patterns;

   – Tuition and institutional aid of primary competition;

   – Key recruitment themes and messages (as seen on competitors' Web sites and in literature); and

   – Market share of your institution compared with primary competition.

3. Review results of recent market survey research, to include:

   – Lost inquiry study;

   – High school counselor survey; and

   – Admitted student questionnaire survey (for enrolled and non-enrolled students).

4. Use data to confirm target markets.

5. If necessary, conduct a program-by-program (major fields of study or concentrations) analysis and establish desired enrollment state and marketing/recruiting needs.

6. Develop a list of recruitment planning assumptions (e.g., staffing, budget, and competition).

Annual goal setting

While SEP calls for three-, five-, or seven-year enrollment goals, recruitment plans call for annual recruitment goals. Recruitment goals must be quantified and understandable to all who are accountable to the achievement of the goals. These goals must also be shared with all members of the enrollment team and the broader campus community.

As stated in Chapter 8, campuses must determine whether they want to increase, maintain, or shrink enrollment. The examples shared in that chapter are worth repeating here, as they should also guide the annual recruitment planning process:

- **Increase** enrollment, because a campus is focused on growing net tuition revenues, has capacity to grow, and has academic programs with growing demand;

- **Maintain** enrollment, because an institution has little or no capacity to grow but may have other enrollment goals, such as improving academic quality, shaping the enrollment in specific academic programs, improving the geographic and/or socioeconomic diversity of the student body, etc.; and

- **Shrink** enrollment, either by design (perhaps due to focusing on higher student academic quality and/or a narrowed set of academic offerings) or by necessity (e.g., the catchment area is regional and there are declining high school graduates, there is declining employer support for students pursuing master's programs, there is increasing competition from a lower-cost provider, or there is declining demand for the academic programs that have been historically offered).

The following points are also important to the goal-setting process:

- Goals are an expression of the outcomes of the recruitment plan.

- Goals are derived directly from the enrollment planning process.

- Goals are most often, but not always, expressed quantitatively and relate to desired enrollment outcomes. If a goal is not measurable, it should at least be recognizable and qualitative in character.

- Generally, recruitment plans contain no more than three to five major goals.

- Goals are stated as simply and concisely as possible.

- Effective recruitment plans begin with a clear understanding of the goals that must be achieved in order to succeed.

- Goals are always supported by one or more strategies.

- Goals are mutually agreed upon by all whose efforts will achieve them.

Table 11-2 provides a framework for setting funnel goals. This framework should be used for setting both the overall new student enrollment goal as well as other subpopulation goals (transfer, honors, graduate, out-of-state, etc.).

Table 11-2: Admissions Funnel Framework: Quantitative Enrollment Goals

Enrollment goals for each funnel stage						
Stage	Year one final	Year two final	Year three final	Year four final	Four- to five-year average	Next year's goal
Prospects						
Progression percent						
Inquiries						
Conversion percent						
Applicants						
Completed applications						
Accept percent						
Accepts						
Yield percent						
Confirms						
Capture percent						
Enrolled						

Table 11-3 provides some examples of the goals that might drive a recruitment plan.

Table 11-3: Examples of Typical Recruitment Planning Goals

Recruitment goals
Overall goal: Enroll a total of 2,200 new students for fall 2012, consisting of 1,500 new freshmen and 700 new transfer students. This is compared to 1,862 new students in fall 2011 (1,190 FTIC/672 transfer).
Goal one: Enroll an entering class with an average high school grade point average of 3.2 or better (versus 3.15) and an average ACT score (or equivalent) of 23 or better (versus 22.5).
Goal two: Achieve 10 percent domestic minority representation in the entering class (150 students versus 125).
Goal three: Achieve 6 percent out-of-state representation in the first-year class, versus 3 to 5 percent in recent years.
Goal four: Increase new student enrollment in the College of Arts and Sciences by 125 students, from 750 to 875.

Recruitment strategies

Once the goals have been established and agreed upon, the strategies to reach those goals should be identified. The strategies should include a connection to the institution's mission and values, which link academic, co-curricular, and enrollment planning and align them with fiscal planning. Effective recruitment plans include a variety of strategies that will vary by institution type and by student population, but some are central to any plan. While the strategies discussed below are not meant to be an exhaustive list, they do represent the essential elements of new student recruitment.

Funnel theory and management

For years, the traditional enrollment funnel model (see Figure 11-1) has been used to manage new student enrollments at college and university campuses across North America. However, rapid changes in student behavior have caused that funnel to become much more chaotic at prospect, inquiry, and applicant stages.

Figure 11-1: Enrollment Model: Traditional Versus Current Student Behavior

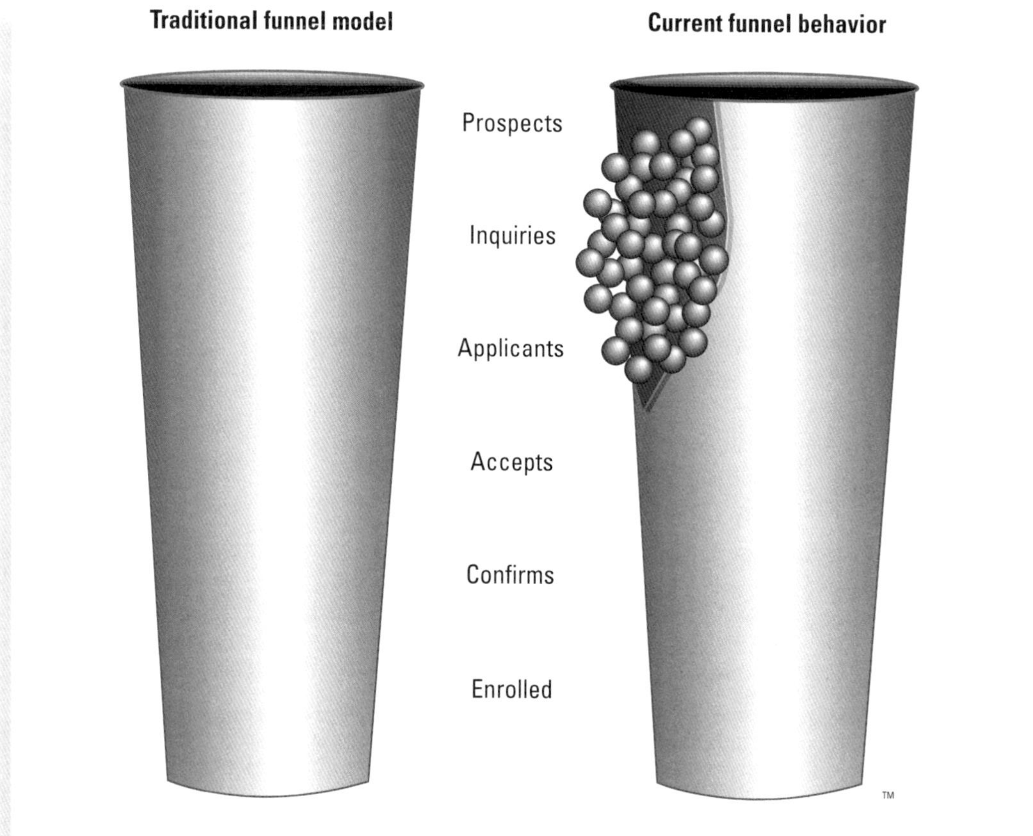

The traditional funnel focused on stages—students advanced from one stage to the next until they ultimately enrolled or opted out of the process. This model enabled enrollment managers to develop marketing and recruitment strategies designed to build sufficient volumes at each stage of the funnel to support desired quantities at subsequent stages. Under this theory, an increased number of confirmed students simply required more accepts, applicants, inquiries, or prospects; a substantial shift in the conversion ratio(s) from one stage to the next; or a combination of these two strategies.

Recent developments in technology and a shift in student college choice patterns have undermined this model, especially at the top of the funnel. Widespread use of the internet to search for colleges and a growing tendency among prospective students to remain anonymous in the college selection process (at least prior to submitting an application for admission) are changing the paradigm, as illustrated in the funnel representing current funnel behavior in Figure 11-1. These emerging trends, as well as other fundamental problems with the classic funnel model and traditional approach to prospecting, have impacted campus results.

The funnel in Figure 11-2 is a better representation of the current metrics that campuses should be using. Under the new paradigm, prospective students will enter at a time and a channel of their choosing and will progress through the funnel at different rates depending on the manner and timing of that contact.

Figure 11-2: Enrollment Funnel With Multiple Entry Channels

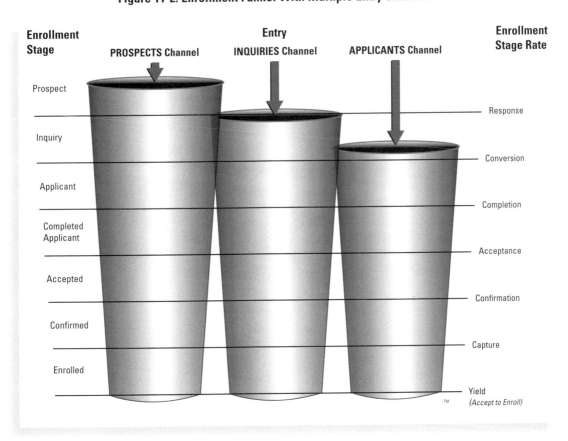

Table 11-4, from the Noel-Levitz *2010 Admissions Funnel Benchmarks* report, illustrates the average funnel rates for both four-year public and private institutions from 2003 to 2010.

Table 11-4: Admissions Funnel Rates

Public universities—FTIC first-year student funnel rates								
Median funnel rates	2010	2009	2008	2007	2006	2005	2004	2003
Inquiry to application	35%	34%	33%	31%	28%	25%	27%	24%
Application to admit (all applications)	66%	65%	66%	67%	70%	73%	70%	72%
Application to admit (completed applications only)	81%	85%	71%	74%	83%	83%	NA	NA
Admit to enroll (yield)	41%	43%	38%	39%	42%	43%	47%	49%
Deposited/ confirmed to enroll	93%	91%	92%	93%	92%	92%	NA	NA
Deposit melt	7%	9%	8%	7%	8%	8%	NA	NA

Private colleges and universities—FTIC first-year student funnel rates								
Median funnel rates	2010	2009	2008	2007	2006	2005	2004	2003
Inquiry to application	15%	15%	13%	13%	14%	13%	12%	10%
Application to admit (all applications)	66%	65%	71%	73%	70%	72%	75%	76%
Application to admit (completed applications only)	86%	86%	87%	87%	91%	87%	NA	NA
Admit to enroll (yield)	29%	29%	31%	33%	35%	35%	36%	36%
Deposited/ confirmed	88%	88%	90%	91%	90%	89%	NA	NA
Deposit melt	12%	12%	10%	9%	10%	11%	NA	NA

When an institution's funnel rates fall below the national average, it typically indicates that new or improved strategies need to be considered for that funnel stage. For example, if a private institution has been converting admits to enrollees at a rate of 21 percent, instead of the national average of 29 to 30 percent, the campus might consider enhancing its post-admit communication plan to include messages of value and outcomes. This may also indicate an opportunity to improve the effectiveness of the institution's financial aid strategy.

As a campus seeks to sync its recruitment and SEP, the understanding and management of the funnel and use of these metrics (and how they are changing) is critical to align action with goal setting and a basic underlying foundation of funnel management. Campuses must focus on all stages of the funnel but need to remain keenly aware of the bottom lines—the numbers of students enrolled and graduated. As the enrollment team works through the funnel, the goal should be to use data about recently enrolled students to build a funnel that will assist an institution in meeting its enrollment goals and to understand how those goals are being accomplished.

Building the inquiry pool

Even with the changing funnel dynamics, the development of the inquiry pool is important to any sound recruitment program. A successful admissions operation will intentionally and consistently manage the development of an inquiry pool to reach the desired goals for new student enrollment. Although the shape, size, and characteristics of inquiry pools are changing (mainly as more students are waiting to make the initial contact with the institution at the applicant stage), it is still essential to understand how inquiry pools are built, which inquiry sources are more predictive of enrollment, and what opportunities for improvement exist to strengthen communication at this fundamental stage of the new student enrollment funnel.

The type of inquiry can be categorized into four distinct areas, each converting and yielding at different rates. Campuses should attempt to develop an appropriate mix of inquiries that will achieve the targeted funnel percentage goal from inquiry to applicant to enrolled.

1. **Student-initiated:** These inquiries often convert and yield at the highest rates, since they come directly from students as they express an interest in the institution. These include standardized test scores, applications as first source, e-mails, phone calls, and campus visits, among others. It is wise for campuses to heavily focus on strategies to get more student-initiated contacts into the inquiry pool.

2. **Travel-initiated:** These are cultivated during counselor travel, including high school visits, college fair programs, community college meetings, off-campus receptions, and other events. They are a direct result of the territory management model discussed later in this chapter.

3. **Solicited:** These are prospective student names that are purchased from a variety of sources (e.g., ACT, College Board, NRCCUA, and CollegeFish.org). Once the prospective student expresses interest, either as a result of a direct mail or e-mail campaign or at any time during the recruitment cycle, he/she should be entered into the inquiry pool. This may also include a subset of search names that are directly loaded into the inquiry pool using a predictive model score or some other qualification technique.

4. **Referral:** These are names provided to the admissions office by alumni, faculty, intercollegiate athletics, churches, and others. Creating a plan for generating or asking for these referrals is an important step in building the inquiry pool.

It is equally important to understand *how* various inquiry sources move through the funnel and ultimately become enrollees. Enrollment officers will want to create a basic inquiry-by-source report that tracks the volume of inquiries by source as well as their funnel rates.

Table 11-5: Example of Initial Inquiry Source Code Report

Source	Inquiries			Applications			Accepts			Confirms/Enrolled		
	Current year	Last year	Diff	Current year	Last year	Diff	Current year	Last year	Diff	Current year	Last year	Diff
High school visit												
ACT test submitted												
NRCCUA search name												
College fair												
Web inquiry												
Application as first source												

Qualification and grading

Funnel qualification is a systematic process designed to determine the level of student interest in an institution's prospect, inquiry, applicant, and confirmed student pools. Students can be qualified through operations and market research, reply mechanisms (including the initial prospect card), by telephone, or through other personal contact. Funnel qualification has two goals:

1. Identify and target students who are genuinely interested in the institution.

2. Remove students with little or no interest in attendance.

An effective qualification system allows the enrollment management team to focus scarce resources on those students with the greatest *propensity* to enroll. See Figure 11-3.

With *funnel grading*, an institution rates the desirability of prospective students at the prospect, inquiry, applicant, and decision stages. This is generally accomplished by examining student characteristics, such as academic profile or racial/ethnic category (objective assessment), and through personal contact (subjective assessment). An effective grading system allows an institution to focus resources on those students it has the greatest *interest* in enrolling.

There are a number of advanced methods, such as statistical modeling or predictive modeling (the Noel-Levitz modeling process is called Forecast*Plus*™), that can identify the best prospects for a campus and make the qualification and grading process much more precise. The data-informed nature of these methods also makes them well suited for the SEP process, in addition to recruitment planning.

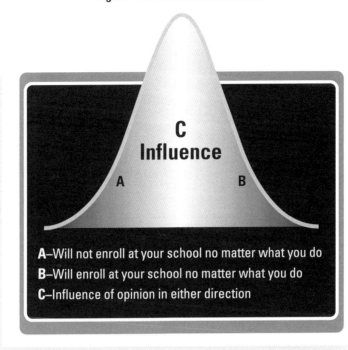

Figure 11-3: Influence Continuum

C
Influence

A   B

A–Will not enroll at your school no matter what you do
B–Will enroll at your school no matter what you do
C–Influence of opinion in either direction

Student search

Student search plans should build awareness of an institution in primary, secondary, and tertiary markets. However, today's student search process needs to be approached differently than in previous years, giving less attention to response rates and more focus on actual enrollment rates. With the increase in secret shoppers (those whose first formal contact with the institution is as an applicant—often called "stealth applicants"), student search has shifted from a response mechanism to a critical process for building institutional awareness. Institutions are finding that, by getting their brand into the marketplace and on the minds of students much earlier, their applicant pools are increasing even if their inquiry pools are not growing as quickly.

Beyond the name purchase itself, institutions are placing increased efforts on direct marketing campaigns for search names. It is not uncommon for today's search campaigns to include multiple messages, in both written and electronic form. The old way of sending a search piece and waiting for a response no longer works. Consider the data in Figure 11-4 from the Noel-Levitz report *Marketing and Student Recruitment Practices at Four-Year and Two-Year Institutions*.

Figure 11-4: Written Communications a Prospective Student Received by Stage

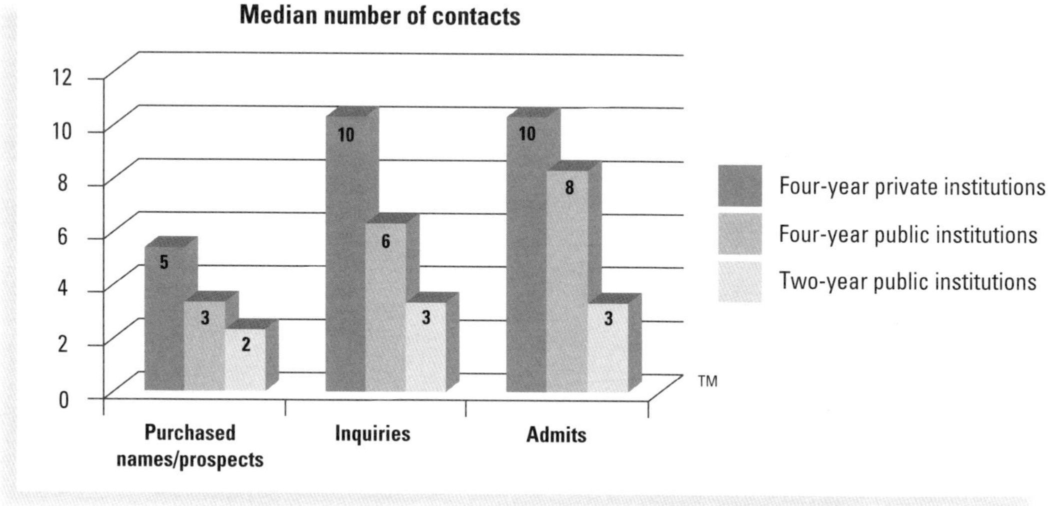

Median number of contacts

Legend:
- Four-year private institutions
- Four-year public institutions
- Two-year public institutions

Categories: Purchased names/prospects (5, 3, 2), Inquiries (10, 6, 3), Admits (10, 8, 3)

The complexity and importance of student search have driven the creation of new metrics for measuring the effectiveness of search. Rather than focusing solely on response rates, campuses are paying more attention to enrollment rates and the prospect coverage rates (PCR) of search purchases. By definition, the PCR is the percentage of the enrolled pool that was in the search purchase.

Marketing and communication

Strong prospective student communication plans begin with an understanding of the institutional image and brand. Branding is generally an institutionwide initiative that involves university relations and enrollment management (at the very least), and should also be part of institutional strategic planning initiatives or discussions. As outlined in Chapter 10, branding is what an institution is known for or wants to be known for—what makes it unique and distinctive. For branding to be effective in new student recruitment, an institution must continually assess how to deliver on the promise of its brand. If a brand communicates "student success is our business," then graduation rates must be well above average, retention initiatives must permeate institutional planning priorities, and alumni successes must be well tracked and documented.

Messaging involves the expression of key strengths that speak to the institution brand and may include some targeted messages for selected audiences. Messaging helps to translate why the brand has value for the audience. Unfortunately, many colleges miss the mark when it comes to selling value. The focus of the key messages tends to be more about the atmosphere of campus (student life, religious affiliation, facilities) than on the actual product—the academic experience and related outcomes. While co-curricular offerings are important and do drive some students' decision making (e.g., playing a sport and/or receiving a scholarship to play a sport), the majority of students enroll and graduate because of the quality and outcome of the academic program.

Once the key messages have been identified, the challenging task of communicating them to prospective students and their families begins. Building effective communication plans for today's prospective students can be daunting, to say the least. While it is clear that students use many forms of technology, including Web, e-mail, social media, and texting to communicate, research also suggests that they still rely on written communication. In the 2012 Noel-Levitz E-Expectations research report, *The Online Expectations of College-Bound Juniors and Seniors*, 71 percent of students reported that printed publications and letters were an effective way for them to learn about an institution's academic program offerings.

One common misperception is that marketing ends when a student is admitted. This is a mistake, especially as more students apply to multiple institutions than before the advent of online applications, pre-populated applications, and the Common Application. Effective communication plans should be integrated with the recruitment process, begin at the search stage, and continue until the student is enrolled. Even after students have made a deposit, it is wise to keep communicating with them and create compelling reasons for them to see their enrollment all the way through.

As with student search, marketing and communication metrics are changing. Given the importance of marketing to recruitment as well as the importance of recruitment to SEP, campuses should consider tracking metrics such as:

- Institutional awareness in primary and secondary markets (how many students in those markets have heard of the campus prior to any contact?);
- Awareness of primary strengths and academic offerings (for what is the institution known?);
- Awareness of the primary strengths and academic offerings of main competitors; and
- Impressions of the value of a degree from the institution (such as job opportunities, post-baccalaureate study, and alumni success).

Some of these metrics, such as institutional awareness, may be quantifiable. Others are more qualitative (such as most-recognized academic offerings), but can be tracked year-to-year to discern whether the campus is reaching its desired state in its target markets. Depending on the research capabilities of the institution, a campus may want to engage outside, specialized market research to periodically examine some areas (at the beginning of the SEP process, then again every two to three years while moving toward the desired state).

Territory management

Territory management assigns the recruitment and enrollment of students from a specific geographic area to one or more admissions representatives. Its objectives include:

- Establishing application and enrollment goals by territory. These goals should be aligned with any new market development goals that are outlined in the SEP.
- Empowering admissions staff to develop territorial recruitment strategies.
- Providing recruitment staff with budget responsibilities within their territories.
- Making certain that the same staff person works with a student from point-of-inquiry through enrollment.
- Assigning responsibility for transfer and adult students to a dedicated transfer/adult counselor(s).

Building relationships is probably the single-most-important duty of the territory manager. The territory manager should build relationships with secondary school counselors, community college advising staff, and prospective students and their families during school visits, college fairs, and receptions. Face-to-face relationships may be time consuming, but they provide great value when it comes to enrollment. By developing personal relationships, the territory manager has the greatest ability to motivate students to take the next steps toward enrollment.

Tracking the funnel metrics for each counselor/territory is an important part of the territory management model. Table 11-6 provides a framework for territory metrics.

Table 11-6: Example of Framework for Territory Analysis Report

Territory/Counselor	Inquiries			Applications			Accepts			Confirms/Enrolled		
	Current year	Last year	Diff	Current year	Last year	Diff	Current year	Last year	Diff	Current year	Last year	Diff
Territory 1												
Territory 2												
Territory 3												
Territory 4												
Territory 5												

Campus visit programming

When a prospective student begins to envision him/herself as a member of the campus community, the likelihood of the student applying and enrolling goes up dramatically. Therefore, virtually every strategy contained within a recruitment plan is designed to attract a prospective student and his/her family to visit the campus, and these campus visit strategies are arguably the most important ones implemented during the admissions cycle.

There are many types of campus visit opportunities, including both individual and group options. Often, the mission and size of the institution will determine which are best for the students they serve.

1. **Individual visits:** Prospective students and their families should be encouraged to visit campus individually. This visit could include meeting with admissions staff, taking a campus tour, sitting in on a class or meeting with a faculty member, meeting with financial aid staff, and spending the night in the residence hall (some of these visit elements will depend on the type/size of the institution).

2. **Group visits:** These events are also very important in the recruitment process and need to be targeted to the appropriate audiences, depending on the time in the recruitment cycle. Group visit opportunities include open houses for inquiries and applicants in the spring and fall, an admitted-student day as a way to increase yield, and a college-planning workshop event targeting high school juniors and sophomores.

3. **Transfer visit days:** For most transfer students, the typical open house events will not be appropriate. It is much more effective to host an event that focuses on common transfer student concerns (transfer of credit, paying for college, availability of classes, introduction to other transfer students, etc.).

The strategic use of financial aid

The current economic climate is certainly adding more pressure as institutions strive to find balance between enrolling the size and type of student body they desire while managing discount rates and meeting net tuition revenue goals. College costs have been rising faster than family resources for decades. As a result, students are borrowing more, and institutional discount rates are on the rise in both the public and private sectors. Cost and the availability of financial aid continue to be primary factors that influence a student's decision to enroll in college (Note: See Chapter 1 for numerous data points related to cost and student/family need).

According to the 2012 Noel-Levitz national research report, *Why Did They Enroll: Factors Influencing College Choice*, the top three factors that influence choice are cost, financial aid, and academic reputation. This was true across all institution types. In the Noel-Levitz 2011 E-Expectations study, *The Online Expectations of Prospective College Students and Their Parents*, 46 percent of college-bound high school seniors reported that the current economic crisis has caused them to reconsider the institutions to which they apply or may attend (up from 34 percent when this question was asked in the 2010 study).

Developing a recruitment plan that does not consider these realities is risky for any institution and its longer-term strategic enrollment plan. Any annual and strategic plan must have an effective financial aid strategy that assists families in overcoming cost as a barrier to enrollment. This strategy must address both the *ability* and *willingness* to pay.

Figure 11-5 illustrates what a strategic investment in financial aid funds can do for an institution as it strives to reach enrollment and net revenue goals.

Figure 11-5: Goals of Financial Aid Leveraging

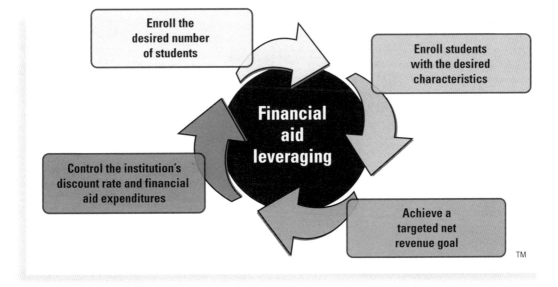

To successfully compete in today's marketplace, institutions need two broad capabilities:

1. **A competitive scholarship and financial aid program** that is designed to enroll the desired number and type of students while simultaneously achieving a targeted net revenue goal and controlling the institution's discount rate. (This is commonly known as financial aid leveraging.)

2. **A strong working relationship between admissions and financial aid** office leadership and staff. Any breakdown in communication between the admissions office, financial aid office, and the prospective student and parent(s) or family members will generally undermine new student enrollment goals. This is true even if a campus has a competitive scholarship and financial aid program in place.

Regarding the first capability, the most effective financial aid strategies use historical enrollment figures, tuition amounts, and award data to pinpoint factors that influence student enrollment. Using this information, the campus can build a financial aid model with the following objectives:

- Understand enrollment yields by need and academic levels as well as within certain student populations (such as first-year, transfer, out-of-state, high-ability, or athletes). Building a plan that focuses on these factors can help an institution reach both annual and strategic enrollment goals.

- Manage the discount rate *and* net revenue and learn about their symbiotic relationship.

- Understand the impact of tuition and aid changes on enrollment behavior through econometric modeling, which can also help a campus understand how non-financial-aid variables affect a student's decision making.

- Determine if the institution is over-awarding some students while under-awarding others.

- Award the right amounts needed to recruit and retain the desired mix of students, and analyze how financial aid affects students' abilities to return each year and complete their educations.

- Track progress toward annual new student and net revenue goals by creating a quality reporting structure to help the campus review key metrics.

Working together to communicate cost and value

In addition to building an effective awarding strategy, it is important to have a strong working relationship between admissions and financial aid. The two offices should jointly create a communication plan for students and parents that explains the details of the financial aid process *and* communicates the value of earning a degree from the institution. This plan might include the following:

- Post a net price calculator on the Web site in a highly visible area so that students and parents can easily find it. Ideally, this calculator will include estimates for merit aid awards as well as federal aid so that it delivers the most competitive net price estimate possible.

- Send early offers of merit aid to all accepted students. Consider including this right on the acceptance letter or in a follow-up letter to arrive within a week of original acceptance.

- Mail financial aid award letters out as early as possible. Include payment plan options in the letter.

- Ramp up financial aid follow-up calling efforts. Train and/or retrain staff on this strategy. As an institution, make sure it is clear to the frontline staff what the policy is when families negotiate and to determine if more aid will be offered to families who need or ask for it.

- Develop creative financing options for students. Are there additional types of payment plans to offer (10-month, 12-month, etc.)? Make sure admission and financial aid staff know how to respond when a family asks for additional assistance.

- Create a cost worksheet and enclose it with the financial aid award. This worksheet will list all of the costs a family may incur during the first year.

- Ensure the bill is accompanied by some type of personalized letter to parents. The letter should include:
  - A personalized message;
  - Statement of value/outcomes;
  - Contact information for questions; and
  - Payment plan options.
- Include more in-person appointments with financial aid staff in pre-summer orientation programs. The one general financial aid session will likely not be sufficient for families this year.

Data and reporting

The importance of data has been discussed throughout this book as it relates to defining the current state and goal setting. It is also important to develop data and reporting structures as part of the recruitment strategy to move the campus to the desired state. Campuses should create a basic package of weekly and monthly reports to monitor the progress of the marketing/recruitment program and evaluate the effectiveness of key marketing and recruitment strategies. This monitoring will also provide data for recruitment-related key performance indicators. Table 11-7 shows an example of a funnel report that can track progress for various strategies outlined in the recruitment plan and, ultimately, the SEP.

Table 11-7: Example of Framework for Recruitment Strategy Report

Report title	Inquiries			Applications			Accepts			Confirms/Enrolled		
Variable*	Current year	Last year	Diff	Current year	Last year	Diff	Current year	Last year	Diff	Current year	Last year	Diff

* Suggested variables to analyze in funnel report format

- Market segments (FTIC, transfers, adults, non-degree, etc.);
- Geographic region;
- Counselor territory;
- Inquiry source;
- Campus visit volume;
- Open house;
- Campus visitors (unique visitors);
- Academic interest;
- Co-curricular interests;
- College fairs (any contact);
- High school visits (any contact);
- Alumni event (any contact);
- Community college visits (any contact);
- Outbound phone calls;
- Student interest (qualifying) codes; and
- Academic profile (high school GPA, rank, and test scores in ranges).

Because of the importance data plays in the marketing and recruitment operation, an increasing number of institutions have created a data analyst position within enrollment services to manage the admissions database, produce reports, and support implementation of all communication streams (direct mail, electronic, and telephone).

Putting strategies into action—Developing action plans

As described in Chapter 7, but important to reiterate here, the final step of the planning process is to devise action plans for each of the key strategies. Each strategy must be supported by one or more specific activities necessary to successfully accomplish the strategy/objective. The activities, taken in total, comprise the action plan. This will be the most detailed and time-consuming part of the planning process. The action plans represent the guts of the plan.

Good action plans always include the following components:

1. **What will be done?**
   Specifically describe a quantifiable and measurable activity.

2. **When will it be done?**
   Provide timetables that clearly show key dates and deadlines.

3. **Who will be responsible?**
   Designate clear assignments of responsibility for performing important tasks.

4. **How much will it cost?**
   Provide budget information showing whether the strategy will save money, increase overall costs, or will be budget neutral.

5. **How will accomplishments be tracked?**
   Establish and list the methods of evaluation or control that will be used to monitor progress and measure success or failure of the actions.

The following reminders help to develop effective activity/action plans, which can be tracked using an action plan report similar to the strategy report shown in Table 11-7.

- One or more action plans may be needed to implement a key strategy (e.g., a separate action plan for each individual student search implemented by the institution and action plans for different types of campus visit events).

- A description of the activity should be provided.

- The timetable should include a date by which each task should be completed. If appropriate, it is also permissible to designate an activity as "ongoing."

- Note responsibility for the implementation of the activity/action plan. This may be an individual, a committee, or a functional area.

- Include in the budget section *any anticipated new or reduced direct expenses not currently budgeted* that will be incurred in implementing the activity.

- Evaluation and control may be as simple as indicating that the activity has been fully or partially accomplished.

- The activity/action plan should be complete enough to provide direction to those responsible for its implementation.

Focusing on subpopulations

As we further advance recruitment practices, development of specific subpopulation strategies is increasingly critical. Given current high school graduation projections, enrolling subpopulations may, in fact, help campuses achieve or exceed enrollment goals.

Like any other element related to SEP, institutions should take a data-informed approach to determine which subpopulations they should pursue, how the enrollment of those populations will strengthen the SEP process and move the institution closer to its desired state, and track key metrics related to their enrollment. The campus should avoid targeting specific subpopulations based on existing assumptions about those students or a general notion that the campus needs a subpopulation, without researching the cost and benefits of recruiting students with those characteristics.

In addition, institutions should develop specific communications tailored to those subpopulations. The campus Web site should have pages dedicated to those student populations, and targeted communication flows should address their concerns and interests. As presented earlier in this chapter, many of the general recruitment strategies for traditional students are also well-suited for recruiting subpopulations.

The following are some of the most frequently targeted student subpopulations and general considerations when recruiting those students.

Transfer students

This significant enrollment market should receive the same planning time, attention, and energy as the first-time-in-college (FTIC) market. In fact, for some institutions, transfer enrollment may well be considered a primary market. Therefore, systems should be in place to ensure that transfer students are not only recruited, but also offered a seamless and easy enrollment process focused on helping them quickly move from entrance to degree completion.

While cost, financial aid, and quality of academic programs are among the primary reasons students enroll in college (Noel-Levitz, 2012), there are three additional motivating factors for transfer students. Paying attention to them is important in building an effective transfer recruitment plan.

1. Maintaining credit for courses they have already taken;

2. Academic advising.

3. Career counseling and placement.

Note that maintaining credit is by far the most important consideration among transfer students. They want to know how much credit they will receive toward their general education requirements for degree completion as well as toward the requirements in their major field.

Online students

Most institutions have recognized the importance of online education as a component of overall enrollment. While many are finding that online courses serve traditional on-campus students, others are seeking to develop new student markets by providing online-only or "low-residency" programs at both the graduate and undergraduate level. The Sloan Consortium (2010) has reported annual growth rates in enrollment in online courses of 10 percent or more in recent years (compared to much smaller rates of overall enrollment growth in higher education as noted in Chapter 1).

The National Online Learners Priorities Report (Noel-Levitz, 2011) has revealed that key enrollment factors for online learners, at both the graduate and undergraduate levels, are program convenience, flexible pacing, work schedule, program requirements, cost and availability of financial aid, and ability to transfer credits. In addition, prospective students are interested in future employment opportunities associated with their chosen degree.

In addition to these topical areas, recruitment tactics, including Web pages, should offer students ample opportunities to connect with a representative, either through a chat function, e-mail, or Webinar (online information session). For prospective students willing to provide their contact information, an extended communication flow, including a mix of media, should also be in place. Since many online learners are adult learners, these communications should extend over a longer decision cycle than traditional students.

International students

The overall international market is too large to be completely covered, so campuses need to focus on specific markets—using research and data to guide that focus. It is important to develop a strong inquiry pool by acquiring prospects earlier in the funnel—as early as the ninth and tenth grade. In assembling prospective student name buys, campuses should use several data sources, each of which can identify unique international students at different times in the process. In addition, institutions should ensure that Web pages and communications reflect not only the admissions process but offer strong marketing messages to international students.

Veterans

Many institutions are beginning to recognize the importance of having new student enrollment plans devised specifically for veterans. Enrollment offices must work in partnership with veterans' services and determine how their funding (often supported by the government), prior learning credit, and transfer credits are processed. As the institution considers marketing to recruit more students with military experience, the campus must review partnership opportunities with the Transition Assistance Program (TAP). The law creating TAP established a partnership among the Departments of Defense, Veterans Affairs, and Transportation, as well as the Department of Labor's Veterans' Employment and Training Services (VETS) to give employment and training information to armed forces members within 180 days of separation or retirement (U.S. Department of Labor, 2011).

Graduate student recruitment

The following section on graduate student recruitment was contributed by Sheila Mahan, Noel-Levitz executive consultant and former assistant vice president for academic affairs at the University at Albany, State University of New York.

This chapter has focused mainly on undergraduate recruitment. The same principles and approach for undergraduate annual recruitment planning and efforts should be applied to graduate recruitment. While graduate recruitment is generally decentralized, maximizing future efforts will likely require institutions to take new approaches to graduate enrollment planning and practices. With traditional student populations projected to decline in many parts of the country, many campuses see graduate education as a way to sustain overall enrollment and fiscal health. At many institutions, graduate recruitment and admissions operations have not received the resources or attention given at the undergraduate level. In addition, the organization of graduate recruitment responsibilities can vary widely, from a highly centralized operation in a single campus office to a completely decentralized model that puts graduate recruitment into the hands of individual academic programs or schools (with most campuses somewhere between the two).

Regardless of the organizational structure, there are several elements that are common to effective graduate recruitment efforts:

1. **Give attention to the top of the funnel** to generate and convert inquiries. Many graduate programs do not begin interaction with students until they apply. Instead, use traditional recruitment methods as well as strategies such as advertising, Webinars for prospective students, and community or employer outreach.

2. **Address the specific priorities of prospective graduate students** when communicating with them, including program quality and reputation; outcomes and student successes; and cost, scholarship, and financing options of the program. Address those same concerns and priorities on any Web pages dedicated to graduate student enrollment.

3. **Design an application review process** that it is streamlined and expedited. Once an application is completed, it should be reviewed as quickly as possible and the decision communicated to the student, along with any financial aid or scholarships that may be available. Admitted students should have an immediate opportunity for advisement and enrollment.

4. **Get faculty involved** as much as possible. This is much more essential in graduate than undergraduate recruitment. Faculty members' research, conference presentations, and other discipline-based work are often sources of initial interest to graduate students. Faculty involvement in communicating with inquiries and responding to questions from them can also be highly effective in the recruitment of graduate students.

It is imperative to give graduate programs rigorous analysis using SEP principles. Graduate programs can be a tremendous asset, not only for recruiting graduate students, building academic reputation, and growing revenue, but also for recruiting undergraduate students interested in pursuing graduate study. However, costs, revenues, enrollment goals, job placement rates, and academic demand are just some of the metrics that campuses need to track to make sure their graduate programs are supporting the overall goals of the institution.

Conclusion

The purpose of this chapter was to share the essential elements of any recruitment plan and unite these elements with the SEP. The recruitment plan follows four very clear steps:

1. **Conduct a situation analysis.** This includes collecting, developing, and/or compiling all pertinent data and information.

2. **Set data-informed goals.** Use the data from the situation analysis to guide the establishment of recruitment goals. Goals should be quantifiable, measurable, and realistic. Most importantly, they should be mutually agreed-upon by all whose efforts must achieve them. Finally, they should clearly be applicable to the overall goals of the SEP.

3. **Develop action plans.** Each key strategy requires a set of action or activity plans, complete with timetables and budgets. The activity plan describes the actions or tactics that will occur in order to implement the strategy and achieve the goal. The action plan should assign responsibility, include clear beginning and end dates, include measurable objectives when appropriate, and include budget information.

4. **Track progress toward goals and the impact on net revenue.** If goals are quantifiable and measurable, tracking will obviously be much easier. Monitor key metrics rigorously and make adjustments as needed. As always, keep a close watch on recruitment-related net revenue. A loss of revenue could signal inefficiencies, goals that are too ambitious or unfocused, problems with financial aid awarding, or insufficient demand for some academic programs. No strategy should be done twice unless there is some proof that it worked.

Dialogue

Annual enrollment planning processes are focused on meeting annual institution-specific goals and objectives. In strategic enrollment planning, we seek to build a long-range enrollment plan that aligns fiscal health and enrollments. In building this foundation of success, institutions need to ensure they advance or integrate commonly held best practices into the plan as a part of their long-term efforts in the area of new student enrollment. One outcome of the planning process should be to ensure new student enrollment essentials remain strong while enhancing initiatives that are embedded into the new student enrollment plans.

Before proceeding, consider whether you have mapped out an institution-specific focus in these five areas:

1. How do you assess the effectiveness of your current new student enrollment strategies? If you are not assessing the effectiveness of these strategies on an annual basis, you are likely not using your operating and human resources in the most efficient manner. In addition, your new student enrollment essentials may be associated with traditional recruitment and admissions activities. Take a critical look at what you do to influence new student enrollment from an operating and human resource standpoint.

2. How do you involve others, outside the offices or division of enrollment management, in new student enrollment planning? It's great to have a coordinated, interdepartmental approach to new student enrollment; however, as in the SEP process, it is even better to strengthen ownership of new student enrollment planning by including the academic- and student affairs-related service areas, as well as the business and finance and other administrative units at your institution. In this approach, new student enrollment becomes more holistic and is viewed as an institutional priority, rather than simply a divisional one.

3. What will your enrollment landscape look like in five years? In 10 years? How will your enrollment composition change during that time period? How will demographics impact your future enrollment? How will employment or career trends influence enrollment adaptations? What type of student will you be serving? If you are not constructing the what-if scenarios for new student enrollment planning, then you should not be surprised when your enrollment objectives don't meet expectations.

4. If you have graduate programs, where does graduate enrollment planning fit into your overall plan development? Often, new graduate student enrollment planning is not integrated into the institution's enrollment planning and management enterprise, as it should be in a carefully considered strategic plan.

5. What are the costs to recruit a student? What are those costs by subpopulation? Where are gaps in resources being spent in comparison to market or demographic trends? (For example, are you continuing to invest more in traditional, new student recruitment when, in fact, you should be building an infrastructure to ease the process for transfer students?)

Writing the annual recruitment plan alone will not ensure that new student enrollment goals are met. Implementation is key to your success.

CHAPTER 12

Persistence, Progression, Retention, and Completion

By Tim Culver

For decades, the major focus of those working in the areas of student success and retention has been to raise overall retention and graduation rates. While these continue to be the most critically important measures, this chapter argues that the traditional measures of fall-to-fall retention and graduation rates within a given number of years are insufficient on their own. What is needed is a more systematic, complementary approach to measurement that keeps educators in closer contact with students; an approach expressed by a new paradigm—the student success funnel (Figure 12-1). This chapter describes the student success funnel and shows how to use it to monitor students' progress, set goals more precisely, and plan more effectively. This planning process should be integrated into your strategic enrollment plan and long-term enrollment management.

Chapter highlights

- **Enrollments grow with focus on persistence to completion**

- **Benchmarks guide effectiveness of efforts**

- **Influence and targeted approaches matter**

Today, the pressure is on to enhance student success in higher education. Demands for accountability and mounting concerns about access are prompting educators to rethink traditional approaches to retention management and look for new solutions. At the same time, higher education is witnessing unprecedented changes in its students, including a lack of preparedness, greater diversity, and "swirl"—the phenomenon described by experts such as Adelman (2006) in which many students enroll simultaneously at multiple institutions, attend classes intermittently rather than go straight through college, are decreasingly part of the traditional-age range (18 to 22), and hold down competing responsibilities, such as part-time jobs.

In response to this new environment, educators must make a paradigm shift toward a more precise model for measuring desired outcomes—the student success funnel. Throughout this book, there have been references to the enrollment funnel. Most of the discussion has focused on "top-of-the-funnel" enrollment, which usually includes the stages students encounter up to or through first registration for courses. The second part of the enrollment funnel, student success, includes the continuing student stages that follow the student from the period between admission/deposit through successful completion of the credential or, for community college students, successful transfer to another institution.

Figure 12-1: The Student Success Funnel

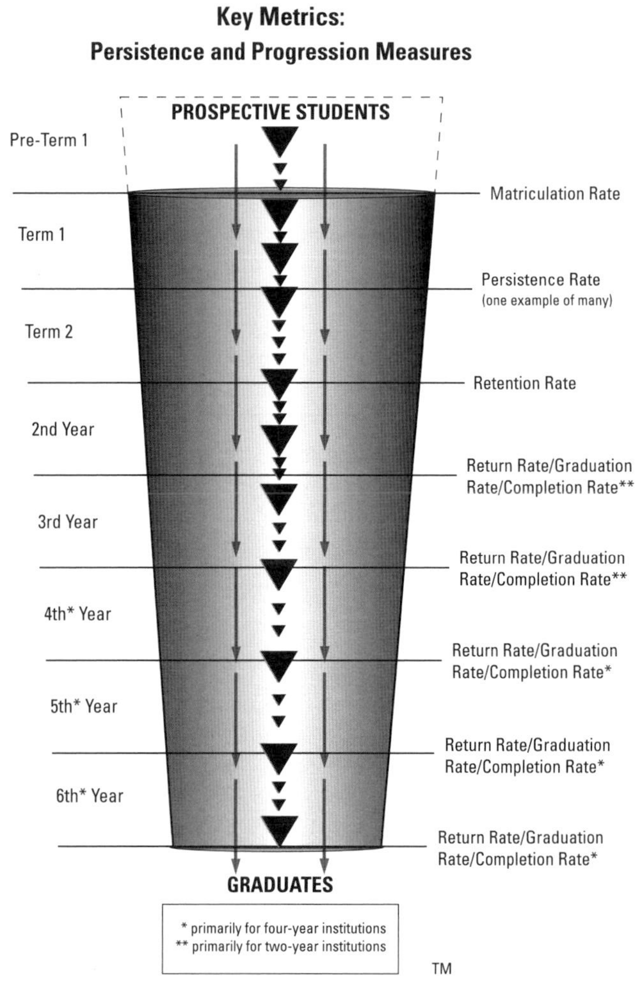

Key Metrics:
Persistence and Progression Measures

```
                        PROSPECTIVE STUDENTS
Pre-Term 1                      ▼
                                ▼
                                                    —— Matriculation Rate
Term 1                          ▼

                                                    Persistence Rate
                                                    (one example of many)
Term 2                          ▼

                                                    —— Retention Rate
2nd Year                        ▼

                                                    Return Rate/Graduation
                                                    Rate/Completion Rate**
3rd Year                        ▼

                                                    Return Rate/Graduation
                                                    Rate/Completion Rate**
4th* Year                       ▼

                                                    Return Rate/Graduation
                                                    Rate/Completion Rate*
5th* Year                       ▼

                                                    Return Rate/Graduation
                                                    Rate/Completion Rate*
6th* Year                       ▼

                                                    Return Rate/Graduation
                                                    Rate/Completion Rate*
                            GRADUATES
```

* primarily for four-year institutions
** primarily for two-year institutions

TM

Essential to any discussion about the student stages of enrollment is the concept that retention begins with recruitment. Enrollment professionals, such as admissions staff, recruiters, financial aid staff, and student success teams, must co-manage the enrollment stages that impact overall completion. A prime example of this is the time between acceptance or deposit and the first day of class. At some institutions, students make decisions to attend many months before classes begin. During the time between this decision and the beginning of classes, students and their families experience many decision points that may impact whether or not they actually begin their chosen course work.

The phenomenon that students commit to a particular college but do not matriculate at that college is known to many enrollment professionals as "melt." Student success teams should be working with enrollment management teams to reduce melt by implementing strategies geared toward reducing the number of students who commit/deposit and then don't attend on the first day of classes. This bridging concept is focused on moving students from one stage of the funnel to the next by working collaboratively to ensure students and their families are prepared with the proper information to commit to their final enrollment and extend the relationship created during the recruitment process.

The continuing student stages of enrollment are: persistence, progression, retention, and completion or graduation. For the arithmetically inclined, consider this theoretical formula:

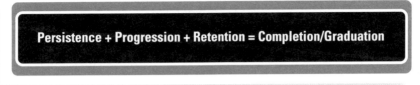

Persistence + Progression + Retention = Completion/Graduation

TM

Persistence

For purposes of this discussion, persistence is defined as term-to-term return. Students who are able to have consistent return patterns from fall to spring to fall and beyond are more likely to complete or graduate within a timely manner. In terms of measurement, persistence is more precisely defined as the enrollment headcount of any cohort compared to its headcount on its initial official census day, commonly measured on day one or the census date of terms two, three, four, and so on, but also measured at ongoing points in time to determine persistence rates on any given day of any given term. The examples below illustrate this concept:

> Example 1: On January 9, 2012, the first day of term two, 90 percent of an institution's fall 2011 first-time-in-college (FTIC) cohort persisted from the cohort's official term one census taken on October 3, 2011.

> Example 2: On August 27, 2011, the first day of term three, 70 percent of the institution's fall 2010 FTIC cohort persisted from the cohort's official term one census taken on October 4, 2010.

At most colleges and universities, students can persist from the first term to the second term without having truly progressed. Almost all institutions of higher education allow students a probationary term in order to show improvement. In effect, students could fail every course in term one and return for term two. While federal financial aid regulations regarding satisfactory progress have recently changed, most institutions continue to allow an appeal term in order for students to get back on track.

Progression

Progression is defined as the rate at which a cohort participates in any activity that an institution has determined to be correlated with persistence, such as course completion rates and academic probation. Students who have successfully persisted have at least satisfied the academic and financial aid policies of the institution. However, in many cases, this is not enough to ensure continuing progress. For example, students who meet the bare minimum requirements for progression may have a much harder time later in their persistence toward completion. This is especially true for students who have developmental education requirements in areas such as math, English, and reading. Students who progress in the math sequence with a grade of C in the first developmental math course may not be as successful in subsequent math courses as if they had achieved an A or a B.

> Example 1: Of the students in the fall 2010 FTIC cohort that took Sociology 101 during term one, 75 percent completed the course successfully (grade of C or higher) by day one of term two, January 10, 2011.

> Example 2: Of the students in the fall 2010 FTIC cohort that were placed on probation at the end of term one, 40 percent were removed from the probation list by the end of term two.

At the very heart of progression is the idea that, if students successfully persist and progress, they will retain to the next fall, barring unforeseen circumstances.

Retention

This stage of the continuing student funnel is defined as the fall-to-fall return rate of any cohort or subpopulation within the cohort. Most campuses are accustomed to reporting this outcome via the Integrated Postsecondary Education Data System (IPEDS) and appropriate state agencies, but retention is really much more complex than that. Some of the seminal work on student retention was completed by Noel-Levitz founders Lee Noel and Randi Levitz. According to Noel, Levitz, and Saluri (1985), "Re-enrollment or retention is not then the goal; retention is the result or by-product of improved programs and services in our classrooms and elsewhere on campus that contribute to student success." Other researchers have also presented reasons why students retain and achieve success. According to the Theory of Involvement outlined by Astin (1999), students who live in residence halls or hold part-time jobs on campus, for example, may show higher retention outcomes than students who do not.

Continuing this thought process leads us directly to completion. As suggested in the formula presented earlier, persistence added to progression added to retention will ultimately assist the college/university in predicting levels of completion. However, this topic should be considered within the context of institution type.

Completion/Graduation

For many years, colleges have focused on the concept of graduation. Since most reporting agencies require institutions to report graduation rates, most benchmarks use graduation as the standard, and the term "graduation" is normative in the higher education lexicon. In the current environment, it makes sense to change this conversation to emphasize completion, rather than graduation, as the standard. Graduation may be the completion standard for some colleges and universities, but not for others. Community colleges and other two-year schools, for example, don't always rely on graduation rates as the ultimate indicator of success.

A 2011 initiative of the American Association of Community Colleges, the Voluntary Framework of Accountability (VFA), developed some preliminary outcomes and success measures that include: percentage of students that earn an associate's degree without transfer; percentage of students that earn an associate's degree with transfer; percentage of students that earn an award of less than an associate's degree (certificate) without transfer; percentage of students that earn an award of less than an associate's degree (certificate) with transfer; percentage of students that transfer to a four-year institution with no degree or certificate; percentage of students that transfer laterally (attendance at another community college); percentage of students that are still enrolled during the sixth academic year; percentage of students that left institution, no award or transfer, but in good academic standing (30+ credits; 2.0+ GPA); and percentage of students that left the institution not in good academic standing. Because graduation is not always the ultimate or best completion indicator, institutions may need to reconsider or redefine completion measures linked to institutional goals as they develop their key performance indicators (See Chapters 5 and 9).

Common data elements

Now that we have defined persistence, progression, retention, and completion, let us discuss the common data elements that colleges and universities should be collecting in order to inform student success planning efforts. The first part of this discussion will focus on data relating to persistence and progression, which in turn lead to retention and completion outcomes. The second part of the discussion will address benchmarking for effective planning.

Leading and lagging indicators

Note that persistence and progression data should be date-, year-, and cohort-specific. Persistence and progression measures are based on concrete behavioral outcomes, such as the acts of registering for, attending, and completing a class. Many institutions have developed a list of subpopulations within the cohort and track them regularly. Consider this example from Montana State University-Billings (2011):

- Main campus
- College of Technology
- College of Arts and Sciences
- College of Business
- College of Allied Health
- College of Education
- Undecided students
- Provisional admits
- AS294 students
- AS101 students
- SOS students
- Residential students
- Full-time
- Part-time

Table 12-1 outlines common data elements that should be tracked for each cohort or subpopulation deemed relevant by the institution. It should be noted that this list is not all-inclusive and should be adapted and customized for each institution.

Table 12-1: Common Data Elements

Persistence data (leading indicators)	Progression (leading indicators)	Retention data and retention outcome	Completion outcome
Weekly tracking of the number of students registered by cohort or subpopulation (once registration is open)	Course completion and course success	First-year student return rates by cohort or subpopulation	Less than a year, certificate, diplomas, transfer; two-, three-, four-, five-, six-, seven-, eight-year outcomes
Persistence at purge for non-payment	Academic probation and suspension	Second-year student return rates by cohort and subpopulation	
Fall-to-spring return rates by cohort or subpopulation	Satisfactory academic progress (SAP)	Third-year student return rates by cohort and subpopulation	
Persistence at drop/add and census	Student achieving less than 2.0 GPA in first term	Fourth-year student return rates by cohort and subpopulation	
Spring-to-fall return rates by cohort or subpopulation	Developmental course completion		
	Major declaration		
	Degree/Completion plan completed		
	Credit hours attempted/earned ratios		
	Student motivation data (first term, end of first term, beginning of second year, etc.)		
	Statistical identification of risk factors and/or student attributes that correlate with retention		
	Student satisfaction data that correlate with retention		
	Engagement data that inform the retention and completion outcomes		

Benchmarking

Any discussion about the use of common data elements for planning should include reference to accurate industry benchmarks. Many agencies such as the Consortium for Student Retention Data Exchange (CSRDE), ACT, and Noel-Levitz provide regularly updated benchmarks relating to aspects of college persistence and retention. Table 12-2 provides examples of persistence, progression, and retention benchmarks compiled by Noel-Levitz (*Mid-Year Retention Indicators Report for Two-Year and Four-Year, Public and Private Institutions*, 2011).

Table 12-2: Examples of Persistence, Progression, and Retention Benchmarks

First-year student return rates							
	Four-year private			Four-year public			Two-year public
	All	Lowest selectivity	Highest selectivity	All	Lowest selectivity	Highest selectivity	All
Persistence rates from term one to term two of 2009-2010 academic year							
25th percentile	87.5%	73.2%	92.7%	88.3%	84.3%	92.4%	77.0%
Median	91.2%	86.4%	94.6%	91.1%	90.0%	94.8%	81.2%
75th percentile	94.0%	92.4%	96.1%	93.7%	91.9%	97.0%	84.3%
Retention rates from fall 2009 to fall 2010							
25th percentile	67.9%	54.3%	79.1%	68.8%	67.6%	81.6%	49.8%
Median	75.6%	64.2%	85.1%	73.8%	71.5%	84.3%	55.2%
75th percentile	83.0%	71.1%	88.4%	82.5%	79.7%	92.7%	63.2%
Second-year student return rates							
	Four-year private			Four-year public			Two-year public
	All	Lowest selectivity	Highest selectivity	All	Lowest selectivity	Highest selectivity	All
Persistence rates from term one to term two of 2009-2010 academic year							
25th percentile	91.1%	84.5%	94.9%	90.6%	89.1%	92.5%	92.7%
Median	94.2%	91.2%	96.3%	93.0%	91.5%	95.3%	85.7%
75th percentile	96.1%	94.2%	97.1%	95.2%	93.9%	98.0%	91.0%
Retention rates from fall 2009 to fall 2010							
25th percentile	76.0%	63.3%	85.4%	77.1%	76.2%	86.1%	NA
Median	83.7%	75.3%	91.0%	83.3%	80.3%	89.7%	NA
75th percentile	88.9%	80.1%	93.2%	87.4%	84.0%	94.3%	NA

Ultimately, each institution must develop its own set of performance measures in response to its distinctive student attrition patterns, while remembering that national benchmarks can provide helpful points of comparison. With this approach, retention teams can link enrollment and budget data to specific activities and programs. For the most effective, year-to-year comparisons, it's advisable to store and analyze three to five years of comparative data, focusing on degree-seeking students.

By measuring and monitoring students' progress every step of the way, an institution is better equipped to accomplish its goals. The advantages of tracking persistence and progression rates in addition to overall retention and graduation outcomes include closer contact with students, more timely identification of student needs, the ability to measure the enrollment impact of specific strategies and tactics, the ability to justify expenditures for student success initiatives, and greater accountability for student success every step of the way.

Integrated strategic enrollment planning

Against this backdrop of retention principles, continuing student funnel stages, completion concepts, common data elements, and benchmarks, it is time to move the conversation into the realm of strategic planning. This begins with a look at the use of data to inform strategies, followed by fundamental approaches for improving completion/graduation outcomes, including academic advising, early- and frequent-alert systems, and student engagement; managing expectations throughout the student lifecycle; and the role of data analysis in planning for new programs or services.

Use of data to inform decision making

Many colleges and universities begin to plan and prioritize before they have the right data and information to proceed. For example, we all believe that effective academic advising and support are strategies that have proven useful at most institutions and are verified by the literature. The use of Supplemental Instruction (SI™), developed by Deanna C. Martin at the University of Missouri at Kansas City in 1973, has been shown to improve course success and eventual retention rates at many institutions, but where should this strategy be placed in our efforts? Should it be in math and natural sciences, because that's where many beginning students have trouble? Or should it be employed in social sciences? A careful analysis of the data will make an institution better informed as it prioritizes strategies.

The concept of milestone achievement and momentum point analysis may be helpful for prioritizing strategic efforts. Leinbach and Jenkins (2008) used a longitudinal approach to determine which milestones at a community college should be achieved in order to increase the likelihood of continued momentum toward completion. Examples included declaration of major, completion of developmental courses, and persistence through sequences. Careful analysis of data will help determine which milestones are not being achieved and thus impeding momentum toward completion. As another example, students who are undecided about a major at the time of admission are less likely to complete than students who have declared a major. If that is the case, then intrusive and intentional advising and career strategies might be prioritized early in the student experience. Thus, the milestone of major declaration may be set as a priority for the institution and a corresponding strategy funded and prioritized in order to encourage student momentum toward completion.

Academic advising

Noel-Levitz conducts biannual best practices research among two-year and four-year public and private institutions across the United States. The 2011 report *Student Retention Practices at Four-Year and Two-Year Institutions* revealed that, in addition to honors programs, mandatory advising was ranked as one of the top retention tools by respondents at all three institution types. ACT (Habley and McClanahan, 2004) found that advising almost always ranks among the top three most effective strategies for retention. In fact, when students are asked to rank the importance of academic advising, it is almost always in the top two, sometimes ranking even higher than instructional effectiveness (Noel-Levitz, 2011). Given this, it is clear colleges and universities must strategically plan for academic advising with respect to the model to be used, related staffing implications, course availability, and degree planning.

Advising models and their implications

Academic advising models can be categorized into one of three organizational structures, as described by Pardee (2004). The models are either centralized, with professional and faculty advisors housed in one academic or administrative unit; decentralized, with professional or faculty advisors located in their respective academic departments; or shared, with some advisors meeting with students in a central administrative unit (i.e., an advising center), while others advise students in the academic department of their major discipline.

According to Pardee, the chosen model should be carefully considered with the following elements in mind:

- What is the enrollment at the institution? For a large college or university, an advising center, either the self-contained (centralized) model or one of the shared structure models, would be an efficient choice with respect to benefits from economies of scale.

- What is the administrative structure of the institution, and what is the reporting line for advising? If the provost, vice president, or dean of academic affairs is responsible for advising, then faculty will very likely be involved with advising, either through a decentralized or shared structure. To what extent is the faculty interested in and willing to devote time to advising? If the faculty are recognized and rewarded for advising, a decentralized structure is feasible. It is also cost-effective, as no space or funding is needed to establish an advising center.

- What is the overall nature of the institution's academic policies, curriculum, and degree programs? A wide range of academic programs, high program selectivity, and complex graduation requirements increase the practicality of a centralized or shared model. In a central office, it is easier for a coordinator to train advisors, thus ensuring that complex policies and program options are understood and accurately conveyed to students.

- What is the institution's mission, and how does academic advising relate to the mission? If the institution and its programs are oriented toward career preparation, a decentralized structure, such as the faculty-only model, would be appropriate. Faculty, as experts in their field, may be better prepared to advise students on course selection, internships, and career options.

- What is the composition of the student body and what are students' special needs? An institution with a sizeable proportion of unprepared, undecided, or re-entry students should devote financial and other resources to specialized advising that is effectively offered in a centralized or shared structure, such as the split model. On the other hand, if the majority of students are academically prepared and have declared majors, then a more decentralized structure would be appropriate.

Pardee concluded that, "There is growing recognition among advising professionals and researchers that a shared structure can incorporate the best features from the decentralized and centralized structures. An ideal shared structure would take advantage of the expertise of faculty advising in their departments (decentralized), while relying on professional advisors in a central administrative unit to meet the special needs of students, such as incoming freshmen, academically at-risk students, minority students, student athletes, or undecided students."

Campuses can use Pardee's three-tiered approach to guide a long-term strategic planning effort that includes consideration of budget implications and the time required to implement improvements to academic advising.

" In addition to selecting an appropriate advising model, colleges should ensure that courses are offered and available as promised."

Course availability

In addition to selecting an appropriate advising model, colleges should ensure that courses are offered and available as promised. If they are not, academic programs should list what courses will be offered when and make sure they are offered in a way that will allow most students to follow the necessary sequence of prerequisites. In rotating course schedules, institutions must determine whether the courses are really offered in such a way that timely completion can occur. If not, are reasonable substitutions made? Only within this framework can proper degree planning occur.

Degree planning

Having an up-to-date degree plan on file for a particular student may be the ultimate indicator of an effective advising relationship. Some colleges call them academic plans, while others call them plans of study or individualized graduation or completion plans. Whatever an institution calls this plan, students and their families must be made aware that the plan is the implicit promise made to them at the time of enrollment. With the guidance of the institution, the credential is the intangible outcome toward which students are striving. Strategically, the advising model must support the degree-planning process via electronic or other methods, making it possible for students to easily track progress toward the ultimate credential outcome.

Early- and ongoing-alert systems

Once strategies are in place to ensure a student has been given accurate guidance for degree planning and set on the path to completion, the next strategic element to embrace is that of early and continuous intervention. Most commonly known as early-alert systems, these activities and approaches provide structure for faculty and staff as they attempt to help students persist and progress.

Early-alert programs enhance student success by identifying students' concerns or challenges as soon as possible and providing them with appropriate assistance so that they can stay on track and accomplish their academic goals. According to the *National Freshman Attitudes Report* (Noel-Levitz, 2012), while nearly 95 percent of incoming freshmen express a strong desire to finish a college degree, approximately half will not achieve this goal.

While students may leave at any time during the student lifecycle, due to a variety of circumstances, the fact is that most students who do not persist leave during the first term or year, or perhaps during the second year. Early-alert systems help campuses:

- Identify at-risk students:
  - In advance of enrollment—dropout-prone students who could benefit from institutional intervention;
  - After enrollment—students experiencing academic, social, and/or personal problems that might be ameliorated by institutional intervention;
- Zero in on motivational factors, including each student's attitude and receptivity to assistance;
- Monitor each student's performance, attendance, and behavior; and
- Intervene when appropriate.

Identifying at-risk students during the first year

There are two approaches that best serve to identify students who might be more at risk for attrition. The first uses historical institutional data and linear regression analysis to produce a predictive model based on how students have retained in the past. The second approach combines the results of the predictive model with the student motivation assessment to provide a powerful prediction, early-alert, and advising tool.

Predictive modeling for early alert and advising during the first year

For many years, colleges and universities have been maintaining early-alert systems that employ a mid-term alert. At some point during the term, if a student shows evidence of not being successful, his or her instructor is expected to send a referral to a student service office. Examples of triggers might include poor test grades, lack of attendance, behavior issues in class, and lack of engagement. While these referrals are valuable and raise issues that should be addressed, they really aren't "early" in most cases. (Think of the "leading versus lagging" indicators discussed earlier in this chapter.) A true early alert can be accomplished by creating a predictive model based on what is known about the student at the time of admission or on past first- or second-term student behaviors related to factors such as enrolled courses or residency. The Noel-Levitz predictive modeling for retention program is called the Student Retention Predictor™.

Using three to five years of historical financial aid and admissions data, appending additional socioeconomic or other data, and using retention as a dependent variable, colleges can establish which variables among the data set have the strongest relationship to retention. In other words, at the time of admission and based on historical attrition patterns, it is possible to predict which students will most likely retain. If an institution possesses this information, it is able to an implement an early-alert system using this identification process. This predictive model allows the institution to prioritize its resources based on the entire risk distribution of the incoming class.

Figure 12-2: Risk Distribution of the Incoming Class

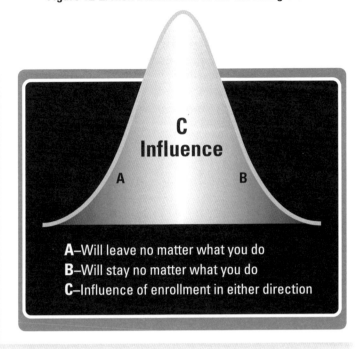

C
Influence

A   B

A–Will leave no matter what you do
B–Will stay no matter what you do
C–Influence of enrollment in either direction

For example, most institutions pay more attention to the upper or lower quartiles in the risk distribution, spending most of their time with the students who are more likely to leave or stay despite any actions they may take (Figure 12-2). The fallacy of this approach is that there are more students in the middle of the risk distribution than at either extreme. Predictive modeling will show the entire range of risk and empower the campus to prioritize resources for the greatest return on investment of time and budget (Figure 12-3).

Figure 12-3: Risk Distribution by Student Model Scale

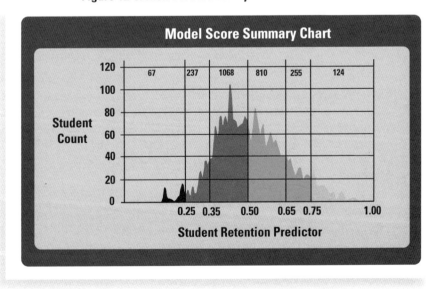

Model Score Summary Chart

67   237   1068   810   255   124

Student Count

0.25 0.35   0.50   0.65 0.75   1.00

Student Retention Predictor

Continuous intervention via understanding of student transitions throughout the student lifecycle

The final question that colleges should consider in developing their early and ongoing intervention services is what students need as they persist and progress to their second, third, and fourth years. From the literature, it is clear that much attention has been paid to first-year and senior-year (for four-year institutions) transitions, but little attention has been paid to second- and third-year transitions. Momentum point or milestone achievement analysis focuses on student persistence and progress throughout the college experience.

As Leinbach and Jenkins (2008) explain, "Understanding how students actually progress through their college programs is essential in developing strategies and choosing appropriate interventions to improve student outcomes. The challenge is to build expertise and capacity in college and state agency research departments to transform raw student unit record (SUR) data into meaningful information of practical use for policymakers and practitioners." As described in an earlier example, if a student achieves the milestone of completing a developmental math course, then that momentum point in time will likely move him to the next math course in the sequence. If not, the momentum has been stopped or delayed.

This same concept can be applied to second-, third-, and fourth-year students. In *Helping Sophomores Succeed* (Hunter et al., 2010), the authors contend that there is little attention paid to the second year. "It is much easier to define the beginning and the ending periods of college, because they are more distinct, pronounced, and therefore amenable to redress." According to the authors, when the second year begins may depend on time in college or credits earned. Noting that the primary objectives of the second year are selecting a major and developing purpose, they recommend institutions focus their intervention and advising efforts with second-year students on these two purposes.

> " Institutions should never assume that, once a student enters his or her last year, decisions have already been made about career or transition to graduate school."

As second-year students develop their purpose and move on to their third year, career closure and making connections between career and academics assumes greater importance. Second-year and third-year student success initiatives typically feature opportunities that focus on academic concerns, degree planning, leadership, majors, careers, community service, finances, and social relationships.

Institutions should never assume that, once a student enters his or her last year, decisions have already been made about career or transition to graduate school. Many fourth-year students find themselves in the predicament of having not taken all the required courses or they need to repeat courses to complete their degrees. Advising and degree checks near the end of the second and third years by faculty advisors and degree audit systems are desirable components of the ongoing and frequent outreach effort.

Student satisfaction and engagement and their relationships to completion

Implicit in this discussion of persistence strategies is the need to conduct student satisfaction assessments and use what our students are telling us. As someone once said, "All you have to do to find out what students need is ask them." One of the basic principles of planning for success is to rely on your assessment results and use them continuously as your students transition through the student lifecycle to completion.

Aligning student and institutional priorities

Each year, Noel-Levitz publishes the *National Student Satisfaction and Priorities Report* by school type and selected learner types. The information serves as a benchmark for colleges and universities and informs the strategic student success planning process. For example, almost every year, students from all institution types rank instructional effectiveness or academic advising as their most important priority. At the same time, faculty and staff within those same institutional types may not rank instructional effectiveness or academic advising as their top priority. This type of incongruence may lead to planning that is misguided, underfunded, understaffed, and ultimately doesn't contribute to the desired completion outcomes.

Engagement influences completion

Similarly, Kuh, Kinzie, Schuh, and Whitt (2005) concluded, "student engagement has two key components that contribute to student success. The first is the amount of time and effort students put into their studies and other activities that lead to experiences and outcomes that constitute student success. The second is the ways the institution allocates resources and organizes learning opportunities and services to induce students to participate in and benefit from such activities." Based on consistent findings among student development theorists (Astin, 1999; Chickering and Gamson, 1987; Chickering and Reisser, 1993), colleges and universities should attempt to create environments where students experience frequent faculty-to-student contact, cooperation among students, active and collaborative learning approaches, prompt feedback, time on task, high expectations, and a respect for diverse ways of learning.

Dialogue

This chapter has discussed the continuing student stages of enrollment, common data elements, and benchmarks needed for the annual and strategic planning process, fundamental strategies for encouraging student persistence and completion, and how satisfaction and engagement levels impact the planning process. Leaders at colleges and universities must now confront a few common myths that may be inhibiting the success of the planning process on their campuses.

First, many campuses adhere to the notion that student success is everyone's responsibility; this is often embraced as a paradigm by most faculty and staff. Even in the unlikely event that this is true, it doesn't mean that improvements in outcomes will automatically happen as a result. These things rarely happen by chance. Campuses must organize their efforts to create better outcomes and appoint a strategic success leader to collaboratively lead the process. It is true that student success does belong to the entire village, but the village cannot make it happen without a chief.

Second, the data needed to inform planning for the continuing student stages must be collected over a four-, five- or six-year period. Having focused on the first year for decades, it is time to focus on the overall completion outcome using data collected throughout the student lifecycle.

Third, those data must be used to plan for the desired ultimate completion outcome. Institutions cannot be fixated on first-year retention rates, even though it is still true that most students who leave the institution will drop out during the first year. Knowing persistence and progression data over the entire student lifecycle will greatly improve and inform planning.

Lastly, as an institution begins to plan for the completion outcomes, these six basic indicators of successful retention approaches as the foundation for planning should be considered:

1. Are retention programs highly structured and integrated with other programs/services?

2. How has the institution assessed student satisfaction, developed a better understanding of student motivation, and integrated data analysis into the process of improving the student experience?

3. What level of quality classroom engagement and outcomes-based learning occurs on campus?

4. What data ensure a student-centered dynamic is embedded into institutional practices?

5. How are faculty, staff, and students empowered to develop relationships with one another?

6. What intrusive and intentional strategies are implemented on campus? Are they effective? This is known as "front-loading" or, as Lee Noel once said, "giving them what they need before they know they need it."

Strategic Enrollment Planning:

A Dynamic Collaboration

Section Four: Conclusions and Our Experience at Work

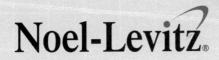

Are You Ready to Eat the Oyster? Strategic Enrollment Planning and Concluding Thoughts

By Craig Engel

Why strategic enrollment planning?

Strategic enrollment planning (SEP): A complex and organized effort to connect mission, current state, and changing environment to long-term enrollment and fiscal health.

SEP is an information-based and ongoing process that effectively:

- Identifies, evaluates, and modifies strategies and enrollment goals;

- Addresses the institution's mission, vision, goals, and capabilities;

- Aligns academic, co-curricular, and support functions with enrollment;

- Analyzes market share, market demand, market need, and degree outcomes/completion;

- Defines how the institution serves students, currently and in the future; and

- Examines how the marketplace and environment may change in coming years.

Tackling these issues and objectives represents a considerable challenge to many institutions. Embarking on an SEP process is, therefore, one of the most significant decisions an institution will make.

In addition, institutions tend to have more ideas than human and financial resources to execute them. How enrollment goals are set, communicated, and achieved is also far from uniform. In the healthiest of environments, institutions arrive at enrollment-related decisions via complex processes that are both mission-oriented and long-range in focus (consistent with what we endorse throughout the SEP process). At struggling institutions, enrollment-related considerations are primarily based on the annual achievement of the net revenue needed to fund operations that year; a highly inefficient and potentially irresponsible way to operate. Most colleges and universities lie somewhere on the scale in between these two poles.

Since traditional strategic planning in higher education is manifested in a variety of ways, it should not be surprising that there is confusion over mission, direction, strategic priorities, and overall market position. Given the dramatic demographic and social changes outlined in the first chapter, it is imperative that SEP be embraced regardless of an institution's current market position or perception of its current state.

Chapter highlights

- **Strategic enrollment planners must honestly examine the current state of the institution**

- **SEP takes strong leadership and skilled facilitation**

- **Successful planners use data to anticipate future enrollments**

The current and projected enrollment demographic situation in Texas illustrates this point. Texas is projecting large increases in high school enrollment until 2020, which would lead many to think Texas is a state free of enrollment worries. Yet upon further examination, fewer than 25 out of the more than 250 counties within the state are expected to grow significantly. Of those counties expecting growth, half are counties where most students graduate from high school under-prepared for college-level work or do not seek to enroll at an institution more than 100 miles from home.

What the reader should have discovered throughout this book is the Noel-Levitz belief, based on enrollment data and work with campuses of many different types, sizes, and missions, that if an institution is to embark on the process of SEP, it must be willing to honestly examine the current state of its institutional culture, mission, vision, and values. This process is not easy, as it may expose institutional shortcomings in leadership, academic programs, and organizational structure. However, it is necessary if an institution is to make an honest assessment of its future and take the required steps to secure the long-term fiscal and academic health of the campus.

The SEP process described in this book seeks to align the institution with its future environment to promote stability, sustainability, growth, and excellence. This process breaks from traditional planning models in that strategies, tactics, costs, and campus readiness must be determined prior to setting goals. An institution must dig a bit deeper into the planning process when creating tactics to understand return on investment (ROI) prior to setting realistic goals. As the SEP team presents recommendations to meet designated goals, administrative leaders must be in agreement with the overarching strategies brought by the committee to meet long-range enrollment goals. This process results in strategies and associated ROI supported by data and careful analysis. The end result is a plan designed to foster long-term enrollment and fiscal health.

> " Colleges and universities are not built to change. In many ways, they are built to resist change. This preservation of the status quo could represent the single greatest threat to survival and success in the future."
> **David Crockett, former Noel-Levitz executive**

As discussed in Chapter 1, at tuition-driven institutions, which applies to most colleges and universities, current tuition revenues will not be enough to sustain them. SEP starts the process of identifying new and enhanced revenue streams to augment and supplement those that are in decline.

Getting started

During my 18 years consulting with several hundred colleges and universities of all types, I have found the SEP process to be the most challenging work that I have done. Annual planning for recruitment, for example, typically rests solely with the office of admissions, without much involvement or oversight from other academic or administrative units. That is not to say that others on campus are not impacted by the outcome of an annual recruitment plan, but that the plan itself is focused on the here and now, with strategies and action plans primarily the responsibility of one department. Clark Kerr, the first chancellor of the University of California, Berkeley, and 12th president of the University of California, once said, "Institutions of higher education represent a variety of decentralized and differentiated disciplinary interests often linked together solely through the existence of a common heating or payroll system" (Personal communication). Here lies the difficulty of SEP—breaking down the silos of an interdependent organizational culture that has existed for decades (if not centuries) while bringing administrative and academic units together to form an institutional future that is unimaginable today. This uncertainty is unsettling to many institutions because, like it or not, when the SEP process begins, they don't know where the journey will take them.

The SEP process also presents a challenge because it involves individuals from all corners of the institution and at all levels who are not necessarily used to working together on such a vast undertaking that can have a far-reaching impact on the institution's enrollment and fiscal health. As discussed in Chapters 2 and 3, SEP is typically centered on institutional mission and the institution's academic and co-curricular programs. SEP requires involvement from the president, whose role it is to promote institutional mission, as well as the chief academic officer and his/her deans and department heads. There is no mission without margin. Because of this the chief financial officer must be heavily involved as well.

Consider SEP as a macro-enrollment planning process where the whole equals the sum of its parts. These parts, which include academics, student affairs, finance, recruitment, financial aid, retention/completion, athletics, and marketing, among others, operate daily in silos. Each has its own micro annual plan. SEP expands on these individual micro plans to create one macro plan that extends three to five years or longer and marshals these silos toward collective, campuswide goals. When done well, however, SEP actually alleviates uncertainty, fosters campuswide cooperation, and becomes an essential part of sustained institutional success.

The first important step in SEP is the formation of the planning committee itself, ensuring an institution has a combination of institutional leaders, decision makers, and content experts. Equally important is the direction provided by the president, or chief academic officer, to the SEP committee. The institutional leader can accomplish this by inserting him- or herself into the process as a chair or co-chair or by presenting a charge to the committee. The SEP leadership must be nimble enough to bring in additional content experts at the subcommittee level as the data is evaluated and the process moves forward.

Several years ago, I was conducting an initial consulting visit at a large, flagship research university and asked my on-campus lead to invite everyone who would be involved in the project to attend an "introduction to planning" workshop. When I walked into the room that morning, I was surprised to see more than 50 people in attendance—usually there would be one-third that number. I was told that this group represented the enrollment management team and that there was representation from marketing, recruitment, financial aid, student life, athletics, campus security, department heads, buildings and grounds, and others. The group started out with fewer than 10 individuals and had grown over time because the team was unable to solve the myriad of problems it was facing without content experts from other departments and offices on campus. As discussed in Chapter 2, this campus had obviously developed a trusting environment wherein there was a comfort level in asking others to join in the process.

Some of the basic questions institutions must answer include: Academically, what should we be offering? How should we offer it? Where should we offer it? When should we offer it? And, what support services are needed to help students succeed? These questions have everything to do with institutional mission, culture, and enrollment. The answers have ramifications for all aspects of the institution, including academic program demand, the marketplace, co-curricular programs, and student life. As a result, it is common for the SEP committee to be chaired by the chief academic officer. However, it is not uncommon for the SEP committee to have co-chairs, with either the chief enrollment officer or chief financial officer sitting alongside the chief academic officer.

Figure 13-1: The Interconnectivity of Effective SEP

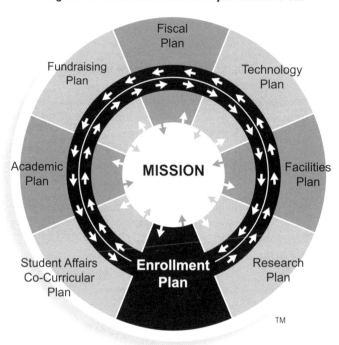

Do not hesitate to combine academic or administrative units within subcommittees to ensure there is enough representation and expertise for the subcommittee to be effective: marketing and recruitment/admissions, academic affairs and adult or graduate programs, finance and financial aid, athletics and student life/affairs, and academic affairs and retention.

As Christiansen and Golden noted in Chapter 2, "The central aspiration of SEP is to empower a collection of talented individuals to bring about a new world of promise they could not have fathomed as individuals and understand that this collaboration leads to a stronger future state." Once the chairs have been selected, the initial subcommittees established, and the charge delivered, the SEP process is ready to begin.

Step-by-step approach

Because each institution's motivation for SEP is different, the phases described below must be aligned with institutional mission and culture and be informed by the data and information gathered during the SEP process. Following are the four planning phases described in more detail in Chapter 4:

1. Phase one focuses on campus preparation, collection of data, identification of key performance indicators (KPIs), and creation of the situation analysis using a data-informed review of the institution's strengths, weaknesses, opportunities, and threats (SWOT).

2. The second phase identifies desired strategies and actions and provides the planning team with the information needed to prioritize these strategies and actions (based on campus readiness and attractive ROIs).

3. Phase three creates quantifiable goals and enrollment estimates for the overall institution and each subpopulation.

4. During phase four, the planning team implements and monitors the plan.

Given the impact of enrollment, it is understandable that urgency often drives plan completion. However, for most institutions, the phases summarized here will take the better part of an academic year, if not longer, to complete.

Patience is particularly critical at the beginning of the process. The first two tasks—preparation and the establishment of KPIs—are the foundation of the plan. It takes time to properly compile and analyze the internal and external data, and this is often where institutions lose patience. Institutions that expect goal setting and strategy development to be similar to annual planning can become frustrated with the pace of SEP. However, if you rush the planning process, you will likely end up with a plan that looks very similar to annual marketing, recruitment, retention, and academic plans that have been developed in the past, rather than a long-range, data-informed, strategic enrollment plan designed to align an institution to its external environment and promote stability and excellence.

As described in Chapter 4, determining the overall scope of the plan at the outset will help define the process, the research to be completed, and the composition of the planning team. The larger the scope of the plan, the longer it will take to complete. To increase the likelihood of success, be careful not to bite off more than can be chewed. For instance, if an institution has both undergraduate and graduate/professional programs, the main focus might be on completing the traditional undergraduate portion first and then phase in graduate/professional planning, rather than trying to do both at the same time.

Academics at the center of SEP

Currently, the development and management of academic programs at colleges and universities rarely involve non-academic units. Academic program review (adding or discontinuing programs and majors) has historically been done within academic affairs. And why not? No one else on campus is better suited to determine how an academic discipline should be taught, or which classes will be offered and how, than the professors who teach them.

The heart and soul of any institution lies within its academic programs, with the students and faculty providing the lifeblood of those programs. While enrollment managers often ask faculty to meet with prospective students in an effort to encourage new student recruitment or to provide feedback on current students in an effort to enhance student persistence and retention, it is less common for faculty/academics to consult with enrollment managers or student affairs personnel on which programs and majors they should offer, and how, when, and where they should be offered.

" He was a bold man that first ate an oyster."
Jonathan Swift

For these reasons, Chapters 3 and 4 recommend having the chief academic officer serve as chair (or co-chair) of the SEP committee. SEP usually includes internal and external research, as well as a thoughtful analysis and discussion of the research specifically surrounding the academic programs at the institution, noting how they currently contribute to enrollment management and how they will contribute to future enrollment. If an institution does not connect academic and co-curricular examination in this process, the institution is only creating a long-term recruitment and retention plan, not a strategic enrollment plan.

In the past 20 years, more and more institutions have adjusted their academic programs and delivery in response to academic demand. Institutions founded in the liberal arts and for-profit institutions are developing programs based on consumer demand, especially for nontraditional students. When I'm on a campus, I often hear, "What are we going to do about X institution that is opening up a satellite campus in our market?" or "Y institution already has seven sites in the metropolitan area," or "Z institution has opened up a center on the Army base, which is costing us students." In response, institutions must be willing to react to student demands by purchasing new technologies for online and hybrid teaching, as well as providing the training and support to faculty so that they can master the use of this technology.

For example, data indicate that, in the next decade, adults will be the fastest-growing new student population, and adults are likely to gravitate toward institutions that not only have programs to meet their educational goals, but ones that consider their work- and home-life needs. Therefore, if an institution wants to attract adult students as part of its overall goals, it should consider not only academic offerings, but how it can make the educational experience convenient for these students in terms of location, time of day, and how classes are taught. For institutions that hope to grow or maintain enrollments, a discussion of new majors, programs, and delivery systems must be part of SEP.

SEP as process

I hear enrollment leaders paraphrase President Dwight Eisenhower, saying "the plan is nothing, implementation is everything." For SEP, this is not necessarily the case. Institutions that have completed SEP often believe the process of planning was as valuable as the final plan itself, because the process brings faculty, staff, and administrators together. It also leads to important discussions in areas that may not impact participants individually, but have profound macro-level effects on the institution.

The downside is that the process isn't easy, and it's a bit frightening, especially for academic units that may see the process as a veiled excuse to phase out undersubscribed academic programs. It takes strong leadership and skilled facilitation to motivate individuals to openly and honestly engage in SEP, which, in most cases, requires them to step outside of their areas of expertise and comfort zones. SEP involves change, and many people dislike or even fear change—even talking about change makes them uncomfortable, especially when discussing change that impacts the routine they have established in their daily work lives.

> " **Communication is the key to any relationship between human beings."**
> **Dr. Robert E. Engel, my father**

This will be most apparent during phases one and two as individual SEP team members and subcommittees evaluate and provide feedback on data and information—often outside of their own area of expertise but, undoubtedly, inside of someone else's realm of expertise. This may be challenging, as there is a tendency to hold back observations and opinions, knowing that the spotlight will eventually be turned toward the analysis of data in one's own area of expertise. At times, SEP can feel very personal, which is why the president or SEP chair(s) must create a planning environment that fosters open analysis, dialogue, and interpretation. Without this leadership and charge, the planning process will end up focusing on obvious issues or minor concerns facing the institution without ever addressing the uncomfortable topics, the "elephants in the room," that must be addressed during successful SEP.

Unlike annual planning, where goals are often set by the administration (top down), simply aligned to a revenue/budget goal, or are a continuation of the status quo (e.g., to enroll more students than last year), SEP goal setting must follow the process. Similarly, annual plan strategies are typically developed to align with goals after they have been established. If potential strategies are properly analyzed, and resources are provided, establishing enrollment goals is an outcome of the strategy development process.

Finally, in order to take full advantage of the SEP process, communication plans and events should be established by the chair(s). Examples of this include sharing the initial data findings, the situation analysis, and the broad themes emerging from the planning process with the campus community. This is particularly helpful if there are discussions surrounding the creation, elimination, or downsizing of programs, services, or activities, in order to gain campus buy-in and explain the rationale behind those decisions. For example, it is not uncommon to have a faculty representative from the SEP team address the faculty senate each month to provide a regular update on the SEP process in an effort to keep faculty informed. The same can be true for administrative SEP representatives as they cascade information to their teams.

Are you informed?

The recruitment and retention of students is often viewed as an art, because enrollment managers work with human beings who sometimes make enrollment decisions based on what we might consider irrational reasons. We've all heard new first-time-in-college (FTIC) students say that they enrolled because "it just felt right," or "my favorite high school teacher went here." However, we are also constantly trying to make sense of the reasons students enroll and stay enrolled through graduation, developing as much "science" as we can through the compilation and analysis of data and other information.

Several years ago, I was meeting with a provost who outlined her goals for our consulting partnership. Clearly, she had thought about what she wanted accomplished, and she quickly articulated that the goal of the project was to increase the average FTIC SAT from 1150 to 1200 and increase the number of FTIC students from 900 to 1,000. She went on to add that this was to be accomplished in the class entering the next fall (this conversation took place in November!). I diligently wrote the goals in my notebook, and then went about the process of collecting data to learn what we would need to do in order to accomplish these goals. Working with the institution's director of institutional research, it didn't take us long to determine that the only way to accomplish the goal in nine months would be to eliminate the bottom 10 percent of the entering class and increase institutional aid in the middle two quartiles in order to increase the enrollment yield from accepted students. However, these strategies had significant consequences. Because of the ethnic and economic characteristics of the bottom 10 percent of the entering class and the increase in institutional aid, there would be a decline in ethnic diversity and an increase of several percentage points in the discount rate. (This second result was due in part to the fact that the bottom 10 percent brought large amounts of Pell and state grants with them.)

Once the data was presented to the provost, we were able to easily convince her to develop a three-year plan to increase enrollment and academic quality without such drastic ramifications for institutional mission, diversity, and revenues. These kinds of tradeoffs are at the heart of a fruitful SEP process.

Much, if not most, of the enrollment strategy implementation in higher education is quantifiable. We have recruitment response rates, conversion rates, acceptance rates, and yield rates; we have continuing student persistence rates, progression rates, retention rates, and completion and graduation rates. We have student satisfaction and engagement data, academic ability measurements, discount rates, market penetration studies, student outcomes data, and surveys on the quality of our faculty. Each of these can be dissected in different ways, by many different market segments, from year to year, and with national benchmarks. Indeed, in the example above, we were able to use data analysis and modeling not only to determine how to reach the desired goals, but also to realize that another path would be more strategic and prudent. Here, science informed art.

While data and information may exist on a campus, it is typically collected and reviewed at the departmental level and rarely shared on a macro level. However, much of the analysis of data for SEP will be conducted by a diverse group of individuals who possess content expertise, but not in the area required by their SEP subcommittee. It is also highly likely there will come a point during the process when the group will question the interpretation of data. The SEP chair will need to look to institutional research or content specialists to provide confirmation of the data. With this in mind, as an institution begins SEP, it will want to have at least one SEP team member with the talent and expertise to mine and assemble data and information, both internal and external, and know what is important to collect. This individual will not only be helpful in the area of data collection, but also in confirming the findings of others within the group who may not be as skilled in interpreting the data.

It can be easy to become paralyzed in the collection and review of data, which can go on for months if you allow it. Institutional leaders can become impatient and lose confidence in the process if the SEP team spends what they perceive to be an inordinate amount of time collecting and reviewing data, delaying strategy development. While more data can always be collected, it is essential that the planning leaders keep the committees focused and understand that the plan is a living document where data continues to be collected as the SEP process unfolds.

As I have stressed, the first two phases of SEP are challenging—fear of change, working outside of comfort zones, discussing difficult institutional issues directly, and the gathering and analysis of seemingly overwhelming amounts of data. It is no wonder that most institutions that fail in the SEP process do so during these two steps. That said, I cannot emphasize enough how important phases one and two are to the SEP process. As with any difficult endeavor, the hard work and perseverance do pay off, and they pave the way to a process that pays tremendous returns when conducted properly.

Strategic direction

While I've used words like "difficult" and "frustrating" to describe SEP, developing long-range strategies for SEP can actually be exciting. With smart, informed, and committed people laying out ways to move an institution forward, ways that maximize institutional strengths and overcome institutional barriers, the end results can be exhilarating. Enthusiasm can be contagious and, suddenly, instead of confronting challenges to mission and vision, institutional colleagues are rapidly charting new possibilities. Noel-Levitz was working with a campus last year on SEP when they experienced an unexpected 20 percent decline in new student enrollment. This was a campus that had enjoyed remarkable enrollment stability for more than a decade so this sudden drop in new student enrollment was very unsettling to institutional leaders. Fortunately, we were already in the process of identifying new strategies when the enrollment decline occurred and this gave the campus tremendous confidence that they could overcome this short-term setback. As the president said at the time, "Imagine how we would feel if we were not in the midst of this process and this had occurred."

As an institution proceeds with the SEP process, it is bound to have more strategies than it can practically implement. As suggested in Chapter 7, once each subcommittee has reviewed the research summary for its content area, it can commence with the development of strategies focusing on the team's specific content or subject area (e.g., marketing, retention, finance, academics). These can be broad, directional strategy statements or more specific action strategy statements, similar to KPIs and PIs. It is not uncommon for a subcommittee to finish its first round of strategy discussions with 10 or more strategy statements. If there are six to eight subcommittees, an institution could have 75 to 100 strategies, which will need to be paired down to a manageable number and linked to ROI and ROM considerations (Chapter 8).

This prioritization process is like standing at an all-you-can-eat buffet; everything looks so good that you want to try to eat a little of everything, but you know you can't. As the planning process diverges via the subcommittees, the planning team needs to scrutinize those ideas through prioritization and return-on-investment analysis to identify which ones should be implemented, as well as create a timeline for that implementation. Chapter 7 provides an example of how a campus might prioritize strategies.

> " This prioritization process is like standing at an all-you-can eat buffet; everything looks so good that you want to try to eat a little of everything, but you know you can't."

Desired state

As described in Chapter 3, SEP is a continuous and data-informed process that provides realistic, quantifiable goals, uses return-on-investment and action-item approach, and aligns the institution's mission, current state, vision, and changing environment to foster predictable long-term enrollment and fiscal health.

At the highest level of setting enrollment goals, an institution must determine whether to increase, maintain, or shrink enrollment. Few institutions want to shrink enrollments. However, the desire to maintain or increase enrollments conflicts with national high school attendance projections, showing almost half of all U.S. states will see declines in traditional enrollment in the coming years. Institutions that are unwilling to redesign delivery methods and create more flexible systems for enrollment will see smaller enrollments in future years.

Adapting to a changing environment is a crucial part of SEP, and future changes may call for institutions to examine their mission, vision, and current state in light of these changes. For example, an institution that says it is a "residential liberal arts institution" located in a rural environment may find it difficult to maintain enrollments that align with such a mission. If it needs to consider satellite sites or adding several online programs, the core academic mission may remain the same, but the overall mission may need to be adjusted to match the changing landscape of higher education and its primary market.

The strategies the SEP team ultimately selects as its highest-priority items must not only point to what the institution hopes to achieve (the desired state), but clearly articulate the financial and cultural implications the strategies will have for the institution once the goal is attained. For example, if an institution wants to grow overall enrollment or increase a specific subpopulation, what will that cost? Will the institution need to expand its market or develop/expand facilities and hire additional faculty and staff? Will the long-term impact of growth justify the cost of goal attainment? Thinking back on the earlier example of the provost who wished to raise academic profile and overall enrollment, will there be unintended consequences such as a loss of diversity or federal aid that supplements institutional aid? The SEP process serves to both identify these potential pitfalls and suggest solutions and/or better alternatives.

After the institution has completed the majority of its research and developed and prioritized its initial strategies, it is time to add other components of the SEP process in order to determine the direction and viability of the plan. This should be based on ROI considerations linked to the growth strategy matrix and projection models.

In Chapters 3 and 8, we introduced the strategic enrollment growth matrix to help institutions view goal setting in the four categories presented in Figure 13-2.

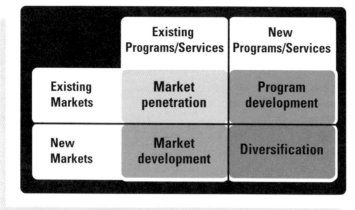

Figure 13-2: Strategic Enrollment Growth Matrix

	Existing Programs/Services	New Programs/Services
Existing Markets	Market penetration	Program development
New Markets	Market development	Diversification

TM

Using new student enrollment as an example, if the data indicate market share could be increased, then an institution might pursue strategies that impact existing programs and services in existing markets in an effort to increase market share by 1 percent over the next five years (this would become the goal). If demographic data show that the potential student population in three counties, in what has been a tertiary market, will be increasing over the next 10 years, strategies should be devised that impact existing programs and services while opening up these new markets/counties. If national/regional competition and student-level data indicate the market would be well served by adding a nursing program, an institution might accept strategies that would develop this new program and add it to existing marketing and communications.

As an institution considers new programs, it must also discuss program startup and ongoing operational costs linked to program capacity. In the nursing example, the start-up and operational costs may be very high, and capacity, depending upon location, may be limited due to the number of clinical or other practicum experiences required by the program. The campus needs to weigh all of these issues carefully when adding new programs, regardless of the opportunity for quick market penetration.

Finally, if the data from the three counties in the tertiary market show that there is a need for a centralized MBA program in this market, an institution can accept strategies leading to the startup of an MBA program away from the main campus in a more accessible location. Of course, the financial implications of growing or adding these programs are also critical to the analysis. In the examples of the nursing or MBA programs, while demand and employment data may show great need, the institution must provide a careful assessment of cost and revenues for adding these programs, linking cost to new markets or market penetration.

" It costs money to make money and to change."

ROI considerations for reaching a desired state

Chapter 7 outlined ways to calculate and understand return on investment, with suggestions for how to fold these new expenditures into the current institutional budgeting process. If this is done well and institutional goals are achieved, the increases in enrollment and/or long-term efficiencies will offset the expenditures in the early years of SEP implementation. Be sure to look for hidden costs, even for actions that appear to have minor fiscal consequences or appear to be cost-neutral. Keep in mind that campus resources are a finite pool, and taking action in one area, even "on the cheap," means moving resources away from other programs. As Marilyn Crone said in Chapter 8, "Consider the difference in ROI between 'do something' and 'do nothing' scenarios." Not funding initiatives could leave the institution at a severe competitive disadvantage.

Enrollment and revenue projection models offer the most useful and definitive way to determine the financial impacts of quantifiable macro goals for enrollment at any institution. They also identify the potential for additional revenues over time as enrollment and revenue grow.

The models presented in Table 13-1 provide examples of three institutional scenarios for traditional undergraduate enrollments. (Models can be developed for multiple market segments and populations, such as graduate, professional, adult, distance learning, etc.). Scenario one represents the result of maintaining market share. Scenario two reflects stable market share along with an increase in first- to second-year retention by 1 percent for the first five years before leveling off. Scenario three combines the first two scenarios, while also including an increase in nursing students.

Table 13-1: Examples of Enrollment and Revenue Projection Models (Three Scenarios)

Three institutional scenarios for traditional undergraduate enrollments (fall)										
	2009	2010	2011	2012	2013	2014	2015	2016	2017	2018	2019
Scenario 1: Baseline											
FR	732	789	777	774	773	773	773	773	773	773	773
SO	477	515	549	545	543	542	542	542	542	542	542
JU	615	579	610	639	638	636	635	635	635	635	635
SR	549	562	538	561	585	587	585	584	584	584	584
Total	**2,373**	**2,445**	**2,474**	**2,519**	**2,539**	**2,538**	**2,535**	**2,534**	**2,534**	**2,534**	**2,534**
Scenario 2: Moderate enrollment increase through retention											
FR	732	789	777	774	773	773	773	773	773	773	773
SO	477	515	557	561	567	575	583	584	584	584	584
JU	615	679	610	646	651	656	663	670	671	671	671
SR	549	562	530	552	582	589	594	600	606	608	608
Total	**2,373**	**2,445**	**2,474**	**2,533**	**2,573**	**2,593**	**2,613**	**2,627**	**2,634**	**2,636**	**2,636**
Scenario 3: Aggressive scenario—increases in FY retention and new students due to nursing											
FR	732	789	783	786	793	801	808	809	810	810	810
SO	477	515	558	568	580	594	610	615	616	617	617
JU	615	579	612	651	665	678	693	707	712	714	715
SR	549	562	538	563	595	610	623	636	648	654	656
Total	**2,373**	**2,445**	**2,491**	**2,568**	**2,633**	**2,683**	**2,734**	**2,767**	**2,786**	**2,795**	**2,798**

Table 13-2: Tuition Revenue Projection Examples (Three Scenarios)

Tuition revenue (in thousands) based on enrollment scenarios										
	2010	2011	2012	2013	2014	2015	2016	2017	2018	2019
Scenario 1: Baseline										
FR	$9,936	$10,176	$10,542	$10,950	$11,388	$11,843	$12,317	$12,810	$13,322	$13,855
SO	$6,606	$7,324	$7,562	$7,835	$8,134	$8,459	$8,737	$9,149	$9,515	$9,896
JU	$8,274	$9,066	$9,877	$10,256	$10,631	$11,041	$11,482	$11,942	$12,419	$12,916
SR	$8,085	$8,050	$8,730	$9,467	$9,880	$10,240	$10,631	$11,056	$11,499	$11,959
Total	**$32,902**	**$34,616**	**$36,711**	**$38,509**	**$40,034**	**$41,583**	**$43,228**	**$44,957**	**$46,756**	**$48,626**
Scenario 2: Moderate enrollment increase through retention										
FR	$9,936	$10,176	$10,542	$10,950	$11,388	$11,843	$12,317	$12,810	$13,322	$13,855
SO	$6,606	$7,431	$7,784	$8,181	$8,629	$9,099	$9,479	$9,858	$10,253	$10,663
JU	$8,274	$9,066	$9,985	$10,465	$10,967	$11,528	$12,115	$12,619	$13,124	$13,646
SR	$8,085	$7,930	$8,590	$9,419	$9,913	$10,397	$10,922	$11,473	$11,971	$12,450
Total	**$32,902**	**$34,603**	**$36,901**	**$39,015**	**$40,897**	**$42,867**	**$44,834**	**$46,760**	**$48,670**	**$50,617**
Scenario 3: Aggressive scenario—increases in FY retention and new students due to nursing										
FR	$9,936	$10,255	$10,706	$11,233	$11,800	$12,380	$12,891	$13,423	$13,960	$14,518
SO	$6,606	$7,444	$7,881	$8,369	$8,914	$9,520	$9,982	$10,399	$10,832	$11,265
JU	$8,274	$9,096	$10,063	$10,690	$11,335	$12,049	$12,784	$13,390	$13,965	$14,543
SR	$8,085	$8,050	$8,761	$9,629	$10,267	$10,905	$11,578	$12,268	$12,877	$13,433
Total	**$32,902**	**$34,845**	**$37,410**	**$39,922**	**$42,316**	**$44,854**	**$47,235**	**$49,479**	**$51,633**	**$53,760**

By utilizing the projection models and ROI worksheets described in Chapter 8, institutions can predict the financial impacts of goal attainment. While initial investments may seem significant, the potential ROI may represent a two-fold increase within the first year.

Always remember that being truly strategic may mean making tough choices. These types of projection and ROI analyses will help ensure that those tough decisions are wise ones that will have a long-term, positive impact on the institution.

The essential elements of enrollment management

When Noel-Levitz first developed our essential elements for enrollment management, we asked ourselves the following question: If you were going to create a new college or university today, what would you need in place to build a state-of-the-art enrollment management program? (This question applies to all institution types: public or private; liberal arts, comprehensive, or research; two-year or four-year; large or small.) During the course of my 18 years with Noel-Levitz, the list below evolved from that discussion, just as higher education and enrollment management have evolved.

In Chapters 10, 11, and 12, the authors shared an overview of the key elements of marketing, recruitment, and retention/completion as they apply to SEP. However, I caution you not to interpret the SEP process as a way to fix your annual marketing, recruitment, or retention programs. What if an institution does not have a strong enrollment management foundation in place? What if there are no effective plans for marketing, recruitment, and retention? Can the SEP process still begin?

Before I explore this dilemma further, let me share with you what Noel-Levitz believes to be the essential elements of enrollment management. We have divided these elements into six categories: institutional mission and values; organizational structure; data, analytics, and technology; planning and implementation; curricular and co-curricular offerings; and relationship management.

> " This isn't rocket science; it's all about building relationships with human beings and paying attention to details."
> **John Dolan,
> vice president
> of enrollment
> management,
> LaSalle University
> (Personal
> communication)**

1. Institutional mission and values:
   - Connect long-range strategic planning with mission and vision;
   - Associate academic, co-curricular, and enrollment planning with mission and vision; and
   - Align fiscal planning with institutional mission and vision.

2. Organizational structure:
   - Make enrollment leadership visible;
   - Engage the entire institutional community and constituents;
   - Create an effective enrollment management council;
   - Build a trained and talented enrollment team; and
   - Provide adequate resources.

3. Data, analytics, and technology:
   - Be committed to data integrity;
   - Make data-informed decisions using metrics that align with goals;
   - Employ a comprehensive prospective and continuing student information system and database; and
   - Produce relevant and accurate reports.

4. Planning and implementation:
   – Create a comprehensive strategic enrollment management plan;
   – Develop annual recruitment and retention plans that complement and meet the needs of multiple populations;
   – Set clear and realistic goals—annual and strategic;
   – Make sure you have effective operational processes in place;
   – Use financial aid strategically to achieve institutional goals; and
   – Collect, understand, and use internal and external research for informed decision-making.

5. Curricular and co-curricular offerings:
   – Start with quality academic programs;
   – Ensure course sequencing that facilitates student progression and completion;
   – Promote an institutional service philosophy with student-centered policies and procedures;
   – Develop proactive developmental advising programs;
   – Establish appropriate intervention programs; and
   – Invest in quality and availability of student support services.

6. Relationship management:
   – Build and manage enrollment funnels for new and continuing students;
   – Undertake proactive positioning and relationship building with new and continuing students;
   – Encourage faculty and staff engagement in student success;
   – Employ relevant and contemporary modes of communication; and
   – Use course management systems effectively.

Without going into detail about each of the bullet points, suffice it to say that most of the essential elements listed above have several layers, as described in Chapters 10 through 12. So the question remains, does an institution need to have a strong enrollment foundation and infrastructure prior to the development of a macro strategic enrollment management plan?

Having fundamentally sound and successful marketing, recruitment, and retention plans in place certainly will benefit the SEP process, as an institution will already have proven outcomes and data upon which to base decisions. In addition, if the institution is not struggling with the "blocking and tackling" of enrollment management, the SEP team will not be distracted with concerns about whether the institution can handle a long-range plan. However, SEP can also greatly contribute to the micro marketing, recruitment, and retention functions on campus by observing challenges in one or more areas and identifying solutions that can simultaneously become part of the micro-level annual plans and the larger SEP. Indeed, it is acceptable for an SEP plan to contain foundational strategies that need strengthening if the institutions hope to capitalize on the opportunities evident in the environment.

SEP is a fluid, ongoing process, much the same as sustaining a state-of-the-art enrollment management program. Figure 13-3 illustrates how the essential elements of SEP lead to constant analysis of what is working and not working. In turn, this informs long-range planning, which then influences the enrollment essentials as the campus seeks to make improvements to its enrollment management enterprise.

Figure 13-3: SEP Process

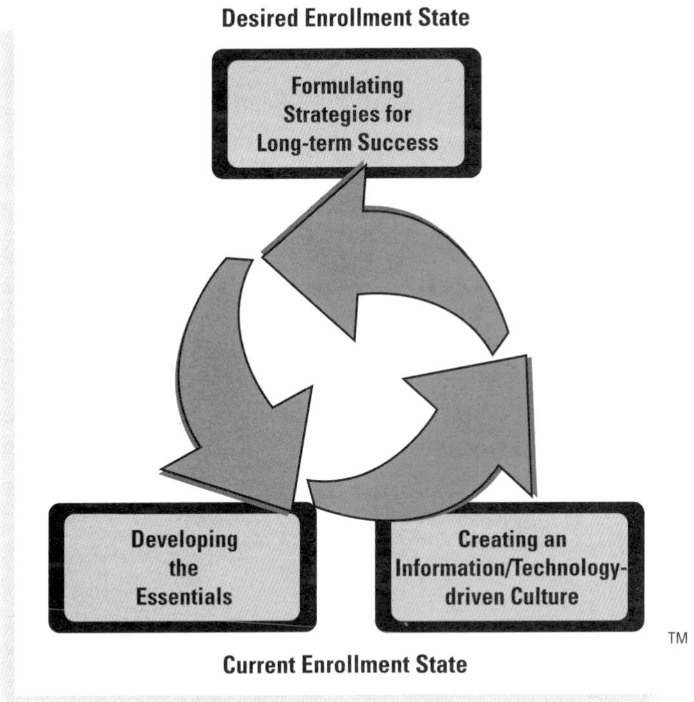

Desired Enrollment State

Current Enrollment State

While it is preferable to have a strong enrollment foundation in place in the form of annual marketing, recruitment, and retention plans, it is not necessary as long as the institution understands the need to develop and fine-tune micro and macro plans simultaneously.

The benefits of SEP

In conclusion, consider the benefits of institutional strategic planning offered by Jonathan Brand, and easily adapted for SEP. Mr. Brand is currently president at Cornell College (IA), and formerly president at Doane College (NE), and assistant to the president and budget officer at Grinnell College (IA) (Brand, 2011).

Institutional benefits of SEP

- Affirms what an institution should and will do to manage enrollment versus what it cannot or should not do;

- Provides a mechanism for affirming institutional mission, vision, and historical culture, while understanding their impact on enrollment management and the future of the institution;

- Supports decision making at all levels of enrollment management so that the institution does not seem chaotic and directionless, but organized and focused;

- Allows for a careful analysis and monitoring of changes in the external environment impacting enrollment so that the institution can proactively respond to change;

- Provides clarity to assessment of effectiveness for deciding how an institution will define enrollment success;

- Gives clarity to messaging and marketing (What should the institution be saying about itself and how can the institution proactively position itself in the marketplace?); and

- Models a healthy decision-making process—teamwork, communication, and collaboration.

Additionally, through SEP, institutions are able to align academic, co-curricular, and support programs to ensure success throughout the enrollment funnel and provide links to employment or graduate school needs and trends for the next generation.

This list summarizes the benefits discussed throughout this book. SEP is a complex, often difficult process. It is also one that offers unparalleled rewards for campuses. Simply put, there is no other process that can help a campus understand its current position, analyze and adapt to a changing marketplace, maximize its resources for the ultimate benefit of the institution, and not only reach its desired state, but discover the optimal desired state.

As is true for many of our best endeavors, the benefits will reflect the amount of effort invested in the process; and, just as any successful strategic enrollment plan should include a clear return on investment, I hope the strategies described in this book demonstrate the unquestionable, favorable ROI of the SEP process. By following the process and employing a consistent pattern of data analysis, strategic planning, and performance measurement, campus professionals can be good stewards of campus resources, institutional direction, and, most important, the futures of the students whose education and enrichment are the ultimate mission of higher education.

Examples of the Planning Process and Results

Over the past five years, Noel-Levitz has learned a great deal about the ways to create a successful planning environment. As we consider lessons learned, we conclude the book with some examples that may be helpful in preparing to launch a strategic enrollment planning (SEP) initiative.

Lesson one: While the process described is effective, institutions often seek to divert from the planning process. We appreciate the need to customize this approach to match institutional priorities, but that customization often leads to disconnecting the link between academic or co-curricular programs with enrollment practices. For a successful strategic view, planners should resist campus political pressures and understand that no program (either academic or co-curricular) is off limits when reviewing data.

Lesson two: If accurate and reliable data are used, strategies easily emerge through the process. To reach a desired future state, both internal and external trends must be analyzed. This data helps you understand and create strategies that align with future market demands, market penetrations, product developments, and areas where diversification is essential to long-term success.

Highlights

- **Resist campus political pressures**

- **Analyze reliable internal and external data**

- **Campus leaders must be involved**

Lesson three: Leadership matters. There is no getting around this issue. In order for a successful plan to be implemented and lived, campus leaders must be involved in the planning process. Leaders must monitor key performance indicators and link the budget with developed action items. As outlined in the following case studies, once the plan is developed, the council and activities must be shepherded by an institutional leader.

Case study: Community college

Over the past decade, a community college had slowly discontinued a majority of technically related programs, seeking to be more transfer-oriented and believing associate's degree programs would raise the stature of the institution within the community. The Board approved the changes. As programs were phased out and discontinued, enrollment slipped slightly, which was attributed to the decrease in technical programs.

Five years later, enrollment had dropped dramatically. Upon investigation, no data had been used to understand market trends or demands, and the campus had not created a plan to recruit students who matched their new profile. Everyone assumed the new, more academically focused changes would naturally enhance their reputation and thus increase or at least maintain current enrollments. Furthermore, no data analysis was completed to understand the community's perceptions of the institution. When the perception study was completed, findings suggested the institution still had a strong reputation as a technical and skills-based institution. Despite several years passing since offering many technical programs, few now knew of the institution as a transfer or liberal arts/general studies program.

As the college began its SEP process, the campus was data-shy. Rarely had data been used to understand student patterns of behavior. Rarely were recruitment practices linked to yield efforts. Even rarer was the monitoring of enrollment funnels linked to academic program offerings. One year, this caused faculty to scramble to find adjuncts to teach extra courses or beg full-time faculty to teach overloads. Two years later, academic leaders still struggled to fill certain courses or programs. No one had examined their academic programs and enrollment trends. Few co-curricular programs were offered, with the exception of sports, which had strong participation (and community support) but no alignment with recruitment efforts or potential links to academic offerings.

The campus conducted a market research study, an image and perception study, as well as a thorough review of its potential market share as traditional enrollments were expected to decline. In addition, due to location, adult markets showed little potential for growth, or most growth (demand) was in associate's degree programs within the allied health areas. To understand their students' profiles and interests in current academic program offerings, the campus also began to study enrollment patterns, such as: geographic locations of students, feeder high schools, student profile (all had assumed incorrectly that it was below average), time(s) adult students take courses, and the number of students enrolled in online courses.

The results of this review led to three conclusions:

1. Reintroduce some technically oriented programs mainly aligned within health-related majors and boost recruitment efforts for technical programs still offered where market demand and interest existed.

   – Discontinue several associate's degree programs that had minimal or no graduates in the past five years, diverting those faculty and dollars to expand core courses to support the growth planned for additional allied-health-related programs; and

   – Solicit grants and other external funding to update and expand lab facilities needed to meet program and accreditation requirements.

2. Expand sports programs to attract traditional students, linking these athletes with a specific academic advisor to help plan a two-year degree program that leads to degree completion and transfer plans to a four-year institution.

3. Realign several recruitment and marketing initiatives that focus on targeted recruitment practices and the establishment of goals and relationship management tools to build and connect prospective students with the quality education offered by this institution.

The results were slow at first. Given state and district budget cuts, staffing and additional resources were tight. Enrollments did increase, but struggled to reach overall enrollment goals. Efforts were refocused and further advancements were made within recruitment efforts, moving to more targeted practices and better utilization of faculty within the recruitment process that could highlight and speak directly to the quality outcomes gained through program completion. Employer surveys to assess recent graduate job performance were administered, garnering positive results for use in marketing efforts. Two years later, enrollments continued to grow, providing dollars for new academic and technical programs.

The key to their success was living the planning effort. Rather than establishing a plan and delegating that task to a committee, the campus leaders realized (particularly when the first two years garnered minimal results) that their role and drive needed to push the entire campus to engage and implement the plan.

Case study: Four-year private institution

This institution is in a state with about 200 competitors—nearly 75 of which are located within 50 miles of campus and more than 100 located within 150 miles. The college is located in a smaller to mid-size metropolitan area and has a president very committed to maintaining and building solid relationships within the city and neighboring towns. Religiously founded, the institution has maintained a more conservative reputation.

Prior to implementing an SEP process, image and perception studies were solid, boasting the college's student-friendliness, quality internships, and positive perceptions about five niche programs with strong reputations. The college had a solid footing in the undergraduate traditional market as well as the adult and graduate markets.

The college offered numerous academic programs and was very resistant to decreasing or eliminating programs. The chief enrollment officer and academic officer frequently quoted two lines: "The only way to grow is to add programs," and "There is no mission without margin." The latter was from a Noel-Levitz presentation they had heard; however, they did not understand that these maxims did not preclude program evaluation or the cutting of programs if such moves were informed by data and shown to be beneficial to the institution.

The institution was aware of the expected dramatic demographic changes in the state and local area for traditional students, with one of their most popular majors expecting to see significant declining demand based on numerous state funding cuts. There was good potential for growth in adult and graduate programs. Concerned about maintaining market share, the college began an SEP process. An initial review of data showed immediate "low-hanging fruit" with opportunities to streamline operations, enhance marketing and recruitment efforts, and increase net tuition.

Despite all the dedicated efforts, and after a review of current data, the institution was unable to answer the following fundamental questions:

1. What did prospective students want (adult and traditional)?

2. What was an unoccupied market position that could easily be accommodated?

3. What programs (academic and co-curricular) could the college provide equally as well or better than their competition?

4. Who was the competition?

5. Why did accepted prospective students choose to attend another institution?

> " *The institution was aware of the expected dramatic demographic changes in the state and local area for traditional students.*"

The SEP process started with a deep dive into research to answer these questions. Knowing they were not in crisis helped but, fundamentally, the college had not reviewed what programs they should add, grow, maintain, or discontinue. The image study had possible answers for their strengths, but they had never examined the success (persistence to completion or employer surveys) of their graduates. An initial review of retention to completion by academic major of interest showed some alarming data, with some programs completing less than 20 percent of students who entered with that area of interest with any degree from their institution. Other data showed average credit-hour completion per term very close to 12 credit hours, demonstrating few students would graduate in four years; adult credit-hour completion was closer to nine hours per term, further elongating their enrollment. Adult persistence-to-degree-completion rates were less than 25 percent, despite having consistent new student enrollments per term. Adult transfer students showed greater completion rates, convincing the leadership at graduation that their adult programs were strong, never separating out adults into two categories—new and transfer. Other data revealed several programs with robust offerings contributing to core course completion, but with very few majors or majors who completed a degree (about five majors did not have a graduate in the last five years). Using an enrollment projection tool, demographic data showed that, at current rates of decline and current market share, the freshman class would decrease by 20 percent before the enrollments would begin to shift upward. Transfer growth would make up some of the budget and enrollment gap for freshmen but likely leave a 10 to 12 percent enrollment shortfall.

The result of the SEP process was a plan that focused primarily on three areas.

1. A five-year plan to reduce academic and co-curricular programs where programs did not match regional interest or expected employment growth/demand.

2. The creation of very defined and targeted marketing and recruitment efforts. This included the use of sophisticated technology, refined communications flows, and enhanced relationship building. This also included significantly increased faculty involvement in recruitment and specialized efforts for populations where the institution had a niche or market research demonstrated opportunity for higher yield.

3. A revision to the academic advising program. The new model moved to a professional advising process required of all students (adult, transfer, and traditional) with intrusive measures, including focus on four-year degree plans, part-time pathways and maps with assured course sequencing for nontraditional students, and stronger articulation agreements with local community colleges.

Finally, the college shifted from a passive to active attitude, and numerous campus community members (particularly the vice president for enrollment management) led efforts to drive the enrollment plan.

Over the next three years, undergraduate traditional enrollment grew every year (despite decreased traditional students), first- to second-year retention increased by 3 percent, and, more importantly, upperclass retention grew by 8 percent.

Unfortunately, adult programs have struggled with increased competition. This decrease in adult students has caused new budget challenges that the administration has begun to address by measuring market demand and asking key questions: What can they do better or as good as anyone else? How do they offer those programs that align with market demand, trends, and employment needs? Are those curricular offerings presented at times and in formats that match changing adult expectations?

Case study: Four-year public institution

The final example is that of a public, flagship university with a long history of student success. Each year during the mid-1970s, enrollment growth continued to be better than the previous year. A majority of campus community members were happy with the current state. State contributions were strong, an emerging athletic program was growing and moving to national stature, and research initiatives (and funding) were gaining strength and momentum. The campus continued to grow and remain strong through the mid-1980s when, now at national stature, leaders asked internally how the institution could recruit better students and raise its academic profile as it continued to raise its state, regional, and national profile. Numerous efforts were introduced, all yielding positive results.

In the early 1990s, the concepts of SEP were introduced, with the creation of a functional mission statement. The mission emphasized stabilized enrollment through careful planning and a focus to position the institution at the top of its competitors based on a number of enrollment indicators.

In the mid-1990s, the enrollment planning leadership moved to a concentrated and analytical approach to support focused, personalized, and customized student recruitment, financial aid, retention, and graduation strategies. The committee accentuated the undergraduate experience, developing strategies and action plans to improve student support and increase student success.

Toward the late 1990s, the university identified additional benchmarks linking academic program growth and demand and expanded recruitment efforts targeting students who had expressed specific co-curricular interests. The institution launched numerous data projects, including an academic program demand analysis. The planning team (now a full-blown, engaged, and active planning council) reviewed individual programs, seeking information to form and draw conclusions related to future and enhanced planning efforts.

Knowing traditional freshmen were a primary market, the institution examined feeder high schools and high school graduation rates while seeking to understand adult program markets. The council reviewed new and emerging job trends/needs and linked those trends with current and potential new academic programs while re-evaluating existing programs where demand or technology had dramatically changed, establishing strategies to reinvent these programs in a contemporary context. The council expanded its work to see new ways to support growth in master/doctoral programs. Building sophisticated enrollment projection tools, and allowing for multiple scenarios of analysis, the council examined net tuition strategies to grow out-of-state and international markets. While quality was of the highest importance, the council also remained mindful of financial aid data and indicators to ensure the institution provided access and affordability to financially able, yet struggling, students. At the council's request, the campus began to focus on retention- and graduation-related efforts, focusing initially on first- to second-year persistence rates, then increasing graduation rates, and finally analyzing data by subpopulations. The analysis of subpopulations provided unexpected results, with some subpopulations showing dramatically different persistence and completion rates and areas of focus for the council and campus in future years.

> " The council reviewed new and emerging job trends/needs and linked those trends with current and potential new academic programs while re-evaluating existing programs where demand or technology had dramatically changed."

The results were remarkable. First- to second-year retention rates grew by 20 percent, and graduation rates increased by 25 percent. The reason: Dedicated leadership constantly monitored and tracked key and other performance indicators, remaining steadfast to the cause of improvement, and created more sophisticated enrollment management strategies. This council ensured the plan was alive and productive. The leadership continuously analyzed new data to make adjustments, modifications, and enhancements to the plan. In particular, the leader of the enrollment management area worked tirelessly to build relationships with academic leaders, using data to demonstrate successes and needs, and helped academic and other leaders create specific action items, filtered through the council, to maximize efforts.

ACT. (2011). *A better measure of skills gaps*. Iowa City, IA: Author. Retrieved from http://www.act.org/research/policymakers/pdf/abettermeasure.pdf

ACT. (2010). 2010 Retention/completion summary tables. Iowa City, IA: Author. Retrieved from http://www.act.org/research/policymakers/pdf/10retain_trends.pdf

ACT. (2010). *What works in student retention?* Iowa City, IA: Author. Retrieved from http://www.act.org/research/policymakers/reports/retain.html

ACT. (2011). *The conditions of college and career readiness*. Iowa City, IA: Author. Retrieved from http://www.act.org/research/policymakers/cccr11/pdf/ConditionofCollegeandCareerReadiness2011.pdf

Adelman, C. (2006). *The toolbox revisited: Paths to degree completion from high school through college*. Washington, DC: U.S. Department of Education. Retrieved from http://www2.ed.gov/rschstat/research/pubs/toolboxrevisit/toolbox.pdf

Allen, E., and Seaman, J. (2011). *Going the distance: Online education in the United States, 2011*. Boston, MA: Babson Survey Research Group. Retrieved from http://www.onlinelearningsurvey.com/reports/goingthedistance.pdf

American Association of Community Colleges (2011). *Voluntary framework of accountability*. Washington, DC: Author. Retrieved from http://www.aacc.nche.edu/Resources/aaccprograms/VFAWeb/default.aspx

Anctil, E. (2008). Selling higher education: Marketing and advertising America's colleges and universities. *ASHE Higher Education Report*, Volume 34, No. 2. San Francisco, CA: Jossey-Bass.

Anderson, L., and Anderson, D. (2001). *The change leader's roadmap: How to navigate your organization's transformation*. San Francisco, CA: Pfeiffer.

Andreasen, A. (1985). Backward market research. *Harvard Business Review*, May-June 1985.

Astin, A. W. (1999). Student involvement: A developmental theory for higher education. *Journal of College Student Development*, 40(5).

Astin, A. W. (2003). From number crunching to spirituality. In *Higher education handbook of theory and research, Volume 18*. London, England: Kluwer Academic Publishers.

Atkins, K. (2010). Strategically planning to change. *New Directions for Student Services*, 2010: 17–25. doi: 10.1002/ss.372

Babcock, P., and Marks, M. (2010). *Leisure college, USA: The decline in student study time*. American Enterprise Institute for Public Policy Research. Retrieved from http://www.aei.org/outlook/education/higher-education/leisure-college-usa/

Baer, M., and Stace, P. (1997). Enrollment management. In J. Martin and J. Samuels (Eds.), *First among equals: The role of the chief academic officer*. Baltimore, MD: John Hopkins University Press.

Baier, A. C. (1995). *Moral prejudices: Essays on ethics*. Cambridge, MA: Harvard University Press.

Barr, M. (2002). *Academic administrator's guide to budgets and financial management*. San Francisco, CA: Jossey-Bass.

Bassis, M. (2009). Reining in college costs. *BusinessWeek,* December 21, 2009. Retrieved from http://www.businessweek.com/print/bschools/content/dec2009/bs20091221_519869.htm

Bean, J. P. (1990). Strategic planning and enrollment management. In D. Hossler, J. P. Bean, and Associates, *The strategic management of college enrollments*. San Francisco, CA: Jossey-Bass.

Bertalanffy, L. V. (1969). *General system theory: Foundations, development, applications* (Revised). New York, NY: George Braziller, Inc.

Black, J. (Ed.). (2001). *Strategic enrollment management revolution.* Annapolis Junction, MD: AACRAO.

Bleich, D. (2008). Globalization, translation, and the university tradition. *New Literary History*, 39(3).

Bobbitt, D. (2011). Rethink higher education: The new University of Arkansas System president's vision for online education. *Arkansas Times*, November 30, 2011. Retrieved from http://www.arktimes.com/arkansas/rethink-higher-education/Content?oid=1957351

Bok, D. (2006). *Our underachieving colleges: A candid look at how much students learn and why they should be learning more.* Princeton, NJ: University of Princeton Press.

Bolman, L., and Deal, T. (1997). *Reframing organizations: Artistry, choice, and leadership* (Second Ed.). San Francisco, CA: Jossey-Bass.

Bolton, C., and English, F. (2010). Exploring the dynamics of work-place trust, personal agency, and administrative heuristics. In E. Samier and M. Schmidt (Eds.), *Trust and betrayal in educational administration and leadership.* New York, NY: Routledge.

Bowman, N. A. (2010). The development of psychological well-being among first-year college students. *Journal of College Student Development*, 51(2).

Brand, J. (2011). *The role and value of strategic planning for Cornell College: A presidential white paper.* Retrieved from http://www.cornellcollege.edu/president/writings-speeches/Strategic%20Planning%20White%20Paper%20Nov%20%202011.pdf

Brown, J. C. (2011). On the nature of change in higher education (Part I): A guest post. Washington, DC: *The Chronicle of Higher Education*, November 9, 2011.

Brown, J. C. (2011). On the nature of change in higher education (Part II): A guest post. Washington, DC: *The Chronicle of Higher Education*, November 9, 2011.

Brown, J. C. (2011). On the nature of change in higher education (Part III): A guest post. Washington, DC: *The Chronicle of Higher Education*, November 13, 2011.

Bryk, A. S., and Schneider, B. (2003). Trust in schools: A core resource for school reform. *Educational Leadership*, 60(6).

Bryson, J. (1995). *Strategic planning for public and nonprofit organizations: A guide to strengthening and sustaining organizational achievement* (Revised Ed.). San Francisco, CA: Jossey-Bass.

Bryson, J. (2004). *Strategic planning for public and nonprofit organizations: A guide to strengthening and sustaining organizational achievement* (Third Ed.). San Francisco, CA: Jossey-Bass.

Carlson, S. (2011). Financial outlook is brighter for some colleges, but still negative for most. *The Chronicle of Higher Education*, January 16, 2011. Retrieved from http://chronicle.com/article/Financial-Outlook-Is-Brighter/125973/

Chhuon, V., Gilkey, E. M., Gonzalez, M., Daly, A. J., and Chrispeels, J. H. (2008). The little district that could: The process of building district-school trust. *Educational Administration Quarterly*, 44(2).

Chickering, A. W., and Gamson, Z. F. (1987). Seven principles for good practice in undergraduate education. *AAHE Bulletin*, 39(7).

Chickering, A. W., and Reisser, L. (1993). *Education and identity* (Second Ed.). San Francisco, CA: Jossey-Bass.

Christensen, C., and Eyring, H. (2011). *The innovative university: Changing the DNA of higher education from the inside out.* San Francisco, CA: Jossey-Bass.

College and University Professional Association for Human Resources. (2010-11). *Mid-level administrative and professional salary survey*. Knoxville, TN: Author.

College Board. (2007). *The college keys compact*. New York, NY: Author. Retrieved from http://professionals. collegeboard.com/profdownload/final-report.pdf

College Board. (2010). *Education pays 2010*. Trends in Higher Education Series. New York, NY: Author. Retrieved from www.collegeboard.org

College Board. (2011). *College completion agenda, 2011 progress report*. New York, NY: Author. Retrieved from www.collegeboard.org

College Board. (2011). *Trends in college pricing*. Trends in Higher Education Series. New York, NY: Author. Retrieved from www.collegeboard.org

College Board. (2011). *Trends in student aid*. Trends in Higher Education Series. New York, NY: Author. Retrieved from www.collegeboard.org

Collins, J. (2001). *Good to great: Why some companies make the leap ... and others don't* (First Ed.). New York, NY: Harper Business.

Complete College America (2011). *Time is the enemy*. Washington, DC: Author. Retrieved from http://www. completecollege.org/docs/Time_Is_the_Enemy.pdf

Cooke, M., Irby, D., and O'Brien, B. (2010). *Educating physicians: A call for reform of medical school and residency*. Carnegie Foundation for the Advancement of Teaching Preparation for the Professions (First Ed.). San Francisco, CA: Jossey-Bass.

Cope, R. (1981). *Strategic planning, management, and decision making*. AAHE-ERIC/Higher Education Research Report, No. 9, Washington, DC: American Association for Higher Education.

Cullinan, M. (2009). Lemonade from lemons: Gaining strength from financial crisis. *The Presidency*, 12(2).

DeAngelo, L., Franke, R., Hurtado, S., Pryor, J., and Tran, S. (2011). *Completing college: Assessing graduation rates at four-year institutions*. Los Angeles, CA: Higher Education Research Institute at UCLA. Retrieved from http://www.heri.ucla.edu/DARCU/CompletingCollege2011.pdf

Deaton, R. (2011). *Tennessee Higher Education Commission outcomes-based funding formula* (blog). The Knowledge Collaborative. Retrieved from http://www.thekc.org/blogs/tennessee-higher-education-commission-outcomes-based-funding-formula

Dickeson, R. (1999). *Prioritizing academic programs and services: Reallocating resources to achieve strategic balance*. San Francisco, CA: Jossey-Bass.

Dickeson, R., (2010). *Prioritizing academic programs and services: Reallocating resources to achieve strategic balance* (Revised). San Francisco, CA: Jossey-Bass.

Doerfel, M., and Ruben, B. (2002). Developing more adaptive, innovative, and interactive organizations. In B. Bender and J. Shuh (Eds.), *New Directions for Higher Education*, 118. San Francisco, CA: Jossey-Bass.

Dolence, M., and Norris, D. (1994). Using key performance indicators to drive strategic decision making. In V. Borden and T. Banta (Eds.), Performance indicators to drive strategic decision making. *New Directions for Institutional Research*, 82. San Francisco, CA: Jossey-Bass.

Dolence, M., Rowley, D., and Lujan, H. (1997). *Working toward strategic change: A step-by-step guide to the planning process*. San Francisco, CA: Jossey-Bass.

Doran, G. T. (1981). There's a S.M.A.R.T. way to write management's goals and objectives. *Management Review*. November 1981, 70(11).

Durkin, D. (2010). Growing with the flows. *Continuing Higher Education Review*, 74, 2010.

Education Trust, The. (2012). *College results online*. Retrieved from http://www.collegeresults.org

Ehrenberg, R. G., and Webber, D. A. (2010). Student services expenditures matter. *Change*, 2010, 42.

Ellis, S. E. (2010). Introduction to strategic planning in student affairs: A model for process and elements of a plan. In S. E. Ellis (Ed.), Strategic planning in student affairs. *New Directions for Student Services*, (132). San Francisco, CA: Jossey-Bass.

Farnsworth, K. (2007). *Leadership as service: A new model for higher education in a new century.* Westport, CT: Praeger.

Gee, E. G. (2009). A call to (link) arms. *The Presidency*, 12(2).

Ginsberg, B. (2011). The strategic plan: Neither strategy nor plan, but a waste of time. Washington DC: *The Chronicle of Higher Education*, July 17, 2011.

Guskin, A. E. (1996). Facing the future: The change process in restructuring universities. *Change*, 28(4).

Habley, W. R., and McClanahan, R. (2004). *What works in student retention?* Iowa City, IA: ACT. Retrieved from http://www.act.org/research/policymakers/reports/retain.html

Haines, S. (2000). *The systems thinking approach to strategic planning and management.* Boca Raton, FL: CRC Press, LLC.

Handy, C. (1998). *Beyond certainty: The changing worlds of organizations.* Boston, MA: Harvard Business Press.

Heifetz, R., Grashow, A., and Linsky, M. (2009). Leadership in a permanent crisis. *Harvard Business Review*, 87(7/8). Retrieved from http://www.ocvets4pets.com/archive17/Leadership_in_a__Permanent__Crisis_-_HBR.org.pdf

Henderson, S. E. (2005). Refocusing enrollment management: Losing structure and finding the academic context. AACRAO, *College and University*, 80(3).

Hunter, M. S., Tobolowsky, B. F., Gardner, J. N., Evenbeck, S. E., Pattengale, J. A., Schaller, M. A., and Schreiner, L. A. (2010). *Helping sophomores succeed: Understanding and improving the second-year experience* (First Ed.). San Francisco, CA: Jossey-Bass.

Ichheiser, G. (1949). Misunderstandings in human relations: A study in false social perception. *American Journal of Sociology*, 55(2).

Immerwahr, J., Johnson, J., Ott, A., and Rochkind, J. (2010). *Squeeze play 2010: Continued public anxiety on cost, harsher judgments on how colleges are run.* The National Center for Public Policy and Higher Education (NCPPHE). Retrieved from http://www.highereducation.org/reports/squeeze_play_10/squeeze_play_10.pdf

Institute of International Education. (2011). *Open doors 2011: Report on international educational exchange.* Retrieved from http://www.iie.org/en/Research-and-Publications/Open-Doors

Jessup, L. M., and Valacich, J. S. (2008). *Information systems today* (Third Ed.). Upper Saddle River, NJ: Pearson Prentice Hall.

Keller, G. (2004). *Transforming a college: The story of a little-known college's strategic climb to national distinction.* Baltimore, MD: John Hopkins University Press.

Keller, J. (2011). As the web goes mobile, colleges fail to keep up. *The Chronicle of Higher Education*, January 23, 2011.

Kennedy, R. (2008). 50 best branding ideas. *University Business*, December, 2008. Retrieved from http://www.universitybusiness.com/article/50-best-branding-ideas

Kinkead, J. (Ed.). (2011). *Advancing undergraduate research: Marketing, communications, and fundraising.* Washington, DC: Council on Undergraduate Research.

Kotler, P. (1999). *Kotler on marketing: How to create, win, and dominate markets*. New York, NY: Simon and Schuster.

Kotler, P., and Fox, K.F.A. (1985). *Strategic marketing for educational institutions*. Englewood Cliffs, NJ: Prentice-Hall, Inc.

Kuh, G. D. (2008). *High-impact educational practices: What they are, who has access to them, and why they matter*. Washington, DC: AAC&U.

Kuh, G. D., Kinzie, J., Schuh, J. H., and Whitt, E. J. (2005). *Student success in college: Creating conditions that matter* (First Ed.). San Francisco, CA: Jossey-Bass.

Lake, N. (2006). *The strategic planning workbook* (Second Ed.). Philadelphia, PA: Kogan Page.

Lane, C. (1998). Introduction: Theories and issues in the study of trust. In C. Lane and R. Bachmann (Eds.), *Trust within and between organizations: Conceptual issues and empirical applications*. Oxford University Press, USA.

Leinbach, D. T., and Jenkins, D. (2008).Using longitudinal data to increase community college student success: A guide to measuring milestone and momentum point attainment. *CCRC Research Tools No. 2*. New York, NY: Community College Research Center, Teachers College, Columbia University. Retrieved from http://ccrc.tc.columbia.edu/Publication.asp?uid=570

Lesick, L. (2009). A Gazette Minute with Larry Lesick. West Palm Beach, FL: *The Greentree Gazette*.

Leslie, D. W., and Fretwell, E. K. (1996). *Wise moves in hard times: Creating and managing resilient colleges and universities*. San Francisco, CA: Jossey-Bass.

Lewin, T. (2011). Official calls for urgency on college costs. *New York Times*, November 29, 2011. Retrieved from http://www.nytimes.com/2011/11/30/education/duncan-calls-for-urgency-in-lowering-college-costs.html

Light, R. (2001). *Making the most of college: Students speak their minds*. Cambridge, MA: Harvard University Press.

Lumina Foundation. (2010). *Lumina Foundation's strategic plan: Goal 2025*. Indianapolis, IN: Author. Retrieved from http://www.luminafoundation.org/wp-content/uploads/2011/02/Lumina_Strategic_Plan.pdf

Lumina Foundation. (2012). *A stronger nation through higher education: How and why Americans must achieve a "big goal" for college attainment*. Indianapolis, IN: Author. Retrieved from http://www.luminafoundation.org/publications/A_stronger_nation.pdf

Lyman, P., and Varian, H. R. (2003). *How much information, 2003?* School of Information Management and Systems. University of California at Berkeley. Retrieved from http://www.sims.berkeley.edu/how-much-info-2003

Massey, R. (2001). Developing a SEM plan. Chapter from J. Black, *The strategic enrollment management revolution*. Washington, DC: American Association of Collegiate Registrars and Admissions Officers (AACRAO).

Matthews, D. (2011). Bachelor's degree attainment up according to new Census Bureau data. In *Getting to sixty: A higher ed policy blog*. Indianapolis, IN: Lumina Foundation. Retrieved from http://www.luminafoundation.org/dewayne_matthews/

Montana State University-Billings. (2011). *Retention plan*.

Moody's Investors Service. (2011). *2011 outlook for U.S. higher education*. Retrieved from http://www.nhhefa.com/documents/moodys2011OutlookforU.S.HigherEducation.pdf

Mora, J. (2001). Governance and management in the new university. *Tertiary Education and Management*, 7(2).

Moskowitz, G. B. (2004). *Social cognition: Understanding self and others* (First Ed.). New York, NY: The Guilford Press.

Nagda, B., Gregerman, S., von Hippel, W., Jonides, J., and Lerner, J. (1998). Undergraduate student-faculty research partnerships affect student retention. *The Review of Higher Education*, 22.1.

National Association for College Admission Counseling (NACAC). (2010). *Special report on the transfer admission process*. Arlington, VA: Author.

National Association for College Admission Counseling (NACAC). (2011). *State of college admission report*. Arlington, VA: Author.

National Association of College and University Business Officers (NACUBO). (2010). *2010 Tuition discounting study*. Retrieved from http://www.nacubo.org/Research/NACUBO_Tuition_Discounting_Study.html

National Center for Education Statistics (NCES). (2010). *Digest of education statistics*. U.S. Department of Education. Retrieved from http://nces.ed.gov/programs/digest/d10/

National Center for Education Statistics (NCES). (2011). *Projections of education statistics to 2020*, 39th Edition. U.S. Department of Education. Retrieved from http://nces.ed.gov/programs/projections/projections2020/

Newman, F., Couturier, L., and Scurry, J. (2004). *The future of higher education: Rhetoric, reality, and the risks of the market*. San Francisco, CA: Jossey-Bass.

Newton, B., and Smith, J. (2008). Steering in the same direction: The importance of academic and student affairs relationships to student success. *College and University*, 84(1).

Noel, L., Levitz, R., and Saluri, D. (1985). *Increasing student retention: Effective programs and practices for reducing the dropout rate* (First Ed.). San Francisco, CA: Jossey-Bass.

Noel-Levitz. (2007). *E-expectations report: Building an e-recruitment network*. Coralville, IA: Author. Retrieved from https://www.noellevitz.com/E-ExpectationsSeries

Noel-Levitz. (2009). *Six essentials and six common mistakes in cabinet level strategic enrollment planning*. Coralville, IA: Author. Retrieved from https://www.noellevitz.com/papersandresearch

Noel-Levitz. (2010). *Back to the present: Strategic enrollment planning for the coming demographic change*. Coralville, IA: Author. Retrieved from https://www.noellevitz.com/papersandresearch

Noel-Levitz. (2010). *E-expectations report: Focusing your e-recruitment to meet the expectations of college-bound students*. Coralville, IA: Author. (Research partners: OmniUpdate and National Research Center for College & University Admissions.) Retrieved from https://www.noellevitz.com/E-ExpectationsSeries

Noel-Levitz. (2011). *National online learners priorities report*. Coralville, IA: Author. Retrieved from https://www.noellevitz.com/papersandresearch

Noel-Levitz. (2011). *National student satisfaction and priorities report*. Coralville, IA: Author. Retrieved from https://www.noellevitz.com/papersandresearch

Noel-Levitz, Inc. (2011). *Student retention practices at four-year and two-year institutions*. Coralville, IA: Author. Retrieved from https://www.noellevitz.com/papersandresearch

Noel-Levitz. (2011). *E-expectations report: The online expectations of prospective college students and their parents*. Coralville, IA: Author. (Research partners: OmniUpdate and National Research Center for College & University Admissions.) Retrieved from https://www.noellevitz.com/E-ExpectationsSeries

Noel-Levitz. (2011). *Marketing and student recruitment practices at four-year and two-year institutions.* Coralville, IA: Author. Retrieved from https://www.noellevitz.com/papersandresearch

Noel-Levitz. (2011). *Mid-year retention indicators report for two-year and four-year, public and private institutions.* Coralville, IA: Author. Retrieved from https://www.noellevitz.com/papersandresearch

Noel-Levitz. (2012). *E-expectations report: The online expectations of college-bound juniors and seniors.* Coralville, IA: Author. (Research partners: CollegeWeekLive, OmniUpdate, and National Research Center for College & University Admissions.) Retrieved from https://www.noellevitz.com/E-ExpectationsSeries

Noel-Levitz. (2012). *Why did they enroll? The factors influencing college choice.* Coralville, IA: Author. Retrieved from https://www.noellevitz.com/papersandresearch

Norris D., and Poulton N. (2008). *A guide to planning and change.* Ann Arbor, MI: Society for College and University Planning.

Pardee, C. F. (2004). *Organizational structures for advising.* Retrieved from http://www.nacada.ksu.edu/clearinghouse/advisingissues/org_models.htm#over

Peters, T. J., and Waterman Jr., R. H. (1982). *In search of excellence.* New York, NY: Harper & Row.

Pew Research Center. (2011). *Is college worth it? College presidents, public assess value, quality, and mission of higher education.* May, 2011. Retrieved from http://pewresearch.org/pubs/1993/survey-is-college-degree-worth-cost-debt-college-presidents-higher-education-system

Poock, M.C., and LeFond, D. (2001). How college-bound prospects perceive university web sites: Findings, implications, and turning browsers into applicants. *C&U Journal,* 77(1). Retrieved from http://www.aacrao.org/libraries/publications_documents/summer2001.sflb.ashx

Prensky, M. (2002). The motivation of gameplay: The real twenty-first century learning revolution. *On the Horizon,* 10(1).

Pryor, J. H., Hurtado, S., DeAngelo, L., Palucki Blake, L. P., and Tran, S. (2011). *The American freshman: National norms for fall 2010.* Los Angeles: Higher Education Research Institute, at UCLA.

Rowley, D., Lujan, H., and Dolence, M. (1997). *Strategic change in colleges and universities: Planning to survive and prosper.* San Francisco, CA: Jossey-Bass.

Samier, E. (2010). Trust in organizational, leadership, and management studies: Theories, approaches, and conceptions. In E. Samier and M. Schmidt (Eds.), *Trust and betrayal in educational administration and leadership.* New York, NY: Routledge.

Schroeder, C. C. (1999). Partnerships: An imperative for enhancing student learning and institutional effectiveness. In J. H. Schuh and E. J. Whitt (Eds.), Creating successful partnerships between academic and student affairs. *New Directions for Student Services,* No. 87. San Francisco, CA: Jossey-Bass.

Sevier, R. (2007). Brand as experience, experience as brand. *University Business,* July 2007.

Sevier, R. (2000). *Strategic planning in higher education: Theory and practice.* Washington, DC: CASE Books.

Sloan Consortium. (2010). *Class differences: Online education in the United States, 2010.* Retrieved from http://sloanconsortium.org/publications/survey/index.asp

State Higher Education Executive Officers (SHEEO). (2010). *State higher education finance FY 2010.* Boulder, CO: Author. Retrieved from www.sheeo.org

Steiner, G, Miner, J, and Gray, E. (1992). *Management policy and strategy* (Second Ed.). Old Tappan, NJ: MacMillan Publishing.

Stewart, A., and Carpenter-Hubin, J. (2000). The balanced scorecard: Beyond reports and rankings. *Planning for Higher Education,* 29(2).

Terenzini, P. T., Pascarella, E. T., and Blimling, G. S. (1996). Students' out-of-class experiences and their influence on learning and cognitive development: A literature review. *Journal of College Student Development*, 37(2).

Tierney, W. (2006). *Trust and the public good: Examining the cultural conditions of academic work.* New York, NY: Peter Lang.

U.S. Department of Education. (2011). *Meeting President Obama's 2020 college completion goal.* Retrieved from http://www.ed.gov/news/speeches/meeting-president-obamas-2020-college-completion-goal

U.S. Department of Labor, Veterans' Employment and Training Service. (2011). *Transition assistance program manual.* Retrieved from http://www.dol.gov/vets/programs/tap/main.htm

Van Der Werf, M., and Sabatier, G. (2009). *The college of 2020: Students.* Washington, DC: Chronicle Research Services: The Chronicle of Higher Education. Retrieved from www.research.chronicle.com

Vanover Porter, M. (2010). When the price is right. *NACUBO Business Officer*, March 2010.

Whitney, R. (2010). Involving academic faculty in developing and implementing a strategic plan. In S.E. Ellis (Ed.), Strategic planning in student affairs. *New Directions for Student Services.* San Francisco, CA: Jossey-Bass.

Zak, P. J. (2011). *Trust, morality and oxytocin.* Retrieved from http://www.ted.com/talks/lang/en/paul_zak_trust_morality_and_oxytocin.html

Zak, P. J., Kurzban, R., and Matzner, W. T. (2004). The neurobiology of trust. *Annals of the New York Academy of Sciences*, 1032.

Zlotkowski, E. (Ed.). (1998). *Successful service-learning programs: New models of excellence in higher education.* Bolton, MA: Anker Publishing.

Douglas L. Christiansen, PhD

Douglas L. Christiansen is vice provost for enrollment and dean of admissions at Vanderbilt University. He also serves as assistant professor of public policy and higher education in the Department of Leadership, Policy, and Organizations at Vanderbilt's Peabody College. In his role as vice provost, Dr. Christiansen serves as the university's chief enrollment strategist, overseeing the offices of Undergraduate Admissions, Student Financial Aid and Undergraduate Scholarships, Enrollment Management Information Systems, the University Registrar, Vanderbilt Institutional Research Group (VIRG), and Honor Scholars.

Prior to his role at Vanderbilt, he served at Purdue University (IN) and at the University of Utah. As an associate consultant for Noel-Levitz, Dr. Christiansen has conducted more than 120 consulting engagements, working directly with presidents, trustees, enrollment professionals, and faculty on enrollment-related issues.

Dr. Christiansen is a frequent conference speaker and an active researcher and professor. He earned his PhD in higher education administration at the University of Utah.

Sarah Coen

Sarah Coen offers two decades of experience in new student recruitment, financial aid, orientation, and staff development. As Noel-Levitz vice president for consulting services, Ms. Coen has served more than 40 institutions in the United States and Canada, including small and large four-year private, two-year public, and four-year public institutions. In addition, she has worked with system-level projects in both Louisiana and Maine.

Before her position at Noel-Levitz, Ms. Coen was director of admissions at Transylvania University (KY). During her tenure at Transylvania, she helped engineer record gains in applications, freshman enrollment, and net revenue. In addition, academic quality and freshman-to-sophomore retention rates increased, resulting in the largest enrollment in the university's 225-year history.

Ms. Coen previously served as director of admissions at Commonwealth College (VA) and director of admissions at the University of Michigan-Dearborn. She holds a master's degree in public administration from Central Michigan University.

Kevin W. Crockett

Kevin Crockett is president and CEO of Noel-Levitz. He consults directly with campuses on effective leadership and strategy development for admissions, marketing, recruitment, retention, and student financial aid. An experienced enrollment manager, Mr. Crockett has served more than 200 institutions and systems throughout North America.

Prior to joining Noel-Levitz, Mr. Crockett served as dean of admissions and enrollment management at Cornell College (IA), where he enrolled the three largest consecutive entering classes in school history—culminating in record opening enrollment.

Mr. Crockett is an inspirational speaker on enrollment management topics and frequently appears at higher education conferences to share significant enrollment trends and innovative strategies. He holds an MA in higher education administration from the University of Iowa with concentrations in policy analysis and leadership studies.

Marilyn Crone

Marilyn Crone offers more than a decade of experience in higher education, serving private institutions in the United States and Canada. She has managed a broad range of enrollment issues, including student recruitment, student retention, financial aid, and marketing and communications. She is currently vice president for enrollment management at Seattle University.

Prior experience includes multiple roles at Trinity Western University (BC) and vice president for enrollment and retention management at Baylor University (TX). As a Noel-Levitz associate consultant, Ms. Crone provided management consulting for Quest University Canada, a newly established private institution in British Columbia. She created and headed the implementation of key enrollment strategies needed to enroll the university's inaugural class until permanent enrollment leadership could be secured.

Ms. Crone holds an MBA from Baylor University. She conducts pro bono consulting for several ministry organizations.

Timothy D. Culver

Tim Culver is Noel-Levitz vice president of retention consulting services, helping institutions develop, implement, and evaluate plans for improving persistence, degree completion rates, and enrollment. He has expertise in a wide range of areas of enrollment management, including retention planning, Title III and Title V grants, enrollment planning, developmental education, and institutional assessments.

Mr. Culver has consulted with more than 50 four-year and two-year institutions across North America, working to strengthen retention initiatives through better planning.

Prior to joining Noel-Levitz, Mr. Culver served as director of the Student Success Center at Shawnee State University (OH). He wrote and received federal Title III grants resulting in the implementation of a new instructional support services model at the university. At Shawnee State, he used his passion for teaching as well, designing a curriculum for and teaching developmental mathematics courses.

Mr. Culver is currently enrolled in a PhD program at Colorado State University.

Craig A. Engel

Craig Engel, Noel-Levitz senior vice president, works with campuses on the effective administration of their enrollment management programs. Offering over 25 years of hands-on experience in enrollment management, Mr. Engel's career has focused on building, maintaining, and shaping enrollments—first on campuses, and now as a consultant.

Mr. Engel's areas of expertise include database and inquiry pool management, staff training and development, transfer and graduate/professional recruitment techniques, and strategic enrollment planning.

Prior to joining Noel-Levitz, Mr. Engel held campus-based positions in admissions and financial aid at Golden Gate University School of Law (CA), the University of Iowa, and Cornell College (IA). Mr. Engel holds an MA in higher education administration from the University of Iowa.

Gary L. Fretwell

As a senior vice president and a consultant for Noel-Levitz, Gary Fretwell has been a strong catalyst for enrollment success on hundreds of campuses throughout North America. His recommendations and guidance have helped institutions establish strategic and tactical enrollment plans for both graduate and undergraduate programs.

In addition to providing consulting services, Mr. Fretwell frequently delivers presentations on strategic enrollment management, development of campuswide retention programs, graduate and professional school recruitment, and mobilizing campus divisions to achieve enrollment success.

Over the course of his 30-year career in higher education, Mr. Fretwell served as vice president for enrollment and student affairs at Millsaps College (MS) and held a variety of posts at Tulane University (LA) and the University of South Florida. Mr. Fretwell holds an MA from Stetson University (FL).

Thomas C. Golden, PhD

Thomas C. Golden has served as senior associate director of undergraduate admissions at Vanderbilt University since 2006. In his role, Dr. Golden leads all aspects of prospective student and family recruitment, including high school relations, on-campus visitation programming, direct marketing, interactive media communications, pipeline development strategy, and management of student, alumni, and Vanderbilt parent volunteers. In addition, he is an assistant adjunct professor in the Leadership, Policy, and Organizations department of Vanderbilt's Peabody College of Education and Human Development.

Prior to his work at Vanderbilt, Dr. Golden served as senior assistant director of admissions and enrollment management projects coordinator at Purdue University (IN).

Golden holds a doctorate in educational psychology from Purdue University.

Jim Hundrieser, PhD

Jim Hundrieser is vice president for enrollment management and student affairs at Plymouth State University (NH). Dr. Hundrieser's enrollment management expertise covers strategic enrollment planning, student recruitment, student retention, strategic planning, institutional planning and assessment, and student life.

As a former vice president at Noel-Levitz, he consulted with more than 50 colleges and universities to create comprehensive strategic enrollment plans, long-range enrollment plans, and recruitment and retention strategies. His recommendations and guidance helped institutions establish comprehensive enrollment management initiatives for both graduate and undergraduate programs.

Dr. Hundrieser has delivered numerous national and regional presentations and conducted campus workshops on topics ranging from building a strong recruitment program to improving the quality of student life and learning.

Prior to his roles at Plymouth State and Noel-Levitz, Dr. Hundrieser served as vice president for student development at Lynn University (FL) and vice president for student affairs and enrollment management at Marymount Manhattan College (NY). He holds a PhD in leadership and education from Barry University (FL).

Joyce Kinkead, PhD

Joyce Kinkead is an acclaimed academic and administrator with 30 years of experience in higher education. She offers extensive expertise in the areas of student recruitment, retention, financial aid, academic advising, institutional research, academic planning and assessment, and classroom instruction.

Dr. Kinkead currently serves as the associate vice president for research at Utah State University. She has enhanced the undergraduate research program, increased the number of students accepted to the National Conference on Undergraduate Research, administered the university's New Faculty Research Grant Program, and created the Utah Conference on Undergraduate Research, among other accomplishments. In addition to her administrative duties, she is a professor of English and a Noel-Levitz associate consultant.

A prolific scholar and writer, Dr. Kinkead has authored eight books and dozens of journal articles and book chapters. She has presented at numerous regional, state, national, and international conferences. Dr. Kinkead holds a PhD from Texas A&M University–Commerce.

Evelyn (Bonnie) Lynch, EdD

Evelyn Lynch has spent more than 35 years in higher education as a faculty member and as an academic administrator. She recently retired as the executive director of the Lehigh Valley Association of Independent Colleges. This academic consortium, governed by the presidents of the six private colleges in the Lehigh Valley, facilitates collaborative academic opportunities and shared purchasing contracts for approximately 18,000 students and 5,000 faculty and staff. She is a Noel-Levitz associate consultant.

Prior to her work at Lehigh Valley, Dr. Lynch served as president of Saint Joseph College (CT) where she created a strategic vision for the college and facilitated a comprehensive plan for student recruitment and retention. Dr. Lynch held previous leadership positions at East Stroudsburg University of Pennsylvania, Arkansas State University, Ball State University (IN), and Minnesota State University-Moorhead.

Dr. Lynch has published and presented on developmental disabilities, teacher preparation, and education. Dr. Lynch received her EdD from Indiana University.

James J. Mager, PhD

With more than 35 years of experience in higher education as an administrator and consultant, James Mager specializes in strategic enrollment planning, student recruitment, student retention, enrollment management research, and operations analysis.

Dr. Mager was associate vice president for Noel-Levitz until his retirement in 2010. In addition to campus consulting, Dr. Mager was instrumental in the research and development of the firm's many national reports and strategic white papers.

Previously, he held a variety of enrollment management positions at The Ohio State University. As associate vice president of enrollment management at OSU, he led the offices of admissions, first-year experience, financial aid, and the university registrar. Previously he served as director of admissions and financial aid and as a systems analyst.

Dr. Mager received his doctorate in industrial systems engineering from Ohio State.

Brian Ralph, PhD

Brian Ralph is vice president for enrollment management at Queens University of Charlotte (NC), where he oversees traditional undergraduate admissions, graduate admissions, student financial services, residence life, student activities, athletics, campus police, multi-cultural affairs, and health and wellness services. He also co-chairs the University retention committee. Previously, Dr. Ralph served as vice president for enrollment management and marketing at Bethany College (WV). As a Noel-Levitz senior associate consultant, he specializes in strategic enrollment planning, recruitment and admissions processes, marketing and promotions strategies, and marketing communications.

An excellent speaker, Dr. Ralph has presented on numerous occasions at national higher education conferences. He completed the Institute for Educational Management at Harvard University and received his PhD in organizational communication and culture from Ohio University.

Ruth K. Sims

Ruth Sims, senior vice president for marketing and research at Noel-Levitz, consults with campuses on market research, marketing strategy, and communications development. She is a driving force behind the firm's national prominence as a center for market research, specializing in image analyses, communication strategies, and market positioning.

Ms. Sims offers a wealth of expertise, having served more than 175 colleges and universities over the course of her 25-year career in higher education marketing. Her responsibilities range from directing market research studies and leading direct marketing consultations to managing publications and Web site development services for clients.

Prior to joining the firm, Ms. Sims managed creative services for a Citicorp subsidiary and served as a marketing executive for US Bank. She holds a master's degree in applied communications from the University of Denver (CO).